MODERN CRITICISM

MODERN CRITICISM

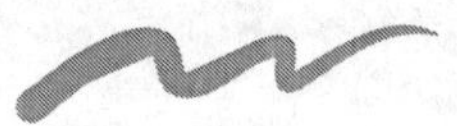

Edited by
CHRISTOPHER ROLLASON
RAJESHWAR MITTAPALLI

ATLANTIC
PUBLISHERS & DISTRIBUTORS (P) LTD

Published by

ATLANTIC

PUBLISHERS & DISTRIBUTORS (P) LTD

7/22, Ansari Road, Darya Ganj, New Delhi-110002
Phones : +91-11-40775252, 40775214, 23273880, 23275880
Fax: +91-11-23285873
Web: www.atlanticbooks.com
E-mail: orders@atlanticbooks.com

Printed & bound in India by Atlantic Print Services

PREFACE

The history of literary criticism in the twentieth century may speculatively be divided into two markedly contrasting moments, each corresponding to one of the century's chronological halves. The nature of these two distinct moments may be seized if we briefly examine what may be considered similar but contrasting episodes from two of the great English-language novels of recent times, Vikram Seth's *A Suitable Boy* and Philip Roth's *The Human Stain*. In Seth's novel, published in 1993 but set in India just after Independence, a young lecturer's promotion prospects at one point hang on the issue of whether or not James Joyce should be included on his university's programme in British literature, despite the hostility of his older colleagues to the modernist aesthetic. A very different accent is struck when, in Roth's fictional portrait of Bill Clinton's America, published in 2000 and set at the time of writing, a lecturer is faced with a student who complains over the presence on a course of two plays by Euripides which she sees as "degrading to women." The contrast that emerges between the academies of 1950 and 2000 hinges on what might be called the shift away from literary yardsticks and towards non-literary criteria in the dominant procedures for understanding and evaluating texts at large.

The schools of criticism which emerged from within the literary academy in the first half of the twentieth century—the linguistically-inspired Formalism of the Prague School, American New Criticism, and, in Britain, the Practical Criticism of I.A. Richards and the stern evaluative moralism of F.R. Leavis—all, despite their differences, had in common the foregrounding of the text itself and an insistence on close readings. Concurrently, the Marxist and the psychoanalytic schools of criticism both underwent a complex evolution over the same period, deploying increasingly sophisticated theoretical tools and combining close textual analysis with the desire to expose the hidden determinations of literary texts through recourse to extra-literary models. At the same time, a "classical" Marxist such as Georg Lukács or an early Freudian like Marie Bonaparte would not have diverged fundamentally from a Leavis or an Yvor Winters over the need for a canon or the objective existence of literary value.

The twentieth century's second half saw an ever-harsher break, within academic circles, with the textual and interpretive emphases of those earlier discourses, and an ever-more insurgent interrogation of such hitherto unassailable concepts as aesthetic value, the canon, the centrality of European literature, and, finally, the very possibility of textual meaning. Formalism mutated into Structuralism, which combined claims to scientific objectivity derived from linguistics with the post-Nietzschean "death of the author" famously proclaimed by Roland Barthes. As the century wore on, new and radical critical positions claimed increasing numbers of adherents—among them, notably, feminist theory, which questioned a canon perceived as a manifestation of male power; postcolonial theory, which sought to build alternative canons for "peripheral" literatures based on redefined criteria of value, or else, as in Edward Said's celebrated studies *Orientalism* and *Culture and Imperialism*, proposed a radical post-imperial re-reading of Western writings; and, above all, Structuralism's unruly heir Deconstruction, the philosophy or anti-philosophy which, with Jacques Derrida as its high priest, aspired to dethrone hermeneutic models of interpretation, in an undifferentiated embrace of an infinite plurality of non-hierarchical meanings. These modes of reading may all, in their certainly very different ways, be said to shift the emphasis away from the literary text and on to a varying series of extra-literary criteria.

At the same time, however, in a development which may not have been sufficiently mapped, criticism of the more traditional kind did not simply lie down and die. Dissident elements such as Christopher Ricks voiced concern that criticism was becoming increasingly divorced from the experience and language of the ordinary reader and, indeed, of most creative writers; and Harold Bloom's rear-guard defence of canonic literature, expressed in his two controversial and much-publicised volumes *The Western Canon* and *Shakespeare: The Invention of the Human*, had the merit of conferring public visibility on the academy's internal struggles. Finally, as the twenty-first century loomed on the horizon, the cunning of history unexpectedly brought the common reader back into the game with the rise of the Internet. Today, any computer-literate reader of books can post a review on any of numerous popular websites or discussion groups, thus becoming his or her own critic and bypassing the academic establishment altogether. The exact implications of these developments remain unknown, but the contours of a new reader-centred criticism are likely to become visible as our new century progresses.

The present volume is intended as a modest contribution to the above theatre of critical debate. It assembles sixteen essays on different aspects of modern criticism, by authors from six countries and four continents. It is divided into three sections. The essays in the first section examine a diversity of general theoretical perspectives; the second section concentrates more specifically on key issues in the area of postcolonial literary studies; and in the third and final section, a series of interdisciplinary perspectives point up new and challenging possibilities for the future of criticism.

Section I begins with two discussions of the still-pregnant issue of postmodernism, with Christine Jones offering a general theoretical overview and T. Ravichandran concentrating more pragmatically on the experience of the postmodernist text in the classroom. Next, Nouri Gana examines the strengths and limitations of a related theoretical model, namely the reader-response approach. The claims of various models deriving from linguistics are then explored, by María Ángeles Ruiz Moneva, who proposes a detailed application of linguistically-defined concepts of irony; Prakash Chandra Pradhan, who outlines the claims of sociolinguistics as an aid to reading fiction; and N. Raveendran, who considers the possibilities of applying linguistic models to the study of drama. The section concludes with a reminder, in Gangadhar Gadgil's eloquent defence of literature's symbolic function, that, for all the attraction of poststructuralist and linguistic models, criticism of a more traditional kind is still very much with us, and is far from having said their its word.

As befits this volume's publication in India, Section II distills a number of theoretical perspectives on postcolonial literatures. The essays by Anthonia Kalu and Mala Pandurang examine some of the problems of defining a culturally appropriate model for the study of African literature; Subhendu Mund overviews the critical issues surrounding the phenomenon of Indian writing in English; and Rajeshwar Mittapalli considers that same "Indo-Anglian" literature from the specific vantage point of psychoanalytic discourse, striking an interdisciplinary note which will recur strongly, in other forms, in the contributions of the final section.

Broadening out the field of argument, Section III opens with two stimulating studies which explore the relatively new terrain of the potential parallels between literary criticism and legal discourse, contributed by Dámaso Javier Vicente Blanco and, again, Nouri Gana. The input of women's studies and feminist theory is represented by N. Geetha's re-evaluation for our times of an ancient genre, namely the fairy tale. Christopher Rollason re-examines the work and theoretical positions of a major twentieth-century critic, Walter Benjamin, in the light of the new vistas opened up for criticism by the electronic networks of the twenty-first century. Finally, Virgílio Augusto Fernandes Almeida, in a daring re-reading of a twentieth-century literary classic, Italo Calvino's *Invisible Cities*, presents a set of analogies between text and network that point towards a qualitatively new way of seeing which could guide both literature and criticism in new directions, as the Internet age evolves.

It is not by chance that we have concluded this volume with this adumbration of how literature can shadow forth a whole new universe of interrelations. Without the Internet and the continuous intellectual collaboration between scholars on different continents that it has made possible, this anthology would not have existed in the form in which it now reaches its readers. Today, the creation of new "invisible cities" of the intellect promises unforeseen and surprising horizons for reading, writing and criticism, whose exact shape the future will tell us—as we ourselves, critics, writers and readers, across the networks that link us, create that future.

—CHRISTOPHER ROLLASON
—RAJESHWAR MITTAPALLI

CONTENTS

SECTION I

1

Postmodernism's Linguistic Turn

CHRISTINE JONES

Introduction

The term postmodern encompasses a wide range of meanings, so that what is referred to as postmodernism varies considerably according to context. However, among the tenets which characterize the debate about postmodernism amongst scholars in the humanities, none is perhaps more prevalent than that which highlights the critical awareness of the mind's fundamentally *interpretive* nature.

A key tool employed in the mind's interpretation or representation of the world is, of course, the human meaning-maker language. For many postmodern thinkers, language, instead of simply reflecting the world, is considered to be actually constitutive or constructive of the experience we have of the world. In this paper, I shall be concerned to explore the impact that the "linguistic turn" has had within the domain of literary studies. But first, in order to more adequately understand how postmodern ideas about interpretive practice have influenced literary-critical discourse, we need to trace the historical factors that gave rise to postmodernism. In other words, we need to explore what it was in modernity that postmodern thinkers wanted to square off against.

Postmodernism: Historical background

Philosophic postmodernism can perhaps be best understood

as centering on a critique of certain modern notions about reason and the autonomous rational subject. The term "modern" in this context is often linked with patterns of thought identified as Cartesian and of the Enlightenment and with those delineated within the German idealist tradition, particularly in Kant and in Hegel.

Characteristic of the modern "enlightened" appeal to reason is the quest for a pure, neutral, disengaged reason, a reason from which all presuppositions have been eliminated. The radically critical modern subject, believing that any recognition of historical contingency would threaten the very integrity of reason, pronounces allegiance to a disinterested and universal reason in the hope of reaching assured foundations for knowledge freed from dogmatic dependence. A distinctive feature of modernity, suggests Jürgen Habermas, one of its contemporary defenders, is that it "has to create its normativity out of itself"[1]; it has no recourse other than itself, no tradition to fall back upon.

Convinced that human beings can regulate and evaluate their beliefs by rational self-reflection, and that the identification of data in the activity of inquiry does not require any prior theoretical commitment, Descartes, near the beginning of the modern project, endeavoured to start with clear and distinct ideas and to suspend allegiance to received wisdom, declaring, "My plan has never been more than to try to reform my own thought and to build upon a foundation which is completely my own."[2]

Likewise, Kant, near the end of the project, supposed that the truly critical and self-determining modern individual was the one who, when reasoning, had freed him or herself from dependence on tradition, or from the interference of passion, feeling, prejudice, and so on, thereby exemplifying the power to rule his or her own beliefs autonomously. Building upon this bedrock foundation, humankind would then be able to arrive at objective, true knowledge of the way things are in the world. And, along with the progress of rational inquiry would come the improvement of human life.

The anthropocentric turn of the Enlightenment, its insistence on an ideal humanity founded on reason and the radically autonomous rational subject (in opposition to the subject in subordination to the authority of the Church, tradition, or Revelation, as had been the case formerly), gave rise to a number of developments which were to become essential features of modern western culture. The emphasis on the autonomy of reason played itself out in many ways: for one thing, reason was increasingly *opposed* to faith, or the "faith seeking reasons" of the medieval era. The new "double-truth" theory of the universe, where faith was seen to have its own object and reason its exclusive right to its own object—the phenomenal world—a right which should be uncontaminated by the encroachments of faith, gave rise to an increased sense of mastery over nature. With the right use of reason, humankind could become, in Francis Bacon's famous (or by now infamous) phrase, "masters and possessors of nature." The link that was formed between knowledge and power promised to bring about unending techno-scientific development. It also gave rise to a distinctly modern conception of subjectivity: as epistemology was given priority over ontology, the individual had a heightened sense of its power as subject vis-à-vis the object which was the world, inert mechanical nature. The modern subject became a consciousness set over against the world, engaged in a supposedly value-free mirroring of nature.

Nietzsche and Postmodernism

It would be foolhardy to downplay the many gains of the modern techno-scientific world-view, but so many things—the ecological crises of the last century for one, the development of weapons of mass destruction, for another—vitiate the story of modernity as one of unsullied progress. And it was this presumption about progress and the way in which the quest for mastery or for totality could so easily convert into totalitarianism that postmodern thinkers, with Nietzsche setting the ball rolling, reacted against.

Indeed, the insistence on the fundamental perspectivism or relativism of knowledge which lies at the heart of the postmodern sensibility derives much of its conceptual impetus from Nietzsche, the original "genealogist." Nietzsche drew attention to the insufficiently historicized conception of reason which modern thinkers proposed. What they took to be principles of rationality *per se* were actually historically contingent, particularist positions. Unmasking the will to power which lay behind claims to neutrality, Nietzsche stressed the way in which all our ideas, most especially our ideas concerning reason, are historically conditioned.

Where Enlightenment thinkers took rational justification to be independent of all partiality and attempted to reach assured foundations for knowledge freed from social and cultural particularity, claiming that they were engaged in a value-free mirroring of nature, Nietzsche, disillusioned with the failure of the attempt to reach rational foundations, and with the presumption of Enlightenment modernity, proclaimed instead the multiplicity of perspectives in the activity of inquiry and the relativization of truth to those perspectives. All those claims about neutrality and for universality turned out under Nietzsche's scrutiny to be particularist forms of power masquerading as universals.

Recognizing that the epistemological subject is necessarily situated, Nietzsche concluded that thought is not external to being, but that "our highest and most daring thoughts are characteristic fragments of reality. Our thought is made of the same substance as everything else."[3] Thus, the world cannot be said to exist as a thing-in-itself independent of the human mind, nor can it be said to possess any features in principle prior to interpretation; rather, the world comes into being only in and through interpretations.

Postmodern Reason

As Thomas McCarthy points out in his assessment of what it means to philosophize "postmodernly," recognition of the contingency of the criteria for what counts as rational "in any given time or place" has now superseded the universality of reason. Postmodern thinkers are concerned to explore "the irreducible plurality of incommensurable language games and forms of life, the irremediably 'local' character of all truth, argument, and validity." To the *a priori*, postmodern thinkers oppose the empirical,

> to certainty fallibility, to invariance historical and cultural variability, to unity heterogeneity, to totality the fragmentary, to self-evident givenness ("presence") universal mediation by differential systems of signs, to the unconditioned a rejection of ultimate foundations in any form—transcendental conditions of possibility no less than metaphysical first principles.[4]

In an attempt to overcome the nostalgia for unity, totality, and foundations, postmodern thinkers reject any form of thinking which legitimates itself through the appeal to some grand metanarrative such as the "dialectics of Spirit, the hermeneutics of meaning" or the progress of Reason.[5] As part of this abandonment of the quest for absolute foundations, it is suggested that all claims to knowledge or truth are made by individuals who are first and foremost embodied in the world, so that knowledge of the world is always grounded in an individual's dealings with it. Knowledge claims are, it is said, advanced from some particular perspective or point of view, and from within what are called variously "conceptual schemes, conceptual frameworks, forms of life, networks of categories, modes of discourse, systems of thought, [and] paradigms."[6]

Postmodern thinkers following Nietzsche's lead, disillusioned with the Enlightenment attempt to reach assured foundations for knowledge freed from all social and historical particularity, are concerned to de-center the radically autonomous epistemological subject of modernity. Nietzsche's legacy has been such that for philosophic postmodernity the autonomous epistemological and moral subject has been decentered and "the conception of reason linked to it irrevocably desublimated."[7]

Rupture or Continuation?

Jean-François Lyotard has suggested that the postmodern project involves a major shift in the modern understanding of reason, and an about-face concerning all those ideals attendant on it—the Grand Narratives such as the idea of progress, and so on. And Lyotard's view seems to be confirmed by defenders of modernity who themselves link modernity and rationality and characterize postmodernism as representing a departure from a distinctively modern conception of rationality (Jürgen Habermas can be cited here as an example).

So from one angle, postmodernism can be understood as looking at reason and its capacities and limitations from a radically new perspective. But postmodernism, in a certain sense, can also be seen as being continuous with the project of modernity, for the seed of postmodern perspectivism can actually be found in the great modern thinkers themselves. Kant himself, who gave every indication of being an absolutist, can be held responsible, for good or ill, for postmodern perspectivism. And this is in part because his guiding principle was that the mind, in organizing sensory data, imposes concepts or categories on these data. Thus, the seed of cognitive relativism is contained in this belief that the mind *determines the form of our experience of the world.*

Yet whether postmodernism is best understood as being continuous or discontinuous with the modern project, it is clear that those operating after the repudiation of the original modern project advance as a crucial insight the idea that the endeavour to reach absolute foundations for knowledge freed from historical particularity is ill-founded. The inquirer is no longer considered to be a participant in a universal, unified enterprise shared by all other reflective human beings, where each contributes to an overall progress, as s/he was according to the modern understanding, but is constrained instead to be tolerant of ambiguity. According to the postmodern conception of rationality, standards of rationality inhere in historical and social institutions, and are mediated through language.

The Linguistic Turn

The belief in the discursive construction of reality, or the idea that language rather than reality is the constitutive agent of human consciousness, received further impetus in the last century from structural linguistics. Ferdinand de Saussure, the founder of modern linguistics, made a distinction between *langue* (the synchronic or internal relational properties of a language system) and *parole* (the diachronic or historically contingent aspects of language-using activity) and insisted that *langue* in isolation from *parole* was the most suitable object of linguistic study. Saussure argued that while "some people regard language [...] as a naming process only—a list of words, each corresponding to the thing that it names," the truth is that the linguistic sign unites "not a thing and a name, but a concept and a sound image."[8] Saussure viewed language as a self-contained system of signs whose meanings are determined by their relation to other signs in the system rather than by their one-to-one correspondence with items in reality. To put the matter simply, we understand the meaning of the word "dog" because of the way in which it differs from "fog" or "log." On this view, the truth of a belief or statement is holistic, or a matter of the internal relations within a self-enclosed linguistic system, and not a matter of a given statement's relation to something extra-linguistic.

For many of Saussure's epigones and their interpreters, if not for Saussure himself, language, no longer considered to be a naming process, cannot be said in any meaningful way to relate to reality at all. Language is instead understood to be anterior to the world, so that what we call reality is but a linguistically-constructed artifact, something that is produced or caused by the different language systems we inhabit. Jacques Derrida's oft-quoted phrase "il n'y a pas de hors-texte"[9] reflects his belief that language cannot adequately represent anything outside of itself. Reality becomes on this view that which the text itself poses as real in constituting it as a referent beyond itself. And, taking Saussure's principle about the differential nature of signs one step further, Derrida highlighted the way in which meaning is always *deferred*: signs of necessity form "an infinite chain, ineluctably multiplying the supplementary mediations that produce the sense of the very thing itself, of immediate presence, of original perception."[10]

The idea that linguistic meanings are determined independently of ontology, or that cognition is essentially linguistic, is one which enables its proponents to express an indefinitely large number of alternative conceptualizations of reality; furthermore, no one conceptualization of reality can be said to be more correct or true than any other because there is no extra-linguistic reality which can be referred to in order to settle matters between rival interpretations of it. As Nelson Goodman claims, since we have "access to the world only through some description or depiction of it," and since "we can only know the world as conceptualized in one way or another [...] what counts as 'the facts' and what counts as 'correspondence with the facts' can vary from version to version."[11]

For many critics operating after the linguistic turn, then, language is no longer considered to be a medium for the transparent representation of reality; instead it is seen to shape our experience of reality and, in a certain sense, to constitute it. Literary theorists who appropriate the idea that cognitive arguments are not grounded in the nature of things frequently suggest that texts are not *interpreted* in the sense that their determinate meanings are ascertained, but that they are instead constructed, there being "no facts independent of interpretations."[12] "Interpretation is not the art of construing, but the art of constructing," suggests Stanley Fish: "Interpreters do not decode poems; they make them."[13] In a similar vein, the post-structuralist critic Roland Barthes characterizes textual interpretation as the art of construing rather than extrapolating meaning, and likewise implicitly puts increased emphasis on the role of the reader in the process of interpretation or even the production of meaning. As Barthes puts it:

> The work is without circumstance and this is indeed perhaps what defines it best: the work is not circumscribed, designated, protected, directed by any situation, no practical life is there to tell what meaning to give to it [...] in it ambiguity is wholly pure [...] [it is] open to a number of meanings, for they were uttered outside of every situation—except indeed the situation of ambiguity.[14]

Conclusion

In this paper I have attempted to give the reader a sense of the impact that the movement from reality to language as the constitutive agent for the production of meaning has had in recent years. I have not attempted to refute the more radical formulation of this position—the constructivist position—by proving the way in which something extra-linguistic exists, nor have I provided an explanation of the referential link between the truth of a statement and what that statement refers to. I haven't done so because I believe that to give priority to epistemological questions inevitably involves one in endless disagreement about these issues since there is no absolute foundation that we could all agree upon as a starting point to adjudicate between them. But the Saussurean or post-structuralist conception of language misunderstands, it seems to me, the nature of what might be called language's embodied or lived logic. In placing the emphasis on *langue* rather than *parole* this school of critics posits a philosophy of language that overlooks our actual use of language within our worldly situations, treating it as something which is absolved from any question of validation in terms of the world we use it in.

Postmodern thinkers have succeeded, it seems to me, in refuting the modern totalizing form of inquiry. It is clear that standards of rationality do inhere in historical and social institutions, and that our understanding of the world is necessarily mediated through language; but it does not follow that we are trapped within the "prison house of language." As literary critic Lee Patterson suggests in response to the common claim that all reality is "textualized" in one way or another, to adopt an interpretive method that assumes that reality is "not merely known through but constituted by language is to act as if there are no acts other than speech acts. But while we can all agree that language cannot be prised off from the world, that whatever nonverbal, non-symbolic reality exists can be known only by means of linguistic mediation, this does not allow us to abandon the category" of the historically real entirely. Historical reality, Patterson continues,

> is impelled by consequential and determinative acts of material production: building cities, making wars, collecting wealth, imposing discipline, seizing and denying freedom—these are material processes that, while enacted in and made known by symbolic forms, possess a palpable force and an intentional purposiveness [...] that stand against the irresolutions and undecidabilities valued by contemporary methods of interpretation.[15]

Notes and References

1. Jürgen Habermas, *The Philosophical Discourse of Modernity. Twelve Lectures,* trans. Frederick G. Lawrence (Cambridge, Mass.: The MIT Press, 1987) 7.
2. Rene Descartes, *Discourse on Method and Meditations on First Philosophy* [1637]. Trans. Donald A. Cress (Indianapolis: Hackett Publishing Co., Inc., 1988) 8.
3. Kroner, ed., *Werke, Grossoktavausgabe,* 2nd ed., 20 vols. Leipzig: Kroner, 1901-13 and 1926: XII, Part 2, No. 2. Quoted in Jean Granier, "Persepctivism and Interpretation," *The New Nietzsche: Contemporary Styles of Interpretation,* ed. David B. Allison (Cambridge, Mass.: The MIT Press, 1990) 190.
4. Kenneth Baynes, James Bohman, and Thomas McCarthy, eds., *After Philosophy: End or Transformation?* (Cambridge, Mass.: The MIT Press, 1989) 3-4.
5. Jean-François Lyotard, *The Postmodern Condition* (Minneapolis: U of Minnesota P, 1984) 87.
6. Paisley Livingston, *Literary Knowledge: Humanistic Inquiry and the Philosophy of Science* (Ithaca and London: Cornell UP, 1988) 63.
7. Livingston 61.
8. Ferdinand de Saussure, *Course in General Linguistics,* ed. Charles Bally and Albert Sechehaye from notes on Saussure's lectures of 1906-1911; trans. Wade Baskin (London: Fontana, Collins, 1974) 65-66.
9. Jacques Derrida, *Of Grammatology,* trans. Gayatri Chakravorty Spivak (Baltimore: 1976) 157
10. Derrida 5
11. Nelson Goodman, "The Fabrication of Facts, *Relativism: Cognitive and Moral,*" ed. Jack W. Meiland and Michael Krausz (Notre Dame and Indian: U of Notre Dame Press, 1982) 8.
12. Stanley Fish, *Is There a Text in this Class? The Authority of Interpretive Communities* (Cambridge: Harvard UP, 1980) 327.
13. Fish 327
14. Roland Barthes, *Criticism and Truth,* trans. Katherine Pilcher Keuneman (London: Athlone 1987).
15. Patterson Lee, *Negotiating the Past: The Historical Understanding of Medieval Literature* (Madison, Wisconsin: The U of Wisconsin P, 1987).

✪✪✪

2

Teaching a Postmodern Text

T. RAVICHANDRAN

I. THE PROBLEM OF DEFINITION

Fixing the Protean

Postmodernism is a polysemantic and self-contradictory term: polysemantic in the sense that it is multiple in its meanings, and self-contradictory as it contains its enemy within, "modernism," which it seeks to revise and/or negate. So before a teacher would plunge into the teaching of a postmodern text, he needs to grapple with the definition of the term as such. Yet with no explicit and ready-made definitions available in the critical market, he needs to fix the untenable, hold the protean and make a stand, though on a slippery ground.

Postmodernism, like the mythical Proteus, is evasive when grappled, assuming all possible varying forms so as to avoid one fixed form that would display its proper identity. As Ihab Hassan perceives, "Postmodernism suffers from a certain *semantic* instability; that is, no clear consensus about its meaning exists among scholars"(1986: 14). The general difficulty is being compounded by the "brash adolescence" of the term and "its semantic kinship to more current terms, themselves equally unstable": "Thus some critics mean by postmodernism what others call avant-gardism or neo-avant-gardism, while still others would call the same phenomenon simply modernism" (1986: 14).

Mapping the Borderless

While some critics (Bradbury 1983: 164) suggest that

Postmodernism has reached its end already, and while some others (Barth 1985) foresee it as a synthesis yet to come, the trend generally accepted by these critics is that it is a reaction against and/or a continuation of Modernism. Hassan also talks about its "*historical* instability." By this he means that the "Postmodern period" must be perceived in terms *both* of continuity *and* discontinuity, the two perspectives being complementary and partial. Hence the Postmodern phenomenon ought to be viewed in terms of both continuity and discontinuity from Modernism. In the former case, it is from Modernism that Postmodernism has spread its tentacles and it is Modernism which it tries to intensify, extend and revise. In the latter case, Postmodernism considers Modernism an anti-model whose versions it frustratingly seeks to subvert/convert/pervert so as to keep its versions incomplete. A related difficulty is that one could not successfully or completely define the term "Modernism" and learn to demarcate it from "Postmodernism." Hassan explains:

> Modernism and Postmodernism are not separated by an Iron Curtain or Chinese Wall; for history is a palimpsest, and culture is permeable to time past, time present, and time future. We are all, I suspect a little Victorian, Modern, and Postmodern at once. And an author may, in his or her own lifetime, easily write both a modernist and postmodernist work (1986: 17).

No General Consensus

In trying to contradistinguish the term postmodernism from modernism, critics are of divided opinion. Therefore some contend that modernism has been superseded by postmodernism while some others consider modernism an extended/replenished phase of postmodernism. Andreas Huyssen opines that "while the postmodern break with classical modernism was fairly visible in architecture and the visual arts, the notion of a postmodern rupture in literature has been much harder to ascertain" (1990: 237). "The different accounts of postmodernist literature and its relation to modernist fiction that have been offered by Leslie Fiedler, Ihab Hassan, and John Barth, among others," in Joel Black's opinion, "hardly constitute a consensus, and none of these views has yet succeeded in becoming a definitive critical statement on the subject" (1986: 96).

Ecriture rather than Literature

The postmodern tendency conjures up a galaxy of writers and critics. To name only a few dominant ones—among the writers: Italo Calvino, Gabriel García Márquez, Umberto Eco, John Fowles, John Barth, Thomas Pynchon, Jerzy Kosinski, William Burroughs, Donald Barthelme, Raymond Federman, John Hawkes, William Gass, E.L. Doctorow, Robert Coover, D.M. Thomas, Salman Rushdie and J.M. Coetzee. Among the critics: Jacques Derrida, Jacques Lacan, Roland Barthes, Michel Foucault, Jean-Francois Lyotard, Susan Sontag, Leslie Fiedler, Ihab Hassan, Paul de Man, Harold Bloom, J. Hillis Miller, Gerald Hoffman and Geoffrey Hartman. As David Lodge comments, "Postmodernism has established itself as an *ecriture*, in Barthes's sense of the word—a mode of writing shared by a significant number of writers in a given period" (1988: 221).

Complicated Theoretical Background: Deconstruction and the Notion of Play

Postmodern difficulty is compounded in its complex theoretic background. In particular, one needs to grasp such complicated concepts as Poststructuralism and Deconstruction. Even some renowned critics have written off deconstruction by saying that it is highly ambiguous. Jacques Derrida himself seems to revel in paradoxes and contradictions. In an interview, he once remarked, "What deconstruction is not? Everything of course! What is deconstruction? Nothing of course!" Nevertheless, Derrida "subverts" or "undermines" the supposition that the system of language provides adequate grounds to establish the boundaries, the coherence or unity, and the determinate meanings of a text or self. Deconstruction attempts to erase the boundaries between oppositions, hence to show that the values and hierarchical order implied by the oppositions are also not rigid. Every word contains every other word by association and beyond that the meaning of every word is always deferred by circumstances. Meaning is that which differs, and which defers. Thus for Derrida, it is made dialectically—it lies always in a tension between the binaries, and there is no central meaning ("absolute signified") holding it all together. Without meaning, then, there can be no Truth and no Authority, and so power relations fall apart. The centre was a "construct," rather than something that was simply true or there. "This is not to say that there are no truths, but to put it in a somewhat convoluted manner, the truth of Truth is that there is no truth; this is Truth's truth" (Wolfreys 1966: 188). Rather than mourning the fixity of meaning, one can play along, rejoice in multiplicity and affirm the provisional nature of all meaning. Thus the poststructuralist is of the view that the object-text can be construed in an almost infinite number of ways, none of which is more faithful to the text itself than any other. In the words of Mark Currie, "where the structuralist was concerned with *structure*, the poststructuralist is concerned with *structuration*, or the ways in which the text is constructed by criticism" (Wolfreys 1966: 59).

No Sense of Centre/Unity

Umberto Eco has suggested that Postmodernism is born at the moment when we discover that the world has no fixed centre and that, as Foucault taught, power is not something unitary that exists outside of us (Hutcheon 1988: 86). Burdened with the overwhelming fatherhood of Modernism, Postmodernism sees the centre as a construct, a fiction, and not a fixed and unchangeable reality. The old "either-or" breaks down and the new "both/and-also" of multiplicity and difference opens up new possibilities. The "mythical method" (of Pound, Eliot and Joyce) of ordering or giving shape and meaning to a fragmented world is displaced by a growing insistence that there is no order, no shape or significance to be found anywhere. In Todd Gitlin's words:

> In the postmodernist sensibility, the search for unity has apparently been abandoned altogether. Instead, we have textuality, a cultivation of surfaces endlessly referring to, ricocheting from, reverberating onto other surfaces. The work calls attention to its arbitrariness, constructedness; it interrupts itself. Instead of a single centre, there is pastiche,

> cultural recombination [...]. Not only has the master voice dissolved, but any sense of loss is rendered deadpan [...]. The implied subject is fragmented, unstable, even decomposed, it is finally nothing more than a crosshatch of discourses. Where there was passion, or ambivalence, there is now a collapse of feeling, a blankness (1990: 15-16).

So Many Labels

The types, rather species, of narcissistic narrative which mushroomed in this condition are labelled "Metafiction," "Historiographic Metafiction," "Parafiction" and "Surfiction." Since all the possibilities of the fiction are used up, abused and exhausted, fiction in its conventional sense becomes impossible. Hence the Postmodern fiction tries to explore the possibilities of fiction as a "fictional construct" than as a mimetic representation of reality. The Postmodern fiction does not aim to hold the mirror up to nature but simply to be true unto its self-reflexive nature. It is, Raymond Federman observes,

> the kind of fiction that constantly renews our faith in man's imagination and not in man's distorted vision of reality— that reveals man's irrationality rather than man's rationality [...]. Just as Surrealists called that level of man's experience that functions in the subconscious SURREALITY, I call that level of man's activity that reveals life as a fiction SURFICTION. Therefore, there is some truth in that cliché which says that "life is fiction," but not because it happens in the streets, but because reality as such does not exist, or rather exists only in fictionalized version (1975: 7-8).

II. THE PROBLEM OF OVERCONNECTIVITY: INTERDISCIPLINARY NATURE

A character in a novel by John Barth remarks: "to understand any one thing entirely, no matter how minute, requires the understanding of every other thing in the world." And in similar vein a character from Pynchon says that "everything is connected." Thus any reader who wishes to comprehend a postmodern text has to first combat with its myriad relations to inter/cross-disciplinary subjects such as the Fine Arts, Mass

Media; Literature, Criticism; Philosophy, Psychoanalysis, Architecture, Cybernetics, Anthropology, Mythology, History, Geography, Mathematics, Social Science and Technology. The problem for a teacher is then not only to be a master of his subject but also a jack of all trades in many others. Even a partial understanding of the novels of Thomas Pynchon, for instance, would call for a knowledge of thermodynamics and of concepts like entropy. Entropy, of course, indicates the declivity of energy or the measure of disorder actualised by it.

Introduction of Innovative Concepts: Cosmopsis

Cosmopsis intimates a cosmic mindfulness in extremity that as a result numbs the mind and the body. "Cosmopsis" is John Barth's ludicrous version of entropy. A portmanteau word coined from "cosmopolitan" and "psychosis," the term indicates a psychological malady. A cosmopolitan belongs to all parts of the world and is not restricted to any one country or its inhabitants; psychosis is a severely disordered or diseased state of mind. In this manner, the person who suffers from cosmopsis grapples with a cosmic awareness; that is all things are possible and equally tenable, and so he does not find himself on a rational ground to choose one particular idea and act. Because he sees the possibilities of everything, he feels nothing for anything. Cosmopsis is a disease of too much imagination, too much consciousness, and it paralyses the mind as well as the body.

An Eclectic Version of Many Versions

While Postmodernism is considered *a* "version," in the way defined above, of Modernism; Postmodernism itself creates *various* versions of its own. But it sets them against one another, without dominance of a single version, constantly implying that every version of perfection is really an image of void. Brian McHale points out that every critic "constructs" postmodernism in his/her own way from different perspectives, none more right or wrong than the others. He observes:

> Thus, there is John Barth's postmodernism, the literature of replenishment; Charles Newman's postmodernism, the literature of an inflationary economy; Jean-Francois

> Lyotard's postmodernism, a general condition of knowledge in the contemporary informational regime; Ihab Hassan's postmodernism, a stage on the road to the spiritual unification of human kind, and so on. There is even Kermode's construction of postmodernism, which in effect constructs it right out of existence (Hutcheon 1988: 11).

Knowledge of Many Languages

In addition to the many subjects one ought to master to understand the pluriuniverse of postmodernism, one further needs to be a polyglot. Especially the knowledge of many foreign languages is presupposed. In this manner, Pynchon is fond of using words from French, Latin, Spanish and German in his novels very frequently. Thus, a knowledge of German is essential for a fruitful understanding of the functioning of a character like Shale Shoenmaker in Pynchon's *V.* "Shale" appears in its English meaning "ugly," and "Shoen" (schön) in its German meaning "beautiful": the reference is to the plastic surgeon that he is, a person who can make ugly things beautiful!

III. UNCONVENTIONAL TREATMENT OF CHARACTER, MYTH, ETC

Unconventional Character Mould: Characterless Personalities

A teacher could not interpret the characters in a postmodern novel by applying the conventional critical tools. Often, he cannot call them characters at all. Throughout Pynchon's novel *V.*, the central character's real stature is unclear. "Disguise is *one* of V.'s attributes" (1975: 385 & 462). Stencil associates V. with a girl named Victoria Wren who appears later as Victoria Manganese, Viola and Venus. Yet truthfully, Stencil himself does not know 'what sex V. might be nor what genus and species' since V. is known to be "a remarkably scattered concept" (1975: 389). The first time when it appears in the novel it is as "mercury-vapor lamps, receding in an asymmetric V" (1975: 11); secondly, as V-note, the name of a jazz club; and thirdly, as Veronica, a female rat. Later, V. is pervasive in place names: Venezuela, Valletta and a strange outlandish region—Vheissu. It is found in ideas as victory, virgin, Virgin, vantage, view, vision, violence, Vatican, various, vagrant, etc; also as energy, the symbol of verb, volt, vector, velocity and so on.

Critics have not only exhausted the probabilities of the letter V. in the novel but also its alternative possibilities: V turned upside down and made 'A' (e.g.: alligator, asexual); double V: 'W' (e.g.: Waterspout, World); and inverted double V: 'M' (e.g.: Malta, Mara) (Greenberg 1969, 58-65). One ingenuous interpretation considers V. just Pynchon's play on words with his readers and V. here represents a reader-surrogate, "for V. is nothing less than interjects the paronomasic encoding of 'V is you'" (Vella 1989, 139). In spite of this surfeit of interpretations, the-he-she-it-they-V. stays, to borrow a term from Salman Rushdie, a P2C2E, that is, *a process too complicated to explain.* As old Stencil claims in his report: "There is more behind and inside V. than any of us had suspected. Not *who,* but *what*: *what* is she" (1975: 53). What V. holds is not an answer to a crossword puzzle, but cross-references to exemplify, as well as to mock what it exemplifies, the complicated identity-formation/ fabrication process in a thoroughly capricious postmodern climate.

Uncanny Treatment of the Myth and the Real

The postmodernists differ largely from the modernists in their use of myth. As David Cowart observes, "where modernists exploit myth as a universal, instinctual truth, their successors either deconstruct myth as an unreliable 'metanarrative' or examine it as a language that, like all language, speaks its speakers rather than the other way around" (1990, 72). Thus if the modernists toil to find a meaning in coherence with myth, postmodernists puncture the mytho-centric-meaning by undermining the much vaunted authenticity/authority attributed to myth to structure reality. Myth no longer "served to explain," as M.H. Abrams defines it, "why the world is as it is and things happen as they do; and to establish the rationale for social customs and observances and sanctions for the rules by which men conduct their lives" (1971, 102). Linked with this distorted vision of myth is also the sense of perception of reality: "if modernism asks, how can we know reality (a reality whose existence is, ultimately, not in doubt), then postmodern asks, how can we know what is real? How can we read the signs and (social) codes that tell us what is real, but in such a way that we are not trapped within the constraint of those codes?" (Madsen 1991, 125).

Pynchon's method of blurring the boundaries of myth and reality is by attributing mythical status to contemporary figures. In this regard, Albert Piela III's comment on the postmodernists' jocular use of myth is pertinent to Pynchon's device. He remarks: "One of the reasons some Modernist authors appropriated myths for their works was that myths provided writers and readers a shared way of speaking about and understanding the world. While Modernists informed their works with classical and Biblical myths, their successors tend to be more playful" (1990, 125). In *Vineland,* Pynchon evokes the myths of popular culture, especially those shaped by television.

Pynchon subverts privileged myths by demonstrating the capacity of television programmes to provide a shared language between author and readers. Rather than seeking to recognise a number of specific allusions to Odysseus or Oedipus, the readers of *Vineland* need to identify such mythic figures as Mr. Spock, Jaime Sommers, and Oscar Goldman who are renowned television characters. The point is that, as Piela III observes, "by recognizing the mythopoeic qualities of television programs and characters, Pynchon upsets a hierarchy that privileges classical and Biblical myths as those appropriate to a high-cultural activity like literature" (1990, 125). Similarly, Pynchon rewrites the stories of Biblical heroes in a technically advanced world. The name of Isaiah 2: 4 given to a character in Pynchon's *Vineland* by his hippie parents, because of the passage's prophecy of peace, takes on an ironic slant interpretation that he is trying to borrow money from his girlfriend's father, Zoyd, to set up a violence amusement park.

IV. THE TEXT PER SE

Subversive/Self-reflexive Text

The postmodern text not only effects the subversion of the received canons of text-manufacturing but also its own "subversion"—that is, it allows itself to undergo a "subversion."

While producing a master version of a story, it provides sub-versions of the master version, thereby invalidating the whole. So the readers are at a loss to arrive at the "total story" and/or "the total meaning" of the text. The text reflects itself to be the product of a highly self-conscious mind. The reader is, inevitably, bound to be the co-creator of the self-reflexive text, yet paradoxically, distanced from it because of its very self-reflexiveness. As Linda Hutcheon explains,

> Some have argued that postmodernist art does not aim, as did modernist, at exploring the difficulty, so much as the impossibility, of imposing that single determinate meaning on a text. Yet it is also true that it does so, not so much by means of textual difficulties alone, but—paradoxically—by overt, self-conscious control by an inscribed narrator/author figure that appears to demand, by its manipulation, the imposition of a single, closed perspective. At the same time, of course, it works to *subvert* all chances of attaining such closure (1980: XIII).

Metafiction refers to fiction which calls attention to itself as an artifact in order to raise questions about the relationship between fiction and reality (Waugh, 1984). In a novel in the realistic tradition of mimesis, we would not have an intrusion by someone outside the text's frame of reference into the very fabric of the novel, nor would we have the form of eternal regress we get in the structure of the novel, in which a segment does not come to closure but instead is repeated, with variation, with a spiraling outward, out of the novel. The various receding and interwoven levels of narrative presented by the postmodern text suggest Derrida's discussion on an endless chain of signifiers, in which there is no final "truth" or transcendental signified: each signifed becomes a pointing signifier.

The Death of the Author and Intertextual connections

Contrary to the traditional, humanist perception of the subject as something represented by the author, the individual who gives life to and nourishes the work, Roland Barthes opines in his essay "The Death of the Author" that "it is language which speaks, not the author" (1968, 143). Barthes shifts the power and authority from the author to the writing itself, and subsequently the reader, who is actively involved in the text-making and meaning-construing process. The text is "woven entirely with citations, references, echoes, cultural languages [...] antecedent or contemporary, which cut across it through and through in a vast stereophony" (1971, 160). Julia Kristéva states in this way: "any text is constructed as a mosaic, any text is the absorption and transformation of another" (1986, 37). Both Kristéva and Barthes caution, however, that this mosaic, the "intertextual" in which every text is held, is not to be confused with some origin of the text:

> to try to find the "sources," the "influences" of a work, is to fall in with the myth of filiation, the citations which go to make up a text are anonymous, untraceable, and yet *already read*: they are quotations without inverted commas (Barthes 1971, 160).

Furthermore, Brenda K Marshall also comments in this context:

> Intertextuality is precisely a momentary compendium of everything that has come before and is now. Intertextuality calls attention to prior texts in the sense that it acknowledges that no text can have meaning without those prior texts, it is a space where "meanings" intersect. There is no such creature as the autonomous text (or work) (1992: 128).

From the perspective of semiotics, Kristéva observes that the term "intertextuality" denotes a "transposition of one (or several) sign system(s) into another" (1986a: 111).

The De-teleological Text

The traditional as well as modern "teleological texts" presupposed the theory that events and developments in life and fiction are due to the *purpose* or *design* that they are serving. The written text as it was with a thematic or structuring principle progressed towards a pre-determined text. The book is, generally, perceived as a discrete physical object and, correspondingly, conceived as a discrete unit of meaning. The postmodern "de-teleological text" decentres this notion and holds no specific purpose or design in its function. It decomposes the object of the book in order to deconstruct the book as concept, and also it retards both that decomposition and that deconstruction. In this respect, the postmodernist authors have done away with plot, character, setting and theme—they view them as the true enemies of fiction. Consequently, the text has taken the pattern of a mosaic.

V. FINAL NOTE: CHALLENGES NOT PROBLEMS!

Most of the difficulties discussed above appear to be problems existing on account of a received pattern of thinking in the conventional reader/teacher's mind, which basically looks for an "answer." Comprehension of a postmodern text is difficult for such a bent of mind, as the postmodernists seem to concur with Murphy's law that states, "there can be no answers, only cross-references." For the same reason, if the teacher would strive, like Pynchon's Oedipa, to look for a one-to-one correspondence between words and "meanings" in the text he may find himself in a state of paranoia. This paranoia is perhaps better than anti-paranoia since it is "a condition," Pynchon says, "not many of us can bear for long, where nothing is connected to anything." What is required, then, is a challenging mind that comprehends postmodernism in its polysemy and accepts the entirely different quality of reading that it demands. The postmodern text and the many texts intersecting within it may not be fully deciphered, completed. Rather, the text calls for an active participation, on the attempted disentanglement of the threads that run through it. As Barthes puts it in his "The Death of the Author":

> In the multiplicity of writing, everything is to be *disentangled,* nothing *deciphered*; the structure can be followed, "run" at every point and at every level; but there is nothing beneath: the space of writing is to be ranged over, not pierced (1968, 147).

Further, the "plurality" of the Text does not yield to a variety of interpretations; rather, it is "an *irreducible* plural" (1971, 159). Finally, the teaching of a postmodern text, in a sense, "begins in delight and ends in wisdom."—as Robert Frost would have explained it: "wisdom"—not of an eternal revelation, or a great clarification of life—but just "a momentary stay against confusion."

Works Cited

Abrams, M. H. *A Glossary of Literary Terms.* Delhi: Macmillan India, 1971.

Barth, John. *The End of the Road.* Harmondsworth: Penguin, 1976.

——. "The Literature of Replenishment." *Postmodernism in American Literature.* Ed. Ihab Hassan. Illinois: U of Illinois P, 1985.

Barthes, Roland. "The Death of the Author." *Image—Music—Text.* Trans. Stephen Heath. 1968. New York: Hill and Wang, 1977.

——. "From Work to Text." *Image—Music—Text.* Trans. Stephen Heath. 1971. New York: Hill and Wang, 1977.

Black, Joel. "Postmodernist Fictions: A Review Essay." *Pynchon Notes* 18-19 (1986): 96-109.

Borklund, Elner. *Contemporary Novelists.* London: St. James Press, 1986.

Bradbury, Malcolm. *The Modern American Novel.* Oxford: Oxford UP, 1983.

Cowart, David. "Attenuated Postmodernism: Pynchon's *Vineland.*" *Critique* 32.2 (1990): 67-76.

Federman, Raymond. "Surfiction—Four Propositions in Form of an Introduction." *Surfiction: Fiction Now [...] and Tomorrow.* Chicago: The Swallow Press, 1975. 5-15.

Gitlin, Todd. "Life in the Postmodern World." *The American Review* 34.4 (1990): 12-18.

Greenberg, Alvin. "The Underground Woman: An Excursion into the *V.* of Thomas Pynchon." *Chelsea* 27 (1969): 58-65.

Hassan, Ihab. "The Culture of Postmodernism." *Postmodernism in American Literature.* New Delhi: United States Information Service, 1986.

Hutcheon, Linda. *Narcissistic Narrative: The Metafictional Paradox.* New York: Methuen, 1980.

——. *A Poetics of Postmodernism: History, Theory, Fiction.* New York: Routledge, 1988.

Huyssen, Andreas. "Mapping the Postmodern." *Feminism/Postmodernism.* Ed. Linda J. Nicholson. New York: Routledge, 1990. 234-77.

Kristéva, Julia. "Word, Dialogue and Novel." *The Kristéva Reader.* Ed. Toril Moi. New York: Columbia UP, 1986. 34-61.

——. "Revolution in Poetic Language." *The Kristéva Reader.* Ed. Toril Moi. New York: Columbia UP, 1986. 90-136.

Lodge, David. *The Modes of Modern Writing: Metaphor, Metonymy and the Typology of Modern Literature.* Delhi: Arnold-Heinemann, 1980.

Madsen, Deborah L. *The Postmodernist Allegories of Thomas Pynchon.* London: Leicester UP, 1991.

Marshall, Brenda K. *Teaching the Postmodern: Fiction and Theory.* New York: Routledge, 1992.

Piela, Albert III. "A Note on Television in *Vineland.*" *Pynchon Notes* 26-27 (1990): 125-27.

Pychon, Thomas. *V.* 1963. London: Picador, 1975.

——. *Vineland.* New York: Penguin, 1990.

Vella, Michael W. "Thomas Pynchon's Intrusion in the Enchanter's Domain." *Twentieth Century Literature* 35 (Summer 1989): 131-46.

Waugh, Patricia. *Metafiction: The Theory and Practice of Self-conscious Fiction.* New York: Methuen, 1984.

Wolfreys, Julian and William Baker, eds. *Literary Theories: A Case Study in Critical Performance.* London: Macmillan, 1996.

3

The Specter of Relativism: A Critical Review of Norman Holland's Models of Reader-Response

NOURI GANA

I. The Transformational Model

In *The Dynamics of Literary Response* (1968), Holland tries to forge a theory of reading that benefits from the insights of psychoanalysis as well as from the New Critical methods of close reading. From the outset Holland does not seem to be interested in the question of validity in interpretation—an issue strongly re-brought to the limelight of literary criticism by E.D. Hirsch's *Validity in Interpretation* (1967). On the contrary, he sets out to describe only the "bi-active" relationship between the text and the reader. But, if his discourse does not explicitly say much about validity in interpretation, it is almost manifestly permeated with what I will refer to as "a theoretical anxiety"—the subjectivity-objectivity dichotomy. Indeed, Holland conceives of this dichotomy as his, as much as it is our, "old *bête-noire*" (*Dynamics* 108). Needless to say that such an appellation—*bête-noire*—is in itself revelatory of the consuming anxiety that the binary of subjectivity and objectivity arouses. I will try to show how in the very act of foregrounding the reader, Holland has been haunted, like many other reader-response proponents, by the *angst* of bordering on relativism, an angst that has almost undercut the initially liberatory vistas he opened for the reader. The broad strokes of my argument will expose Holland's ambivalent treatment of the reader—a treatment that oscillates between insistence on, as much as resistance to, the reader.

Since Holland elides a direct account of validity in interpretation, I will try to extract his discursive and fragmentary "position" on the subject from his fatalistic wrestling with the subjectivity-objectivity *bête-noire*. In *Dynamics*, his treatment of this polarity was shaped by his love for New Criticism and, especially by his admiration of the behaviorist school of psychology, and of eminent behaviorists such as Skinner and Bloomfield. No wonder, then, that he conceives of the text (the objective artifact) as the stimulus to the reader's subsequent response. The text is central to his "transformational theory" as developed in *Dynamics*: it is *in* and *through* the text that transformations take place. The reader responds to those transformations by releasing his/her own repressed drives. This whole reader-emancipating activity is, however, predicated upon the reader's "willing suspension of disbelief." I will, for the time being, suspend my reactions to this attitudinally behaviorist conception of the act of reading, and will examine the nature of "transformations," as well as the adequacy of the "willing suspension of disbelief" to the complexity of the reading process.

In *Dynamics*, Holland conceives of literature as transformation. Such a conception is arrived at through a marrying of New Critical procedures of close reading with the tactics of psychoanalytic psychology. Holland's theory of transformation is highly extrapolative: he reaches it by expanding his reflections on a very simple joke from the habitual world of everyday interpersonal exchange into the realm of the literary reader-text dyadic interaction. The joke tells of a young executive who had appropriated money from his company's safe, played the stock market, and lost it. Desperate, helpless and certain to be caught, he went down the river where he met "an ancient crone in a black cloak, with wrinkled face and stringy gray hair," who, upon learning about his predicament, proposed to grant him "three wishes for a slight consideration." The crone said she was a witch, passed her hand before his eyes, and said she had doubled his personal bank account. After passing her hands over his eyes once again, she informed him that the money he had lost had been put back in the company vault, and that he had been elected vice-president right after. Taken in by the witch's magic and eager to reciprocate her generosity, the young executive asked her what she wanted him to do for her in return, to which she responded: "You must spend the night making love to me." Although the thought of making love to the crone revolted him, he considered it worthwhile, given that he had already redrawn the course of his future life on the basis of the veracity of the witch's crucial intervention in it. Thus, he retired with the witch to a nearby motel.

> In the morning, the distasteful ordeal over, he was dressing to go home when the old crone in the bed rolled over and asked, "Say, Sonny, How old are you?"
>
> "I'm forty-two years old," he said. "Why?"
>
> "Ain't you a little old to believe in witches?" (DY 3-4)

For Holland, this joke is ripe not only with moral and didactic dimensions, but also, most importantly, with psychological underpinnings. Through the metaphorical bargain, it shows how one who aspires to get something for nothing may ultimately be got for nothing: the young executive wanted to get something (money and promotion) for nothing (sex), but it was him who was eventually got (sex) for nothing (words/promises). Being more inclined to belabor the matter from a psychoanalytic perspective, Holland avers that such a didactic meaning does not give as much pleasure as the psychoanalytic one. Like New Critics, psychoanalysts excavate the text, but not so much in search of a central and unifying point or statement "as for a central fantasy or daydream, familiar from couch or clinic, particular manifestations of which occur all throughout the text" (DY 7). In the context of this joke, Holland adumbrates that "It is not hard to recognize a nurturing mother-figure in the crone who magically offers 'sonny' all the sustenance he needs at the moment he needs it most" (DY 9). This sustenance is related to an unconscious fantasy: "being nurtured by a mother as against making love to her" (DY 12). That repressed primary fantasy is "transformed" or "sublimated" in and through the joke such that it has become unfamiliar, and unrecognizable. "We can call the joke's meaning," Holland goes on to say, "a transformation analogous to a sublimation, for it makes the unconscious fantasy intellectually, morally, and socially acceptable and even pleasurable; more technically, it makes the fantasy ego-syntonic" (DY 12). But, for the fantasy, transformed or abstracted through the joke, to be ego-syntonic—in conformity with the demands of the ego—, it is incumbent upon the reader to respond positively to that transformed fantasy to the extent that s/he believes it to be his/her own. In other words, the fantasy in the text of the joke has to be brought to bear on a repressed fantasy, dormant in the reader's unconscious.

The reader is related to the text on two levels: consciously and unconsciously. Consciously, the reader knows that the text is no more than a joke, a fiction from which s/he can extract a moral meaning, an insight or an intellection.[1] Unconsciously, the reader is consumed by the central myths or fantasies the fictional text presents him/her with, such as to find in them an outlet for his/her repressed fantasies. Thus, s/he gratifies those fantasies through a pleasurable and gratifying fusion with the text. Consciously, the reader is interpreting, perceiving, or understanding the text; unconsciously, s/he is dealing with the "unconscious mind of the literary work" (DY 62). A psychoanalytic approach to reading is perforce directed to account for the paradox of reading: we may not believe in witches, yet we cannot help but doing so whenever we read, or listen to, our joke. Why? In "Poetry and Beliefs," I.A. Richards regards poetry as a "pseudo-statement" about reality as opposed to a scientific and factual one. Because we always "hunger after a basis in belief," that pseudo-statement becomes "justified entirely in its effect in releasing or organizing our impulses and attitudes" (Richards 23). For Kenneth Burke, that pseudo-statement strikes us by its "verisimilitude" to reality and to scientific truth. Thus, "only verisimilitude, not truth," Burke argues, "can engage a reader who does not believe in hell, but who derives aesthetic pleasure from Dante's Inferno" (Burke 31). Clearly, these two accounts seem to foreground the make-believe character of the text: pseudo-statement that it is, the text strikes us by its proximity to factual statements. Earlier than these two accounts of the subtleties involved in engagements with and responses to texts is Coleridge's doctrine: the "willing suspension of disbelief"—a doctrine that thematizes the make-believe nature of literary texts as much as the prerequisite willingness and readiness of readers to believe in pseudo-statements. According to Coleridge, when we read we momentarily suspend our disbelief, and behave "as if" what we read were real, as if witches, in this joke, existed.

Holland's study of response starts from this given—the "willing suspension of disbelief"—but ultimately departs from it. When reading, not only does the reader suspend his/her disbelief, but s/he also "fuses" with the text. That fusion is of paramount importance to Holland's model of transformational theory inasmuch as it blurs, as we will see later, the dividing lines between subjectivity and objectivity. Prerequisite to reading literature is a hypothetical "as if" concomitant with a "basic trust" in what will be told. Once this condition is met, the text will more or less keep to its promises of pleasure, wish-fulfillment, and gratification. According to Holland, the reader is "free," but "bound" to choose between plunging into the world of the text or "snapping out of it" in case its central fantasy does not match the reader's.[2] The young executive could have turned down the witch's proposal from the outset, but he did not. In the same manner, we could have snapped out of the text of the joke at anytime (when we, for instance, discovered that the crone was no more than a witch), but we did not. It is because we have adopted a position of *trust* and done *as if* what we read were real that we engage with texts, after all (WSDR 5). Once that contract of basic trust is made, we no longer reality-test our hypotheses, as is the case in everyday life: "We do not reality-test because, in part at least, we ceased to feel we are separate from external reality. To some extent," and this is Holland's major development on Coleridge's suspension of disbelief, "we *fuse* with the literary work. In absorbing it, we become *absorbed*" (DY 80, italics mine).

We experience literature as a dynamic process, as a transformation of an unconscious meaning into a conscious one and vice versa *ad infinitum*. In other words, we experience literature as a dialectic of what is happening "out there," in the text, and "in here," in the reader, such that the "out there" merges into the "in here" (DY 80). We become "rapt" and "taken into" the text and "out" of ourselves (64); we are "gathered up," "carried along" and "absorbed" by the text; we "lapse" (83) and immerse in fantasy as if we were "hypnotized" or "dreaming;" we simply become as "engrossed" in the text as "regressed" to an earlier period of childhood in which we passively suck our mother's breast, and "merge" with our mother—the source and end of desire (87-89). "Literature creates a hunger in us and then gratifies it" (76). "And thus literature does make suckers of us all" (WSDR 6). But suckers that we are, we are passive only outwardly. After all, "To be active in the inner world, we must be passive toward the outer, for action outward binds us to reality; inaction lets us lapse into our most primitive method of gratification" (74).[3] Compelling as it may sound, such an account of the reader's response to literature in terms of fantasies and the gratification of fantasies, in terms of hunger and devouring, may well sound very reductive of the reader's role, not to mention the text's function.

Writing retrospectively, in an article entitled "A Transactive Account of Transactive Criticism," Holland speaks about his transformational model presented in *Dynamics* as a "bi-active" one. It "proceeds from the assumption that the text and the literant (the hearer, watcher, or reader of literature) each cause part of the response" (179). Further, it is suggested that the model was not to grant entire freedom to the reader, as one would expect of psychoanalytically-grounded models; on the contrary, the reader is said to be still 'working' within the limits of the text. But, this claimed activity of the reader is puzzling because it seems to be predicated upon an oxymoron—*passive activity*. On the one hand, the reader is said to regress to an early infantile period of passive gratification; on the other, s/he is said to be actively engaged and stimulated by the text to act on his/her inner drives. In order to aspire to, and perhaps sustain, credibility for the transformational model, Holland was somewhat obliged to play down the role of the reader, to the benefit of the role of the text.[4]

The text seems to cover a thicker part than the reader in the transformational process of reading developed in *Dynamics*. This statement can be evidenced by reference to explicit as well as to implicit material in *Dynamics*. Explicitly, not only is the text said to supply the fantasy, but also its transformation. Implicitly, the reader is said to "introject" that fantasy within him/her, which means that he/she is eventually considered as no more than a receptacle. Holland is, however, aware of his prudent hamstringing of the reader by the text, although his sometimes spectacular and discursive tendency to background the text is evocative of an attempt at balance inflected by the pressure both ends of the binary—text-reader—exert. As a result, Holland oscillates between the two, an oscillation that has not allowed the bringing together of reader and text, and has therefore resulted in the failure of the transformational model.

After having foregrounded the text, Holland occasionally surprises us with statements that play down its role, such as "meaning is not simply 'there' in the text" (DY 25), or "The text itself is only a series of words" (DY 310). Even if we concede that, the text can, by and large, be said to have played in Holland's transformational model a major constraining agent on the reader's introjection; the reader cannot, for instance, be said to force any fantasy on the text. For, the fantasy s/he brings to the text must match the one supplied by the text. Meanwhile, Holland postulates that the fantasy the text abstracts, or transforms, has to be in resonance with the reader's, that is, it has to match a transformation familiar to the reader (96). Even if the reader constructs and introjects the central fantasy the text offers him/her, s/he does that "within the limits of the text" (25). So, at one moment, everything seems to be supplied by the text; at another, fantasies seem to be constructed by the reader in the light of the text. Thus instead of outflanking the subjective and objective positions, Holland has occupied both at different times.

Doubtlessly, Holland's wrestling with the subjectivity-objectivity binary is far from being resolved in *Dynamics*. This restless wrestling is all the more aggravated by the ghostly fear of a potentially inadvertent, but enormous in all likeliness, lapse into the swirl-whirl of relativism. Several defenses[5] (defense mechanisms) have been deployed by Holland in order for him to preclude such a looming disaster: they range from fusion through introjection and identification to denial, which is, as we will see in the following part, a major defense mechanism in operation in his "transactive model."

Having been lured by his *bête-noire* into a tangled jungle of difficulties, Holland found no alternative but to carve out from the archive of psychoanalysis all the tactics necessary to brace his passage. Holland's consuming passion is to demonstrate persuasively that reader and text, subject and object, do merge during the experience of reading—a merger or fusion comparable to an earlier "at-oneness" with the mother. We have earlier spoken at length about the reading process as built on a "basic trust" that reaches its zenith when we become totally taken into the text and out of ourselves, when we lose ourselves in the text, when we mix fiction and reality, when we are "engulfed, overwhelmed, drowned, or devoured" and "buried alive" (DY 35); that is, when we *fuse* with the text. This tendency to fuse text and reader stems from a desire to "mingle subjectivity and objectivity," "to build a conceptual bridge from literary texts objectively understood to our subjective experience"—to resist that overwhelming danger and fear of relativism (DY xiv). But, these clear-cut aims are often clouded throughout the book by the recurrent distinctions Holland makes between three levels of discourse: "subjective, objective, and 'commonly experienced'" (xv). At one moment, Holland heaves a deep sigh of relief—"boundaries blur" (DY 83)—at another, he distinguishes between an "objective text" and a "subjective experience," and, still at other times, between a "fixed" core of meaning and "varying" responses (DY 108). Surprisingly enough, Holland has treated the text as a *fixed* entity, while it has been treated by fellow reader-response theorists as "poem" (Rosenblatt) and as "concretization" (Iser). I was no less surprised to find that Holland regards reading less as an event in time like Rosenblatt, Iser and Fish than as a spatial process in the Schlovskyan formalist, and later New Critical, sense of it. But, when I realized he was mingling, next to objectivity and subjectivity, psychoanalysis and New Criticism, the surprise waned, and gave way to a conviction that *mingling* is the nub of Holland's theory of transformation.

The attempt, however, to mingle, to collapse and fuse binaries may foster, as is the case with Rosenblatt (see Rosenblatt 1978), other distinctions, other binaries; and may eventually reproduce the theoretical fears and anxieties rather than help dissipate them. In *Dynamics*, Holland invested so much in warding off the subjectivity-objectivity theoretical anxiety that he did not pay heed to the rise of another, no less anxiety-ridden binary. If for Holland fusion with the text requires our prior consent to be taken out of ourselves, to suspend our disbelief, to resist reality- testing and intellection, it is ultimately an unconscious journey into the unconscious of the text, an indulgence into fantasy, and an enormous departure from, or exclusion of, the real. This enterprise gives rise to other dualities, other binaries such as the conscious/unconscious binary: Holland insists that the conscious engagement with the text should be kept separate from the unconscious one. This distinction is crucial to Holland's model because he wants to fuse subjectivity and objectivity—a fusion that takes place at the unconscious level of reading. Thus, in pursuit of that fusion, Holland had to maintain a parallel distinction between two moments of reading: the unconscious moment and the conscious one. The question that patently follows is: how can we consciously decide to become unconscious, to fuse with the text, and where can we draw the boundaries of consciousness? Is not lapsing into unconsciousness a very slippery and undetectable slip? If only consciousness could tell me when/ where I am unconscious! One thing, however, is clear: the fusion of text and reader, subject and object, can, according to Holland, take place only at the level of the unconscious, while the distinction between them is sustained tightly at the level of the conscious (DY 310).

We can hardly fail to sense here the exacting pressures which the theoretical anxiety of subjectivity/objectivity has exerted on Holland's theoretical formulations. Holland is ready to sacrifice self-integrity (which he will, as we will see later, recover under the concept of "unity") for the sake of overcoming and mastering this duality—a mastery inhabited at its very heart by the fear of the unmasterable. To solve a conflict between subject and object, between reader and text, Holland is ready to create another within the reader, who is now torn between two moments of response: one conscious, the other unconscious. We are again and again reminded throughout *Dynamics* of this split. It is as if a psychoanalytic response to the text (in the sense of unity with the central fantasy/transformation abstracted by the text) would not obtain unless consciousness is asleep. Indeed, for Holland it really cannot: "*Unconsciously* or half-consciously, we introject [the text], taking it *into us*, at the most *primitive level* of our being [...]. *Consciously*, however, we perceive the text as *separate*, think about it, judge it [...]" (DY 310, italics mine). A split self aspires always for unity. Unable to find it within, it looks for it without; unable to project it, it introjects it. It is the text—in the sense of a conscious management of an unconscious fantasy—that is the prodigy of the unity that the self needs the most. It is in the hope of achieving that unity that a reader is said to "introject," to "fuse," and to unite with the text. Yet, as we have seen before, unity with the text is obtainable only on an unconscious level. The process seems, then, uncompromisingly incommensurate to the rudimentary exigencies of fusion.

It is probably in response to this impasse that Holland has shifted the center of attention from text to reader, to the so-called "identity." It is, after all, the assumption that texts have unity, fantasies, and defenses that has plagued the transformational model. Therefore, starting the other way round—assuming that readers/identities/selves have unity—seems the only way out of the contradictions and inaccuracies the earlier assumption has led to. Apart from that, Holland preserves all the techniques and tactics he developed in *Dynamics*.[6] But even though in the "transactive model" of response the center of attention has, as we will see, changed, the fear of an abysmal lapse into relativism has persisted, if not been aggravated: Holland will be struggling, trying to exorcise, the ghost of the old crone of subjectivity-objectivity.

II - The Transactive Model

> *Whatever form it takes, any [...]* toehold *into* objectivity *makes it possible for some human being to* feel *he has* protected *his self against* falling *into some Other, human or inhuman, a* fear *to which the non-legendary Robert Frost was no stranger,* nor am I. Nor, *I suspect, is* any literary critic.
>
> Please *recognize that in establishing an inextricable proportionality among unity, identity, text and self, and so* denying *claims of* objectivity *that would separate them, I am not positing an isolated,* solipsistic *self.*
>
> —Norman Holland, "Unity Identity Text Self"

Although Holland avers that "interpretation is a function of identity" (TC 340), he obstinately maintains that such a formulation can hardly mushroom into a relativist and solipsist stance in which every interpretation, however far-fetched and unjust, has to be accepted. The above epigraphs testify to the characterologically "hauntological" fears of relativism inherent in literary theories that prize the subjective, the reader, but are anxious to lose, and probably nostalgic to recover, the objective, thc tcxt, as well as othcr objective toeholds such as Fish's interpretive community. In the first epigraph "objectivity" is advanced as a necessary "toehold" or security blanket that helps to mollify the "fears" of falling into "some Other, human or inhuman." In the second epigraph, "objectivity" has become itself the danger one has to avoid, without necessarily sliding into solipsism. Although Holland places a high premium on the reader, his position is that of permanent avoidance of the subjective, of a void dance down the slope of the reader identities. That strategy of avoidance, however, is itself a-void-dance since it serves to claim the dancer, the reader, only to disclaim the dance. In other words, the ontological act of enthroning the reader becomes paradoxically the hauntological idea that undercuts that very endeavor. Thus, Holland's thesis ends up championing as much as spectralizing the reader—that "some Other, human or inhuman."

Holland's address is itself predicated on a primary

sympathetic and acquiescing gesture that we, readers of his theory, have to make. His pleading style and hushed ("please") tone undermine the rigor that is said to sustain his formulations. Harping on the audience is the only alternative left for a theorist to reassure himself and calm the theoretical anxieties generated by subjectivism, solipsism, and relativism combined. Once objectivity is turned into a theoretical fear, the only determiner of Holland's "identity theory" is the timid and trembling "Please." I will argue that, though Holland's "identity theory" has struggled to *insist* on the subjective elements in reading and interpreting as well as to *resist* the theoretical anxieties inherent in such an insistence, it has only provisionally succeeded in fusing such anxiety-ridden binaries as subjectivity-objectivity, and has therefore remained largely determined by the conundrums it has risen to circumvent in the first place. What is even more unfortunate is that much of the 'success' of Holland's postulations would very much depend on whether or not we accept the "Please" of the second epigraph.

Perhaps the emotionally inflected style with which Holland's and also Fish's writings are larded (see the latter's *Is There a Text in This Class?*) stems from their almost waning hope to solve anxiety-ridden questions by either announcing them solved (Fish) or denying their existence (Holland). It becomes all too clear that the more a theory of reading is not anchored in such constricting agents as the author and, especially, the text, the more it begs its own critique, the more it is to be haunted by re-creating that which it seeks to master, outflank, or overpass. Wayne C. Booth might, after all, be right to have cautioned: "A critic who denies the authority either of author or text is trying to fly without a supporting medium" ("Exemplar" 422). But, both Fish and Holland have seen to it so as to fly safely: if Fish has been flying within the orbit of the shared interests and principles of his "interpretive community," Holland has intermittently and ambiguously propelled his theory on notions such as the "feedback" of the text, "the universal DEFT principle," and on the "inter-subjective community." While Fish has dedicated his theoretical postulations to mitigating and deflating the theoretical anxieties that provoke his fellow Anglo-American pluralists into their periodic assaults on reader-response theorists and other deconstructionists, Holland has been very much absorbed in assuaging the anxieties his "identity theory" had given birth to, rather than in responding to his critics. In what follows, I will examine Holland's argument for what he variously calls "identity theory," "transactional theory," or what I would call "sobjectivity."

Starting from *Poems in Persons* (1973), Holland had ceaselessly journeyed into the so-called "transaction," "identity," "identity themes," "feedback," "self," "unity," etc. In an article titled "Unity Identity Text Self," he regards "unity" as something no longer only existing in texts but extending to persons (through introjection). Thus, "unity" has become a characteristic of "identity": "*Identity* is the *unity* I find in a *self* if I look at it as though it were a *text*" (UITS 121, original italics). "Identity" is one of the key tenets of Holland's theoretical thinking after *Dynamics*. In my examination of this term, I will try to interrogate its implications for validity in interpretation and for the subjectivity-objectivity dichotomy, which are, by now, Holland's predictable and recognizable theoretical fears. Holland's concept of identity is very much indebted to Heinz Lichtenstein's explosive work on mother-child identity. For Lichtenstein, every newborn develops, in relation to his mother, to her style and, by definition, to her identity, a "primary identity"—an identity which, albeit "irreversible," remains "capable of infinite variation" (UITS 121).[7] Identity is a mixture of sameness and change, of repetition and difference, of perpetuity and transience, of fixedness and looseness, and of variations on a constant and central "identity theme." Subsequently, every individual can be seen to be "living out variations on an identity theme much as a musician might play out an infinity of variations on a single melody" (120). "'Identity' then equals," for Holland, an "identity theme plus a personal history of variations the individual has played and is playing upon it" (CT 247). In "The Miller's Wife and the Professors," Holland presents us with a seemingly more sophisticated definition of identity: "Identity is ARC—agency, representation, and consequence" (MWP 174). This threefold definition of identity is not, however, very different from the first one, especially in its emphasis on representation, since representing an identity is "not just [a listing of] events but somebody's narrative of those events" (MWP 175). The *narrative* is of paramount importance because it is the only source of variations on an identity theme, variations from which the identity theme is to be ultimately abstracted.[8] Indeed, Holland's identity theory purports to get to a person's identity theme, to formulate a constancy in a person's style by means of "abstracting it from its variations" (120).[9] In "Human Identity," he speaks of "empathy" as a means of studying someone from without, notwithstanding that such a study would always be mediated, and most likely clouded, by the identity of the person performing the study, by the analyzer rather than by the analysand whose paradigmatic shifts in identity might be hammered forcefully by the analyzer into mere variations on a central and permanent theme. As such identity becomes built on the illusion of permanence, and remains thus a permanent illusion.

Response to literature is, for Holland, one way amongst many other *principled* possible ways for individuals "to symbolize and finally replicate" themselves (TC 342). "The overarching principle is: identity re-creates itself, or, to put it another way, style—in the sense of personal style—creates itself" (UITS 124). Within this general principle, Holland isolates four specific modalities whereby readers "perceive DEFTly—through *d*efenses, *e*xpectations, *f*antasies, and *t*ransformations" (NP 338).[10] The reader is said to respond negatively or positively to a work of art. A negative response means that the reader "has not been able to use the work to reenact his own style" (*5RR* 114). Holland neither reflects on the possible objective correlatives that might eventuate in such a failure, nor offers it a cure, but simplistically dismisses it as a failure of transaction, as if transaction were to be exclusively reserved to successful acts of reading. Foreclosing the many corridors for thought that a negative reading experience can give birth to, Holland devotes his interpretive acumen to rewarding experiences of literature—positive responses. When readers respond positively to a text, they are said to actually shape it such that it passes through their adaptive and defensive strategies: readers either adapt their drives to the text, or oppose the pressure those drives exert on them by means of defenses. According to Holland, *defenses* are mechanisms or strategies readers use to ward off anxiety, to deal with fears and wishes, and to ultimately fulfill their *expectations.*[11] Readers have to feel that they are closely matching and bribing into tranquility their defense mechanisms by means of the text; otherwise, they will begin to fend themselves off against it (the text), which might lead them to decline to sign the contract on which the reading transaction is predicated. "This matching is therefore crucial. Without it the individual blocks out the experience. With it the other phases of response take place" (UITS 125).

Contrary to defenses, which have to be matched with minute exactitude, *fantasies* may be gratified with much more leeway. The point is that fantasies proceed in tune with the continuing pressure from the cluster of our drives and desires for gratification while defenses and adaptations "have to oppose and redirect those pressures" (UITS 125). As we match our defenses, we clear out a space for our fantasies to be nurtured and satisfied.[12] Readers are said to project their fantasies on to the work such that the work becomes invested, possessed, and disarmed by them. Fantasies are no longer to be transformationally ensconced in texts and then *introjected* by readers as Holland argues in *Dynamics,* but are now to be rather *projected* by readers on to prostrate texts. Transformations are to be now inwardly carried out by readers rather than outwardly brought about by text: unconscious fantasies that boldly represent adult desires or the childish more bizarre imaginings do normally arouse guilt and anxiety such that readers end up *transforming* them, always by means of the already built-in defenses, from raw fantasies into esthetically, intellectually, morally, or socially decorous experiences. All these four principles or phases are so interlocked and interrelated that Holland compresses them under the single overarching principle, or motto: "identity re-creates itself" (UITS 126). Holland often uses "identity—recreation" and "DEFT" interchangeably. Instead of saying that the reader "reads," or "interprets," the text, Holland would say, somewhat musingly and idiosyncratically, that the reader, or the "literent,"[13] "DEFTs" or "transacts" literature. Thus we end up with such dictums and refrains as: "*literature is transacting literarily, which is rewarded*" (LT 216); "*interpretation is a function of identity*," or "*interpretation re-creates identity*" (TC 340-52).

At this stage, it becomes obvious that Holland's move beyond the axiomatics of transformation developed in *Dynamics* is a shift in focus from the *transformational* model of response to the *transactive* one. In more straightforward terms, this shift is at heart no more than a reversal of emphasis from *introjection* to *projection*, from *text* to *reader*: after having conceived of the text as a force-field of unconscious drives (stimuli) which the reader introjects, or absorbs (response), he now sees the reader as the one who projects (stimulus) his/her own "identity theme" on the text such that the text (response) will submissively respond to it in a form which is ultimately "sensory," and the way the reader feels about it will determine the success or failure of his/her projections. "It is not the book that absorbs us; it is we who absorb the book" (*5RR* 18). In other words, Holland regards the text as "a certain configuration of specks of carbon black on dried wood pulp" until the reader, in the words of Louise Rosenblatt, "poems" it (Rosenblatt 12). But, if for Rosenblatt the reader is contained by the text, it is the text which is, for Holland, contained by the reader. The text as such does not exist; it exists only in terms of each reader's "recreation" of it "in his own mind" (*5RR* 13). If for Fish the text vanishes into the community which is always already in possession of preordained "recipes" for dealing with it, it melts, for Holland, into the reader who ego-syntonically recreates it in astonishingly variable ways. The reader plays the part of "a prince to the sleeping beauty": s/he brings his/her "desires," "lifestyle," and "unconscious loves and fears" to bear on the text.

At this stage, Holland's Transactive theory has to field three questions if it is to swing to its anchor without a flutter. The three questions are raised by Holland himself in his article "The Miller's Wife and the Professors":

> Doesn't this make every reading totally subjective, so that any one reading is as good as another?
> In teaching what do you do about misreadings?
> Don't people change their readings? I know I read *Huckleberry Finn* differently now from the way I did when I was a child (167).

Holland's article undertakes to answer these questions referring to "The Mill"—a poem of his own choice. Obviously, I am most interested in Holland's answer to the first question, partly because it directly addresses the subjective-objective theoretical anxiety and partly because it is the key to answering the other two, which can simply be seen as no more than variations of/on it. The key to Holland's answer to the first question is, however, as I will demonstrate, a psychoanalytically well-established mechanism of defense—*denial*. In *Dynamics*, he ostensibly (and perhaps generously?) provides us with that key: "*Denial can turn anxiety into reassurance*" (299, italics mine). I will argue that Holland's grappling with the subjectivity-objectivity *bête noire*, whose existence he would in the final analysis utterly deny, does not totally lay to rest the still operative and functional distinction between the subjective and objective. "Rigorous" and "scientific" as he claims, his attempt to fuse and blend both horns of the dilemma—which I will capture under the term "*so*bjectivity"—leaves in its wake another dichotomy between the unconscious fusion of the two, sobjectivity, and the unyielding conscious distinction—subjectivity-objectivity—of the two, against which the fusion is to be affirmed and maintained. Meanwhile, it has to be pointed that the denial of the dichotomy has, on the part of Holland, been as much a resort as a logical result following from the other overlapping phases in which Holland aimed at enmeshing or merging subjectivity and objectivity by showing how individuals (subjects) relate to other individuals (the community of subjects),such that an individual's experience of the world, or text (object), no matter how subjective it might sound, is ultimately part and parcel of a collective (intersubjective, transpersonal) experience of the world and, by definition, a valid—in the "obsolete" sense of "objective"—one. Striking a chord between an individual and his community is the argument that Holland ultimately trades on in order to strike another chord between personal experience and objective experience, since the latter is, ontologically speaking, no more than another's (individual) personal experience of the world.

Holland's denial of the dichotomy is the crowning of a lifetime-undiminished hope to make subjectivity and objectivity *relate* to one another. An exclusive espousal of either of them is the danger Holland wants to avoid. Their fusion can, however, ultimately be seen as the version of 'objectivity' one has to stick to, lest one should fall into "some Other." Again and again Holland disassociates himself from either extremes of the dichotomy that has dominated systematic thought since the Cartesian cleaving of the world in twain: the "objective," "out there," and the "subjective," "in here" realities.[14] For Holland, that cleavage has been nurtured by the "illusion of objectivity" as well as by the fear of "dead-end solipsism" (NP 335-39). Although, thanks to the acknowledged feedback of David Bleich, Holland has become more and more aware of the "subjective experience" of "objective texts," such that we sometimes get the impression that he has opted for an extremist subjective stance, he has nonetheless set himself the task "not to sort out subjective from objective but to see how the two combine when we have experiences" (PP 99). But, as adumbrated earlier, the attempt to combine subjectivity and objectivity, and to ultimately deny both of them, was preceded and paved by the contextualization, so to speak, of the reader within a collectivity, a move to which I now turn.

In "The Miller's Wife and the Professors," he avers that transactive criticism aspires to blur the dividing lines between subjectivity and objectivity, to embrace a "fusion tactic" instead of a "fission" one.[15] Accordingly, a reading may start immersed in subjectivity, but will end up striking a cord with objectivity. Citing David Bleich, Holland reiterates that an answer to a given question—for instance, "what is the most important single word in the poem? Why?"—"begins in complete subjectivity and is then transformed into judgments that appear to be objective" (MWP 168). Still, Holland sees more in the answers to such a question than Bleich was able to infer: "There must be more helpful metaphors than 'begins' and 'ends' for developing the relation" (MWP 169). After a detailed study of the professors' answers to such a question, Holland concludes: "*Both objective and subjective responses emerge from a process in which subjectivity shapes objectivity*" (MWP 173, original italics). The reader re-creates his/her identity theme through the experience of the text, rather than simply filling in the gaps the text leaves by means of the text itself, which is supposed to bring within its core the blueprint of its later concretization(s). For Holland, Iser's model, a model in which "the bulk of the response [is] controlled by the poem and the reader simply fills in some inessential gaps," does not adequately and accurately capture what actually goes on in the act of response: readers may simply refuse to fill in the gaps left by the text, and even when they do, they will hardly feel or act within the limits of the text. As such, readings will proliferate and differ depending on the peculiarities of each reader's identity and the contingencies of the act of reading, but they will still end up in resonance with the principles, techniques, and strategies of a given "interpretive community" (the latter concept has been popularized by Fish).[16] We end up with a reading that "*feels right*" (MWP 173), but is not necessarily the only right one.

> I suggest that we all, as readers, use shared techniques to serve highly personal, even idiosyncratic, ends. We put hypotheses out from ourselves into the text [...] what the poem "did" depended on what we asked it to do. That in turn depended on what we brought to it: what questions what expectations, what prejudices, what stock responses, what trust, what codes and rules (MWP 174).

Thus, if Fish sees response, or interpretation, as already decided, beginning and ending within the hold of strategies and principles of a given interpretive community, Holland sees it as dynamic and circular, starting from shared techniques, dissolving into the idiosyncrasies of each reader, and finally emerging in a community of subjectivities.

To move from the "subjective" to the "collective" to "consensus," Holland accepts, albeit provisionally, Bleich's "negotiation" as a bridge (*5RR* 291).[17] But, he seems to confer more emphasis on "tenacity" rather than on "negotiation"— "Tenacity, not negotiation, is the human style, for we use the ideas we hold to re-create our very identities" (NP 342).[18] By virtue of its resoluteness or tenacity, an interpretation comes to be intersubjectively accepted or validated. Furthermore, an interpretation gains in tenacity not only through intersubjective negotiation, as Bleich would argue, but notably through its consideration of the "re-active" "feedback" of the text in question. It is ultimately, as Bleich astutely points out, this persistent clinging to a certain "objectivity" that makes him and Holland part company. Yet, Holland would not consider the recognition of the "objectivity" of the text as separate and different from the assertion of the subjectivity of the reader. It is neither subjectivity nor objectivity the focus of Holland's transactive criticism, but the commingling and the blending of the two—that which I have called "sobjectivity."

I think that the terms on which Holland makes claims to validity in interpretation are, if any, the terms of sobjectivity: "The question is not *whether* interpretation is objective or subjective but *how* it is both" (TC 337, original italics). On the one hand, we get the impression that Holland is not explicitly concerned with validity in interpretation even when he situates the reader within a collectivity of subjectivities; on the other hand, we sometimes come across passages where he forcefully speaks of text and reader as fusing into each other such that that fusion—sobjectivity—becomes the only granter of a "valid interpretation." Rather than speaking of collectivity in relation to validity in interpretation as Fish did, Holland exuberantly speaks of it to further stress the collectivity's difference against itself: collectivity is sameness in difference: because we are all different from each other, at least we share that difference. But that "sharability" enhances differences instead of reducing them. Therefore, it provides no breakthrough for interpretive disputes. For Holland, to look for a "correct" reading is tantamount to believing that there are "correct" and "incorrect" desires, or fantasies. Hence, Holland does not seem to be very cooperative and sympathetic to quests for validity in interpretation because he deems it useless to attempt to regulate reading, given the privacy and irreducible difference of each reader's mind and drives.

By and large, in "The Miller's Wife and the Professors" interpretation is still regarded as a function of identity tried against the "feedback" of the text: "subjectivity questions objectivity, thereby enabling objectivity to respond to and shape subjectivity" (MWP 174). Allowing for feedback, he now calls his identity theory the "identity-cum-feedback model": "identity frames the hypotheses, identity hears the return, and identity *feels* the discrepancy between that return and one's inner standards" (MWP 176). Stimulated by the reader's hypotheses, the poem responds favorably or unfavorably: in both cases it is the reader who figures out whether the response rights his/her hypotheses or not. In very broad terms, the reader starts with what is publicly available as a "sharable promptuary"—the words-on-the-page—and ends up with an interpretation that looks as much idiosyncratic as sharable, as much original and resonant with his/her identity theme as common and resonant with the widespread resources such as conventions, other critics, common sense, literary history, and the dictionary.[19]

In the final analysis, Holland escapes (or so he claims) the tension of the first question by characterizing it as irrelevant:

> It is equally falsifying to assume that a reading could be totally subjective or more subjective than another reading, as the question does. Hence, there is no way to answer such a question. Probably, I am not saying all readings are equally or totally or even partially subjective. *I am claiming that one cannot characterize readings as subjective or objective at all* (MWP 177, italics mine).

A lifetime meditation on and wrestling with an anxiety-ridden dichotomy has taught Holland that both subjectivity and objectivity are chimerical concepts we will never be in full possession of, and therefore we will do ourselves a favor if we just deny their existence.[20] For Holland, since one is always committed to "an honest search for a 'valid' interpretation, one that will command assent from others besides [oneself]," one is by definition pursuing an "objective" goal, "yet at the same time [one knows that one] can only [reach it] in a way which is wholly authentic for [one]—'subjective'" (TPP 231). Subjectivity and objectivity are inextricably intertwined, inter-animated and interlocked such that the vestiges of their autonomous existence can hardly be identified. In a nutshell, subjectivity and objectivity as two separate entities do not, for Holland, exist.

Surely, "*Denial can turn anxiety into reassurance*," but a denial of this kind is too radical to be reassuring. Holland himself conceives of this denial as a more radical enterprise than the extremist, subjectivist project undertaken by David Bleich. "Bleich," Holland writes, "has simply not been radical enough" (NP 339). Not only is Holland's enterprise radical in nature, but also in aspirations: it claims to talk "rigorously" about individuals, to abstract their identity themes from their literary responses and interpretations.[21]

Holland does indeed in *5 Readers Reading* study five readers' interpretations of short stories, and manages to extract their identity themes. But, if we agree to Holland's fundamental principle—identity re-creates itself through experience—how can we 'scientifically' and 'rigorously' draw the lines between the identity being abstracted and the identity performing the abstraction? In other words, if we concede to Holland's givens that a reader reads a text, and his/her reading, so to speak, reads him/her, does not that put the whole enterprise—abstracting the reader's identity theme—in peril, given that the analyzer's abstraction of a given reader's identity theme will in turn be determined, and possibly clouded and distorted, by the analyzer's identity theme? Any interpretation of a person's identity theme becomes thus itself an interpretation of the identity theme of the interpreter: the reader reads, and his/her reading reads him/her, the psychoanalytic interpreter analyses the reader's personality to abstract the reader's identity theme, and his/her analysis analyses him/her, and so on we go regressively *ad infinitum*.[22] Holland has grown aware of this confused and confusing state of affairs, but he scarcely accounts for its deep implications for his identity theory. On the contrary, he contents himself with calling it "mutual interpretation" while

I think it should be called "mutually exclusive interpretation": the identity carrying out the abstraction process of another's identity does ultimately threaten to undermine the analysand's identity in the very process of mastering and re-presenting it. If interpretation is a function of identity as Holland claims, then he has to admit that the identity interpreting would always, being at once the filter and the filtering identity, tamper with the identity of the reader, if not override it altogether.

Can we possibly speak, let alone *rigorously*, about individuals under the assumption that our speech will have to be filtered through, and traversed in variable degrees by, our identity theme?[23] As I have shown, one would even be more skeptical about such an enterprise with such an assumption in mind than a wholehearted subscriber. Yet, Holland would still obstinately hold to his position by introducing a new device, which he calls "empathy": "It is entirely possible," he claims, "to formulate a constancy in your personal style—from outside you but through empathy" (HI 454). Here, Holland leads us into a contradiction: after assuming that each person has a unique idiosyncratic style, he now conceives of the possibility of getting to that style through empathy such that the personal, once we assume we can get to it, becomes divested of the personal.[24] Apart from that, the endeavor is even more complicated by the following assumption: "since we *can* talk rigorously about individuals, we lose no rigor by being personal" (HI 454, original italics). But, do we not lose rigor by being personal? In being personal we may, it bears repeating, lose the identity we are after by confusing it with our own. But, let us examine more closely Holland's quasi-scientific outburst and the claimed rigor of the personal constituent of it.

Contrary to his claims to vigor and scientificity, Holland is constantly eaten up by fear of anarchy and possessed by losing his toehold on objectivity, such that he has always to square up every new problem born out of his lifetime entanglement with the subjectivity-objectivity binary, but it is as if with every new problem the search for the key comes, as T.S. Eliot would have it, no more than a confirmation of a prison. Although he intends his identity theory to amount to a science of personal relationships, he is reluctant to admit of the solipsistic and subjective turn it will logically slide into. He, therefore, oscillates between the demands of the personal and the exigencies of the impersonal: he is both *insistent* on and *resistant* to the personal. Having already illustrated the many ambivalent, shaky, but sometimes extreme ways in which he insists on the subjective, I will now turn to expose his resistance to the reader by examining some of the concessions he makes in favor of the impersonal. Such concessions undercut his claims to studying individuals rigorously.

First, the rigor is vitiated by his admittance of the possibility of misreadings.[25] But, having been broached explicitly only lately in his career, in an article entitled "The Miller's Wife and the Professors" (1986), his conception of misreading does not seem to have been among the assumptions of his identity theory. On the contrary, it seems to have come at a later stage when identity theory has been well-developed without allowing a space from which misreadings could be dealt with. This can even be deduced from his fuzzy and circuitous account of misreading: like Rosenblatt, Holland claims that, "a misreading would correspond to a wrong hypothesis or a wrong application of a right hypothesis" (MWP 179). To avoid misreadings, therefore, Holland recommends that teachers teach hypotheses and put students on an equal footing: "Reader-response teaching addresses the person as an applier of hypotheses, how that person feels, and what that person says when those hypotheses are applied. Hence reader-response teaching points away from a critique of the hypotheses themselves or the ways they are applied" (MWP 178). But how can one teach students to make relevant hypotheses without distinguishing them from the irrelevant ones? By and large, Holland minimizes the occurrence of misreadings because "Too often teachers take it for granted—as part of a residual belief, I think, that modes of reading are self-evident, not to be questioned, eternal verities, linguistic completeness, objective" (MWP 179).

Second, to claim to be able to study rigorously texts as/and individuals, and vice versa, is further attenuated by the possibility of change in one's reading of a given text over time. Holland argues that one changes one's reading of *Huckleberry Finn* over time without necessarily having to change one's identity. Studying the points of sameness and difference would still be accounted for within the same pattern—identity: "It is not the phraser who can affect an AC-identity but the person with an AC-identity who can affect its phrasing" (MWP 175). This argument is very similar to Hirsch's monolithic explanation of the plurality of readings: Hirsch argues that authorial meaning is constant and single while its *significance* may change through time. In the same manner, Holland argues that for every individual there is a constant essence—identity theme—on which s/he plays variations through time. But, if Holland's identity theory purports to be capable of abstracting an author's identity, through which the meaning of his/her texts can later be grasped, it does not preclude the possibility of abstracting that identity differently, according to the abstracter's identity. Here we confront again the residual difficulty accompanying any attempt to get to an author's original meaning. Even identity theory is helpless in front of this difficulty: if Holland claims to be able to abstract my identity theme and my essence through my readings, without precluding the fact that his identity theme might come into play in that very assay, then my identity will be constructed differently according to the differences in the identities of the abstracters—so much so that I will end up with so many accounts of my essence (identity theme) that I would hardly put my fingers on the right theme pertaining to my identity without myself deploying in the very process my own identity, and the vortex widens and devolves into an *ad infinitum mise en abyme*. What is more, perceiving of identity as a dyad of an unchanging identity theme compounded by changing variations rules out the possibility of any changes of the identity theme itself through the constant play of the variations and the "formative" feedback of the text.[26] Finally, if Holland claims to read selves as texts, to holistically abstract from texts that identity a theme which confers unity on them, he is pretty much reasserting and reappropriating precisely that unity postulate he sets out, in the transactive model, to import from the realm of the textual to the realm of the individual. In other words, if Holland attempts to treat personal behavior as a text from which he can abstract an identity theme, he will eventually be replaying the motto of textual unity dear to American New Criticism, a motto which he started by rejecting in favor of the unity of the self dear to American ego-psychology.[27] Holland textualizes the self as a step toward presenting its unity that which he will ultimately translate into identity: "*Identity* is the *unity* I find in a *self* if I look at it as though it were a *text*" (UITS 121, original italics).

Third, although Holland is insistent on the necessity of acknowledging the personal in literary interpretation and criticism, his insistence does not dawn without casting a certain gloom on the validity of his theoretical foundations, a gloom he would constantly be pressured to dispel by hamstringing the reader at the very act of reasserting his/her centrality to the model of transactive response. Holland has been, as we have argued, wrestling throughout his career with the subjectivity-objectivity *bête noire*, a dichotomy whose existence he has denied, repressed, and ironically eternalized, edified, and propagated. The subjectivity-objectivity dichotomy—the repressed/denied—has returned: Holland has never ceased to make his transactive theory answerable, in a quasi-moderate way, as much to the 'subjective' as to the 'objective' exigencies. Reading through his numerous articles, one can spot several variations on a constant claim: to view his transactive model of response as an acknowledgement of the *inseparability* of the personal and the impersonal, the subjective and the objective, the individual and the communal. But, to acknowledge that the personal and impersonal are inextricably mixed should proceed by demonstrating that they are treated on an equal footing by the transaction. Yet, has Holland treated the impersonal and personal equally in his polemical theorization of their transaction? Or has Holland actually taken for granted the inevitability of the impersonal and gone on defending the necessity of the personal?

It seems that Holland has been more insistent on the personal than on the impersonal. When, however, he senses that the personal has become overwhelming, he forcefully, though casually, provides us with instances of resistance to the personal.[28] Instead of allowing subjectivity and objectivity to fuse, he has actually bivouacked on both extremes at different times. Thus, when he speaks about the share of the personal in transaction, we get the impression that everything is ultimately personal (a function of our identity), and when he speaks about the share of the impersonal (in the sense of inter-personal and objective) in that very transaction, we get the impression that Holland's reader is as much the plaything of his/her community as Fish's. Jockeying for an in-between position has been Holland's ultimate goal, yet the realization of its practical unfeasibility has but energized the desire for it, which has eventually made the belief of having already attained it all too desirable and ego-syntonic. Sometimes, Holland's tone loses the rigor and scientism characteristic of the so-called "science of personal transactions," and lapses into a pleading and soliciting whisper.

In "Unity Identity Text Self," Holland tries to fill in the gaps between these four terms, and implores us in an anxiety ridden tone to accept his enterprise:

> Please recognize that in establishing an inextricable proportionality among unity, identity, text, and self, and so denying claims of objectivity that would separate them, I am not positing an isolated, solipsistic self. Just the opposite, in fact I said I would try to fill in the white spaces in my enigmatic title. Let me now reassure you that I am indeed filling them in, and you are too, and all people are, all the time—including the hardest of 'hard' scientists (131).

The least we can learn from this quote is that Holland has qualms about the "tenacity" of his argument and the success of his already-in-place endeavor of filling in the gaps between the above-mentioned concepts. Further, if we follow Holland's logic that when one interprets, one's interpretation interprets one, we can safely and analogously maintain that Holland theorizes, and his theory 'theorizes' him; that is, reads, interprets and re-enacts his identity theme. If for Holland one can read identity as a text and abstract another person's identity theme from the variations he plays on it, one can by now conclude that Holland's identity theme is to mingle, mix, commingle, fuse, interrelate, etc., self and text, identity and unity, the personal and the interpersonal, the subjective and objective. These inclinations to fuse are, as I have argued, variations on the pattern of *insistence* on and *resistance* to the reader. Insistence and resistance have to be checked constantly in order to prevent any inadvertent imbalance. But, it seems to me that the overarching stress falls more on subjectivity than on objectivity, especially in passages in which Holland ghostly writes on the edge of solipsism. Feeling that the "tenacity" of his argument has been vitiated by his unbalanced handling of subjectivity and objectivity, Holland wants to compensate for that through his Fish-like reassuring style.

Certainly, a tenacious argument set on terra firma would hardly need any kind of appeal to the audience (to us readers and critics alike) to command recognition and acceptance. Phrases such as "Please" and "Let me now reassure you" remind us of Fish's anxiety-eaten "consoling—not to worry" (Fish 321), which smack respectively of stumblings and fumblings. One may ask: why should Holland and Fish feel the urge to reassure us? Rather, why should they be concerned such that they directly ask us to be reassured? This is most probably an indirect avowal that they have failed to come to terms with the theoretical anxieties they have set out to mollify. Opting for such reassuring styles is ultimately nothing but symptomatic of anxiety itself. Of course, one does not expect wrestling with theoretical anxieties to be an easy matter; much less a game one can win. Battalions of critics have not been able to pronounce the final word on questions of validity, objectivity, and the likewise theoretical anxieties. Each critic or school has tried to answer these anxieties from its angle of vision, which has resulted in different, disputable, yet often incommensurable, answers. Each answer remains therefore incommensurate with the exerting and exacting complexity of these anxieties.

Notes

1. Holland does not seem to draw clear-cut distinctions between texts of literature and jokes. Indeed, he always reminds us that his theory is,

more than anything else, an extension of Freud's analyses of jokes to literature.

2. In "Literature as Transaction," he states: "The literary transaction is like a contract: you are always free to break it, but when you signed it, you changed the price of that freedom [...]. We humans are always, paradoxically, both free and bound to choose" (215).
3. Holland's psychological approach to literature is by and large concerned with the function of literature inwardly, "in persons," and not on the outward reality.
4. In *5 Readers Reading*, Holland speaks retrospectively of his transformational model as a fiction which he no longer deems useful because it squarely put the stress on the text to the detriment of the reader: "I often spoke in *Dynamics* as though [...] *fantasies and their transformations were embodied in the literary work*, as though the work itself acted like a mind. This, of course, is no more than a useful fiction and maybe less. A useful fiction certainly. Useful? I now think not" (*5RR* 19 my italics).
5. I have taken the term "defenses" from Holland's "dictionary of fantasy." He employs it (more so in *5 Readers Reading*) to describe those defensive mechanisms which the reader adopts to mollify tensions and anxieties. The implication behind this is that if a reader has recourse to those defenses, why not Holland himself, he being in the grip of a theoretical anxiety? We shall be commenting on this turn Holland's logic falls back on whenever he finds himself in front of a major theoretical anxiety.
6. In *5 Readers Reading*, he says: "Essentially, *Dynamics* has stood up rather well, requiring only the modification—or reminder, really—that psychological processes like fantasies or defenses do not happen in books but in people" (xii-xii). In the same book he dramatically moves to categorize his *Dynamics*'s theory as a "fiction" that he no longer deems altogether "useful" (see 17). Here and there, he owes much to David Bleich who aptly pointed out to him that, "people do not fantasy [...] stories do not have defense mechanisms, and plays do not sublimate—but people do" ("A Transactive Account of Transactive Criticism" 181).
7. According to Lichtenstein, entertaining a kind of a relation or a "meshing" with the mother creates "in" the infant a "primary identity," "a zero point which must precede all other developments" and "an invariant whose transformations would provide the developmental sequences with an unchanging inner form or core" (see HI 452). For Lichtenstein, a study of the "character" or "personality" of another person proceeds by abstracting an invariant from "the infinite

sequence of bodily and behavioral transformations during the whole life of an individual" (qtd in UITS 120).

8. In addition to identity as "representation," identity as "agency" consists of "putting out hypotheses from our bodies into the world," or the text which answers them back in a way, the way we feel will about which determine the success or failure of the hypotheses. "Identity is so therefore the culminating *consequence* of those perceptions and actions" (MWP 174).
9. Here, Holland is much inspired by Yeats' "fancy that there is one myth for every man, which, if we but knew it, would make us understand all he did and thought" (qtd in "Human Identity" 453).
10. Holland offers a detailed account of these principles in chapter five of *5 Readers Reading*. In a later article titled "A Transactive Account of Transactive Criticism," however, he comes up with a larger list of ten principles that purportedly govern transactive criticism. I prefer to stick here to the former four because they translate aptly and adequately the core thought from which the other ten are developed. We must remember that even these four principles are, as Holland himself would have it, only variations on a constant, unchanging essence, theme, or principle: identity recreates itself through experience.
11. For Holland, adaptation is "the progressive, constructive, and maturational mastery of inner drives and outer reality," while defense is the "mechanism put into action automatically and unconsciously at a signal of danger from within or without. Thus, the two terms may overlap in any given situation" (*5RR* 115).
12. Fantasy and defense are, according to Holland, "interlocked" in literary response because of their deep-seated relation in the mind: our early stages of development are ambivalent; we witness love and hate; we wish things as much as we fear them (*5RR* 120).
13. In "The New Paradigm," he complains that the concept "reader" remains very restricted to what can be read, and therefore, preempting the spoken. Further, Holland is in search of a term that captures someone responding re-creatively to literature, and he suggests the term "literent" (336) inasmuch as it "defines a person as person-in-relation-to-text" (LT 216).
14. For a detailed account of his disassociation with both extremes of the dichotomy, see his article, "The New Paradigm: Subjective or Transactive?"
15. To adopt a "fission tactic" is to assume that "whatever is subjective or personal subtracts something from objective reality and therefore the subject has to be taken out." To adopt a "fusion tactic" is to assume

that there is a gap between mind and nature, and between subject and object, which one is to close. Holland will adopt the fusion tactic for a certain time before he, radically enough, refuses the existence of the gap altogether, as we will further demonstrate: "Is there a gap? I think not" (see TC 34-335).

16. "The paradox of my existence is that I am sole and whole—yet dual;" "I feel self-contained, yet I am de-centered, displaced, merged into others outside myself;" "I have an experience that is wholly and uniquely my own. Yet I feel the need—and I *necessarily* do—to set that experience in a community of others" (CT 250).

17. By provisionally accepting "intersubjective negotiation," Holland falls partly into line with David Bleich, who strongly believes that "negotiation regulates whether any experience is considered the same or different among different people." Having "the subjective paradigm" as the "operating assumption," Bleich believes that "The degree to which knowledge is not part of a community is the degree to which it is not knowledge at all" (see his *Subjective Criticism* 295-96). But, Holland will disassociate himself from such utter regression into subjectivity since it threatens to become for Holland no more than "a thought-stopper" (NP 339).

18. Holland, here, draws on Max Planck's "wisdom": "A new truth does not triumph by convincing its opponents and making them see the light, but rather because its opponents die" (qtd in "The New Paradigm" 342). One can now clearly distinguish between three supposedly different ways through which an interpretation comes to be accepted by the community from which it has emerged: Fish's "persuasion," Bleich's "negotiation," and Holland's "tenacity." Thus, if for Fish we usually proceed by persuading other members to the principles and strategies our interpretation has adopted, and if for Bleich we simply "intersubjectively negotiate" our interpretations so that a "consensus" may be reached, for Holland the "tenacious" interpretation will simply predominate.

19. In "Literature as Transaction," Holland seeks to merge the "out there" with the "in here" in the process of transaction, which ultimately mingles choice and destiny, freedom and responsibility: "At the highest level, then, in transacting literature I assert my own destiny. I re-assert my free, personal re-creation of self and text precisely by requiring of the text consequences of my freedom. I plunge myself into a dialectic; yet, however the text replies, I retain final responsibility, for I am always free—and bound—to do with the materials of the work what will express my inner nature" (LT 216-17).

20. Realizing that "subjectivity and objectivity lie along a kind of win-here-lose-there continuum" in which the more objective you are, the

more removed from pure experience you tend to be and vice versa, Holland opts for a categorical denial of the existence of the dichotomy altogether: "'objective reality' and 'pure experience' are themselves only *useful fictions, vanishing points* we approach but never reach" (PP 2, italics mine).

21. In an article titled "A Transactive Account of Transactive Criticism," Holland claims that as long as identity theory uses a theme "to search for new evidence or to frame new hypotheses," it is a "scientific" theory "even though it does not lead to numbers or predictions" (183). On several other occasions, he refers to his theory as "the science of personal relationships," or "the science of personal transactions" (187).
22. Susan Suleiman speaks of a "worm in the apple": "if identity replicates itself in interpretation, and if identity itself can only be arrived at through interpretation, then the enterprise whereby the analyst seeks to demonstrate the validity of the first statement is hopelessly circular—it can never fail but it can never be proven either, for proof would require that the identity of the reader be definable independently of the interpreting identity of the analyst" (30). Clearly, Suleiman's remark cuts the ground from under the kind interpretation Holland postulates.
23. In another instance, Holland speaks of identity itself as a barrier: "Identity is a way to be you or me, and only in that sense is it limiting" (TC 339).
24. Holland seems to follow earlier arguments by either rectifying or correcting them: identity is, for instance, no longer regarded as unique: "Identity [...] is not unique" (TC 339). Thus, the same identity theme may obtain for different persons. But, whether an identity theme can be both unique and sharable is a question Holland does not trouble himself to answer.
25. Holland does not seem to make a difference between misreading a text and misreading a person's identity, because he vigorously wants to read persons as texts whose unity is formulated through identity. He often speaks of his study in relation to holistic and New Critical theories (sometimes Hermeneutics) inasmuch as these schools are at least concerned with the unity of the parts with the whole (design/text). In identity theory, the unity is formulated through identity, through variations on a single theme.
26. Mark Bracher and Marshall Alcorn maintain that "the variations of one's identity theme are at least as important as the theme itself; in fact such variations constitute nothing less than a *reformation of the self*" (343, italics mine). These writers complain that Holland's model of identity re-creation tends to understand all response to literature

as projective, pleasure-gratifying, yet not formatively influencing the self. They maintain that reading is as projective as it is introjective, as pleasure-gratifying as it is didactic and reformative of the self. Thus, the variations are as important as the identity theme, in the sense that their variation may eventuate in a paradigmatic shift in a given identity theme.

27. In a "Prolegomena to a Theory of Reading," Culler criticizes Holland for his hammering appropriation of the New Critical tenet of "textual unity" so as to fit it to the exigencies of American ego-psychology: "Rejecting as a fallacious oversimplification the notion of a literary work as a harmonious whole in which everything expresses a central theme, Mr. Holland proceeds blithely to treat the behavior of an individual as the expression of a consistent central essence. This is, of course, the way of the American ego psychology, which can be shown to be a vulgarized and sentimentalized version of the New Criticism" (55).

28. In "A Transactive Account of Transactive Criticism," he avers that transactive theory is, first, precisely the opposite of a theory that assumes that only the self can be known—solipsism. Second, "it squarely contradicts the idea that literary knowledge takes place wholly within an individual's mind, unaffected by the external world (is 'subjective')" (185). Yet, to what extent does Holland's theory contradict the solipsistic or subjective traps if it unflaggingly assumes that interpretation is a function of identity and if it insists that that identity is unique? Holland's self-assured triumphalism over such traps does not resonate: it only amounts to a simple and dry answer that may ultimately contradict itself. Even the limits he puts on individuals do not so much spring from the "objective text" as from other individuals—"intersubjective validity" (NP 345).

Works Cited

Barthes, Roland. *S/Z.* Trans. Richard Miller. New York: Hill and Wang, 1974.

——. "The Death of the Author." *Modern Criticism and Theory.* Ed. David Lodge. New York: Longman, 1988. 168-72.

Bleich, David. "The Subjective Character of Interpretation." *Twentieth Century Literary Theory.* Ed. K.M. Newton. New York: St. Martin's Press, 1997. 200-03.

Booth, Wayne C. "Notes and Exchanges [with René Wellek]." *Critical Inquiry* 5.4 (1977): 203-06.

——. "'Preserving the Exemplar': or, How Not to Dig Our Own Graves." *Critical Inquiry* 3 (1977): 407-23.

Bracher, Mark and Marshall Alcorn. "Literature, Psychoanalysis, and the Re-Formation of the Self: A New Direction for Reader-Response Theory." *PMLA* 100.3 (May 1985): 342-54.

Burke, Kenneth. "Formalist Criticism: Its Principles and Limits" *Twentieth Century Literary Theory.* Ed. K.M. Newton. New York: St. Martin's Press, 1997. 33-34.

Culler, Jonathan. "Prolegomena to a Theory of Reading." *The Reader in the Text.* Ed. Susan Suleiman and Inge Crosman. Princeton: Princeton UP, 1980. 46-66.

Fish, Stanley Eugene. *Is There a Text in This Class?* Cambridge: Harvard UP, 1980.

Hirsch, Eric Donald. *Validity in Interpretation.* New Heaven and London: Yale UP, 1967.

Holland, Norman. (*5RR*) *5 Readers Reading.* New Haven: Yale UP, 1975.

——. (CT) "Criticism as Transaction." *What is Criticism?* Ed. Paul Hernadi. Bloomington: Indiana UP, 1981. 242-52.

——. (DY) *The Dynamics of Literary Response.* New York: Oxford UP, 1968.

——. (HI) "Human Identity." *Critical Inquiry* 4 (1978): 451-69.

——. (LT) "Literature as Transaction." *What is Literature?* Ed. Paul Hernadi. Bloomington: Indiana UP, 1978. 206-18.

——. (MWP) "The Miller's Wife and the Professors: Questions about the Transactive Theory of Reading." *Contexts for Criticism.* Ed. Donald Keesey. San Francisco: Mayfield Publishing Company, 1987. 166-94.

——. (NP) "The New Paradigm: Subjective or Transactive." *New Literary History: A Journal of Theory and Interpretation* 7 (1976): 335-46.

——. (PP) *Poems in Persons: An Introduction to the Psychoanalysis of Literature.* New York: Norton, 1973.

——. (TC) "Transactive Criticism: Re-creation through Identity." *Criticism: Quarterly for Literature and the Arts* 18 (1976): 334-52.

——. (TATC) "A Transactive Account of Transactive Criticism." *Poetics: International Review for the Theory of Literature 7* (1978): 177-89.

——. (TPP) "Three Phases of Psychoanalysis." *Critical Inquiry* 3 (1976): 221-33.

——. (UITS) "Unity Identity Text Self." *Reader-Response Criticism.* Ed. Jane P. Tompkins. Baltimore: The Johns Hopkins UP, 1980. 118-33.

——. (WSDR) "The 'Willing Suspension of Disbelief' Revisited." *The Centennial Review* 5.12 (1966): 221-31.

——. "Reading and Identity: A Psychoanalytic Revolution." *Twentieth Century Literary Theory.* Ed. K.M. Newton. New York: St. Martin's Press, 1997. 143-47.

——. "Stanley Fish, Stanley Fish." *Genre* 10 (1977): 433-41.

——. "Literary Interpretation and Three Phases of Psychoanalysis." *Critical Inquiry* 5.3 (1976): 221-33.

——. "Re-covering 'The Purloined Letter': Reading as a Personal Transaction." *The Reader in the Text.* Ed. Susan Suleiman and Inge Crosman. Princeton: UP, 1980. 350-70.

Iser, Wolfgang. *The Implied Reader: Patterns of Communication in Prose Fiction from Bunyan to Beckett.* Baltimore and London: The Johns Hopkins UP, 1974.

Richards, I. A. "Poetry and Beliefs." *Twentieth Century Literary Theory.* Ed. K.M. Newton. New York and London: St. Martin's Press, 1997. 22-26.

Rosenblatt, Louise Michelle. *The Reader, the Text, the Poem.* Southern Illinois: UP, 1978.

Suleiman, Susan R. "Introduction: Varieties of Audience-Oriented Criticism." *The Reader in the Text.* Ed. Susan R. Suleiman and Inge Crosman. Princeton: UP, 1980. 3-45.

✪✪✪

4

Irony in Relevance Theory: Recurrent Features, Critical Stances and Possible Research Trends

MARÍA ÁNGELES RUIZ MONEVA

Irony has been one of the recurrent topics of research and of immense interest to relevance theoreticians for more than two decades (1978-2000). Although the theory has been consistently proposed (Sperber & Wilson 1986), the standpoints reached or maintained so far can be hardly considered conclusive. This paper attempts a brief analysis of the main recurrent features of the relevance approach to irony and focuses upon the contributions that can be made to shed light on and improve the analysis and comprehension of such a complex communicative phenomenon as irony.

1. A Panorama of the State of the art Relevance Approaches to Irony

The discussion of irony within the framework of relevance theory is in fact one of the earliest developments of this approach, previous to the explicit formulation of the theory itself as a whole, which has continued up to the present moment. It is probably not by chance that the topic of irony, a rhetorical device characterised by its great versatility,[1] has been one of the major concerns of a theory of meaning and communication which insists upon the need to overcome the shortcomings of the traditional or code model. This has led relevance theoreticians to adopt as one of the central tenets of their approach the need to rely on inference when it comes to accounting for the way in which the addressee attempts to grasp the meaning conveyed by his interlocutor. The role of inference has been one of the central tenets in contemporary pragmatics, ever since Grice (1971, 1957) distinguished between what he termed as *natural* and *non-natural meaning.* Relevance theory has tended to insist upon the necessary inferential nature of communication, whereby the addressee does not limit himself to decoding the message conveyed or encoded by the speaker—as traditional theories of communication had assumed—but goes further to infer the meaning which may have been intended by his interlocutor. Nevertheless, this assumption further sets the problem that it may be questioned how far the addressee is assumed to follow and infer the meaning intended by the speaker, or else derive his own interpretation and reach his own conclusions. As Leo Hickey notes: "Once the Speaker has placed an utterance at the disposal of the Hearer, it can be used by the latter in any way and for any purpose he chooses (within very broad limits of semantic and pragmatic meaning), irrespective of the purpose for which it was first intended" (Hickey 324-25).

In this paper it will be assumed that context, and its access and choice by the communicators, as the theory of relevance predicts, can be the possible means of accounting for the way in which both the communication and understanding of irony unfold, and also for the processes undertaken by addresser and addressee, so that their perception and knowledge of the world improves as a result of the communicative process. But before these points are developed, a survey of the main contributions to the study of irony from the perspective of relevance theory is introduced in the present section.

A basic claim maintained by Sperber and Wilson, which will exert some influence on their approach to irony and to rhetoric in general, is their rejection of the traditionally established dichotomy between *literal* and *figurative language.* This distinction goes back in time in fact to the origins of rhetoric, and has been questioned, for different reasons, by authors such as Sperber and Wilson (1981) or Stanley Fish (1989).[2]

The reasons why Sperber and Wilson reject the notion of

figurative are: if the intended, "figurative" meaning of an utterance is taken to rely upon that of a previous, "literal" one, as a result, the intended meaning would be redundant, uninformative, and would not be accessible unless the addressee were acquainted beforehand with the speaker's opinion.

Authors such as Fish (1989) have also questioned the notion of figurative meaning. The reasons for this are that for him both literal or figurative meanings are interpretations, which in turn implies that the literal meaning is often a reading which is imposed upon a text by the canon: it is, therefore, just another reading and cannot be taken as the basis for any other interpretation.

In their earliest proposals on irony, Sperber and Wilson (1981, 1978) rely upon a certain distinction referred to by Lyons (1977) so as to account for the mechanisms by which the speaker expresses her attitude of dissociation towards the propositional content of her utterance.[3] This contrast, which Sperber and Wilson apply to irony, is between *use* and *mention*: "USE of an expression involves reference to what the expression refers to; MENTION involves reference to the expression itself" (1981: 303, capitals as in the original).[4] The third term which is important to understand Sperber and Wilson's concept of irony is *echo*, very closely related to the expression of a certain attitude, which allows the speaker to make manifest her reaction towards the information she has been acquainted with:

> These interpretations achieve relevance by informing the hearer of the fact that the speaker has in mind what so-and-so said, and has a certain attitude to it: the speaker's interpretation of so-and-so's thought is relevant in itself. When interpretations achieve relevance in this way, we will say that they are *echoic* [...] (Sperber & Wilson 1995: 238).

With this notion Sperber and Wilson share a crucial tenet with other pragmatic approaches, such as politeness (Brown and Levinson 1978), what may be termed Classical Pragmatics (Leech 1983; Levinson 1983), or speech act theory (Haverkate 1990), which also approach irony in terms of attitude. In fact, their notion of *echo* captures the aspect of an attitude of dissociation shown by the speaker. Echoic utterances are thus "meant to indicate that the preceding utterance has been heard and understood, and to express the hearer's immediate reaction towards it" (Sperber & Wilson 1981: 306). The notion of echo, however, is not clarified or defined any further.

Sperber and Wilson's approach to irony has been criticised precisely in relation to the notion of *echo*. Thus, Robert Martin claims: "We can say, ironically, *What lovely weather*! even though no actual prior utterance is involved" (1992: 80-81). The problem with their notion of echo lies perhaps in that it is a concept based on gradation, but offers neither a discrete definition nor a clear-cut distinction between what is to be taken as echoic and non-echoic respectively.

In any case, Sperber and Wilson have followed a somehow inconsistent path with regard to the terms *echo* and *mention*. In their 1992 paper on irony, they seem to reject the notion of mention, or, at least, they replace it with the notion of *interpretive resemblance*, which is characterised by a resemblance of content: "We reanalyse echoic utterances as echoic *interpretations* of an attributed thought or utterance, and verbal irony as a variety of echoic interpretation" (Sperber & Wilson 1992: 65). This feature may have been motivated by the criticisms made against the notion of mention: thus, authors such as Récanati (1981) or Ducrot (1984) argue, contrarily to the position of Sperber and Wilson, that the mention present in reported speech is of a different kind to that of irony.[5] On the other hand, some authors approaching irony from a linguistic point of view (for instance, Lapp 1992) admit that Sperber and Wilson's theory of irony has shed light on the function of commentary often displayed by irony.[6]

A whole alternative theory is put forward by Clark and Gerrig (1984), the so-called *pretense theory of irony*. Even though both theories agree that irony is closely related to the expression of a certain attitude, usually of dissociation, the main debate between Sperber and Wilson's *mention theory of irony* and Clark and Gerrig's *pretense theory of irony* regards whether irony is to be approached as either *pretense* (as Clark and Gerrig suggest) or as *echoic* mention (as Sperber and Wilson maintain). These authors, who in contrast to Sperber and Wilson tend to follow Grice's tenets, even quote directly from him to refer to the meaning of irony: "To be ironical is, among other things, to pretend (as the etymology suggests), and while one wants the pretense to be recognized as such, to announce it as a pretense would spoil the effect" (Grice 1978: 125; quoted in Clark and Gerrig 1984:121).

If the notion of *pretense* and its relationship with irony goes back to the ancient Classical period, a brief historical review shows that the Classical authors did not hold such a unanimous opinion on it as Clark and Gerrig seem to suggest in the quotation above. It may be remembered here that in the *Republic,* Plato had described irony as a debate between two characters, the *alazon* and the *eiron,* both of whom pretended to be somebody or something other than they really were: thus, on the one hand, the *eiron* pretended not to know, whereas he did know; on the other hand, the *alazon* knew much less than he claimed to. Significantly, in his *Nicomachean Ethics,* Aristotle had explicitly associated the attitude of pretense with the *alazon* (boastful man), who stands in opposition to the ironist or mock-modest man (*eiron*):

> The boastful man, then, is thought to be apt to claim the things that bring glory, when he has not got them, or to claim more of them than he has, and the mock-modest man on the other hand to disclaim what he has or belittle it, while the man who observes the mean is one who calls a thing by its own name, being truthful both in life and in word, owning to what he has, and neither more nor less (Book III, 18, 1419b).

It was with Cicero that the sense of irony as *pretense* or dissimulation became fully established, when he claimed as follows:

> A jest of this sort is rather trivial, and, as I said, fit for farces, but now and then even we orators find room for one of them, with the result that even a man who is no fool says something in the manner of a fool, but not without humour [...]. These jests provoke hearty laughter, and so most assuredly does everything that is said ironically by

> the wise, and somewhat absurdly, but not without humour. Another jest from this class is pretending not to understand what you understand perfectly [...] (55-45 B.C.: 407).

Coming back to the central tenets of the pretense model, Clark and Gerrig claim that their theory manages to explain three important defining traits of irony, which, in their opinion, seem to be insufficiently accounted for by relevance: asymmetry of affect, the victims of irony, and the ironic tone of voice. The first aspect refers to the fact that ironists are more likely to make positive pretenses (e.g., *What a clever idea*!) rather than negative ones. As for the victims of irony, Clark and Gerrig point out that relevance theory cannot distinguish between the two possible kinds of victims that may exist: on the one hand, the mask that the ironist assumes to be, as a kind of injudicious person; on the other hand, the audience who fail to unmask the pretense. It will be shown below that the relevance notions of *context choice* and *context accessibility* can account for the relationship to be established between the different participants in irony, even though it is also true that no author of relevance theory has applied them to this aspect in a consistent way. Thirdly, pretense theorists claim that a tone adequate to express the speaker's distancing attitude "seems to be mandatory" (Clark & Gerrig 122). However, nothing is said by pretense theorists about the way to account for *written* samples of irony, where the addressee—at least the reader or external addressee—cannot sometimes rely on any indices which may indicate the tone of the utterance.

The relationship between both theories has been assessed by some authors. Critics generally claim that the theories are not so different from each other as their authors claim (Clark and Gerrig 1984; Sperber 1984), and that probably they may be more complementary than excluding, and perhaps neither can be taken to be wholly explanatory of such a complex phenomenon as irony (Williams 1984; Mariscal Chicano 1994).

Sperber and Wilson's major work, *Relevance* (1986, 1995), also devotes a section to irony. There is no revision of the trends of analysis of irony put forward in 1981 (1978), but their proposal is limited to the application of the general tenets of the theory to the explanation of irony. For Sperber and Wilson, communication is always oriented or geared to the maximisation of relevance, which is understood in terms of the balance between the effort required by the subject to process certain information in a certain context and the effects to be attained by such information in that particular context.

If the 1995 (1986) research carried out by Sperber and Wilson on irony stands for the application of the general tenets of their theory of relevance, it may be said that their next paper on irony, "On verbal irony" (1992 [1990]), attempts to make a synthesis of their first contributions and the general framework of the theory devised by them. They claim that the approach proposed in their earlier paper was too restrictive "because certain types of irony do not fit in the analysis of irony as echoic mention proposed in 1981" (Sperber & Wilson 1989: 96). This would not happen if their *Relevance* model of irony as echoic interpretive use is followed, they will claim. Their thesis here is that the distinction established between *use* and *mention* is but a special case of a more general one, related to the notion of *interpretive resemblance*: "We will argue that the use-mention distinction is merely a special case of a more general distinction" (Sperber & Wilson 1992: 62). Irony is then analysed, following the general framework of relevance, as a balance between *cognitive efforts* and *contextual effects*: "the presumption of relevance has two parts: a presumption of adequate effect on the one hand, and a presumption of minimally necessary effort on the other" (Sperber & Wilson 1992: 68).

Other relevance theoreticians such as Blakemore have stressed "the indeterminacy of ironic utterances" (1992: 165) which cannot be accounted for by the traditional explanations of irony. She tends to follow the model provided by relevance theory in a much narrower sense than Sperber and Wilson themselves, by trying to apply the distinction drawn between *strong and weak communication* to the production and understanding of ironic utterances. For relevance theoreticians, communication may be more or less strong depending on the responsibility that the addressee has to take in the fulfilment of the communicative act: the stronger communication is, the more commitment is to be expected from the speaker to the truth conditions of her utterance. On the other hand, in weak communication utterances are assumed to achieve relevance through a wide array of weak implicatures, whose meaning is underdetermined, and which can be completed by the addressee. All this points to a shared responsibility of addresser and addressee for the success or failure of communication, which authors such as Pilkington (1994, 1992, 1989) also maintain: "The reader/hearer inevitably takes a large part of the responsibility for the context accessed, context which, in some cases, is difficult to retrieve beyond the meta-represented cultural/social interpretations that we often use to think with" (Pilkington 1994: 44). In contrast, Sperber and Wilson have claimed that the responsibility of the success or failure of communication lies within the speaker, by referring to communication as an "asymmetrical process."[7] Blakemore follows Sperber and Wilson's main guidelines regarding the analysis of irony at the stage of *Relevance* 1995 (1986) and "On verbal irony" 1992 (1989). She also devotes special attention to the notion of echo, and some of her comments might have been motivated by the critical issues put forward by pretense theory: for her, the echo characteristic of ironic utterances does not necessarily refer to the immediately preceding context: "Notice too that an ironic utterance is not necessarily an interpretation of a thought which the speaker has actually expressed. It is frequently an interpretation of a thought which the speaker attributes to someone else" (Blakemore 1992: 167).

In synthesis, I have sketched some of the main assumptions of the relevance analysis of irony, from a historical point of view. They show some recurrent concerns about irony, which become characteristic of the model put forward by relevance theoreticians. The most significant aspects will be analysed in greater detail in the following sections of the paper. First, the relationship between irony and intention will be analysed; then, the issue of whether irony is necessarily echoic or not will be dealt with; this will be followed by some proposals concerning the way in which non-echoic instances of irony might be approached on a "relevance" theoretical basis; next, attention will be focussed on the role of context in the interpretation of ironic utterances, an aspect which, agreed upon by relevance theoreticians though it may be, could be further developed, as the latest analyses by Yus (2000a, 1999) show.

2. Recurrent Traits of the Relevance Analysis of Irony

The analysis of irony carried out by relevance theoreticians has shed light upon some aspects of its processing and comprehension, and has also tended to concentrate on concrete fields such as the echoic nature of ironic utterances, but seems to have left other aspects insufficiently explained. For the rest of the paper, I will try to analyse some of the shortcomings that the approach seems to present after more than twenty years of research, and point at possible guidelines for further development. The areas dealt with here are the following: first, the relationship between irony and intention; second, whether irony is necessarily echoic or not; third, whether relevance can account for some of the instances of irony described by Sperber and Wilson (1998) as *non-echoic* or *non-ostensive*; and fourth, some possible applications of the relevance approach to the context so as to clarify the roles of the different participants in ironic communication.

2.1 Irony and Intention

The consideration of meaning as intentional has been a recurrent tenet in the pragmatic analyses from Grice (1957) onwards, and irony has been no exception. It is generally assumed that whenever expressing any utterance, not only does the speaker usually refer to a certain state of affairs, but she also expresses her attitude towards it, and whatever is said is done so with the intention of provoking a certain change either in that state of affairs, or in the perception that the addressee may have of it, or even in both. This is captured, for instance, in Austin's tripartite distinction of locutionary-illocutionary-perlocutionary speech acts (1962), and has been a recurrent tenet in pragmatic analyses. In general, the speaker that employs an ironic utterance usually does so with a certain intention in mind, and to provoke a reaction in her interlocutor.

Barbe comments the following about the relationship

between irony and intention: "Given the right circumstances, speakers want other participants to 'read between the lines' in order to recognize their utterance was to function as a criticism. But these intentions will not always be recognized by all participants" (Barbe 1995: 10). This shows that communication is often characterised by its *asymmetry*, although not in the sense described by Sperber and Wilson (1995) when they claim that the speaker is the only responsible agent for the success or failure of communication, but rather in the sense that the addressee may access contexts other than those intended by the speaker. Another instance of asymmetry can be found in what happens in certain instances of dramatic irony, where events may turn out in a way which could not be predicted by the speakers, who remain unaware of the ultimate consequences of their own actions, in contrast to at least some of the external addressees, who may have foreseen in advance what was to become of those speakers or characters. Littman and Mey have made reference to the fact that irony may exist regardless or independent of—or even without—the speaker's intention, which would apply especially to non-verbal instances of irony: "In short, we believe that ironic situations exist independently of linguistic context and can be referred to by speakers to achieve many linguistic goals" (Littman & Mey 1991: 132). Here, these authors do not specify any further whether the context has to be approached only in linguistic terms, or whether the context would cover wider areas, but it is clear that they point to the need to distinguish forms of irony other than verbal. Next they refer to three possible instances of irony which are not subservient to language alone, but they also explicitly point out that there may be many more. The three cases distinguished by them are the following:

(i) *intentional goal/plan irony,* in which an actor executes a reasonable plan to achieve a goal, but suffers when the plan succeeds;

(ii) *serendipitous goal/plan irony,* in which the actor performs an action which incidentally results in the possibility of fulfilling the goal, even though s/he had already given up the goal of overcoming the problem;

(iii) *competence irony,* in which a competent actor fails to use the capability s/he has, and must suffer some undesirable consequences s/he should have been able to avoid.

Nevertheless, it may be set as a hypothesis that the relevance theoretical traits of *context choice* and *accessibility* may shed some light on this aspect, and proves that some insights into the interpersonal component of communication are necessary if one is to understand the meaning of irony in communication. It may be assumed that if communication is an asymmetric process, it is because the context choices made by addresser and addressee may differ, either due to the inaccessibility of the speaker's intended meaning, or because the addressee searches consciously—or not—for an alternative interpretation which may best suit his purposes.

2.2 Is Irony Necessarily Echoic? A discussion[8]

One of the main fields in which the relevance proposals on irony have shown a certain hesitation has to do with the notion of echo and with whether irony is *necessarily* echoic or not. The notion of echo may be said to have been designed by Sperber and Wilson to indicate that a certain attitude on the part of the speaker towards the propositional content of her utterance was made *manifest* to the audience.[9] Therefore, the notion of echo would capture the aspect of the attitude of dissociation which for most contemporary pragmatic theories is characteristic of irony. *Echo* is "meant to indicate that the preceding utterance has been heard and understood, and to express the hearer's immediate reaction towards it" (Sperber & Wilson 1981: 306). Curcó emphasises that echo does not refer to the literal repetition of previously uttered words, and specifies what echo is meant to be in the context of relevance theory: "What is echoed need not be what someone has said, but something they have assumed or implicated, or the thoughts and expectations of a group. Hence, the notion of echoic utterance is not restricted to the echoing of actual words" (Curcó 346).

In their earliest proposals, Sperber and Wilson seemed to suggest that all irony was echoic, since they claimed to have located many problems with the dichotomy echoic/non-echoic irony:

> It might be suggested that there are two distinct types of irony: "echoic" irony [...] whose interpretation involves a recognition of its status as mention, and "standard" irony, whose interpretation involves a recovery of its figurative meaning. The problem with this suggestion is that there is a whole range of intermediate cases between the clear cases of echoic irony and the "standard" cases [...]. If there were two totally distinct processes, one based on mention and the other on figurative meaning, each resulting in a different type of irony, such intermediate cases should not exist (Sperber & Wilson 1981: 309).

In *Relevance,* Sperber and Wilson do not specify any further whether all irony is to be taken as echoic or not. They introduce the concept of *second-degree interpretations,* which show the speaker's attitude or opinion about some facts which correspond to the way somebody else thinks about some state of affairs in particular. Hence, those are not just facts as presented by somebody else, but they are also filtered through the speaker's view about them. Echoic utterances are second-degree interpretations which show the speaker's attitude towards those facts.

It is in their 1992 paper "On verbal irony" that Sperber and Wilson seem to start doubting whether all irony is necessarily echoic. They admit that echoic utterances can express a great variety of attitudes, and also that the approach to ironic utterances in terms of echoic mention is too restrictive, "because certain types of irony do not fit in the analysis of irony as echoic mention proposed in 1981" (Sperber & Wilson 1992: 53). No further specifications are made regarding what varieties or kinds of irony would not fit in that analysis. The distinction between *use* and *mention* is regarded as a specific instance of a much more general one, established, already in their book *Relevance* (1986), between *descriptive resemblance* and *interpretive resemblance*[10]: "We reanalyse echoic utterances as echoic *interpretations* of an attributed thought or utterance, and verbal irony as a variety of echoic interpretation" (Sperber & Wilson 1992: 65).

In this paper, however, Sperber and Wilson identify mentions with literal interpretations[11]; this suggests a rather different notion from that of 1981, where they defined *mention* as reference to the expression itself (1981: 303).

Nevertheless, in the most recent debates on this question, the approach to irony as echoic is taken up again by Sperber and Wilson, who now tend to consider irony to be *necessarily* echoic. This approach will come to be questioned by some other authors. Nevertheless, in their response, Sperber and Wilson remain attached to this view, thus leaving some of the main issues of irony unresolved, as shown below.

Thus, Ken-ichi-Seto (1998) discusses whether irony is necessarily echoic, as Sperber and Wilson claim, and refers to a detailed list of basic mechanisms by which echoic irony may be conveyed, such as emphatic words (*such, truly, indeed, of course, really, actually, certainly, definitely, evidently, obviously, merely*). Nonetheless, his main claim is that there is non-echoic irony, based upon semantic reversal; he also provides a classification of the main devices by means of which irony can be conveyed, depending on what aspect of linguistics they have to do with most: lexical, syntactic, stylistic and prosodic. For Seto (1998), there are two basic types of irony: on the one hand, *echoic irony,* characterised by quotation, and associated with tropes such as allusion, parody, exempla, fable, parable or proverbs; on the other hand, *non-echoic irony,* characterised by a semantic reversal of some kind, and expressed through rhetoric devices such as oxymoron, euphemism, antiphrasis, verbal taboo, banter, antinomy, paralipsis, paradox, litotes, meiosis, or sarcasm.

What both kinds share, for Seto, is that they express implicit criticism. This leads him to define irony in the following terms: "Irony is a way of expressing implicit criticism by means of echoing and/or semantic reversal" (Seto 1998: 253). It may be noticed that for this author both echo and semantic reversal do not exclude each other, and both can be used jointly to convey irony, a view to which probably Sperber and Wilson would not subscribe themselves. For Seto, the main point that characterises both types is that the criticism expressed remains *implicit,* as it is part of the interest of irony to fail to announce itself as such. This view is also shared by both pretense and mention theorists: "Part of the charm of irony is to leave the hearer a little up in the air as to whether or not the speaker is ironical. If irony is transparent, it would simply fall flat" (Seto 252).

In a similar way, Hamamoto (1998) also questions whether the relevance approach to irony as echoic can account for all possible instances of irony, and she refers to a list of instances which similarly the echoic theory could fail to explain:

- vagueness of echoed source. Here it is not clear what is being echoed: e.g. *You look perfectly in your new hair style.*
- ironical utterances which show a dissociation from an echoed opinion or a state of affairs: e.g. *I love children who keep their rooms clean.*
- ironical utterances which describe a state of affairs. The speaker is then being ironical and yet she holds the view expressed by the propositional content of her utterance. In other words, the speaker is being ironical not because she says the contrary or something different from what she thinks, but because she spells out her own opinion, which criticises some existing situation or state of affairs: e.g. *Friends are always there when they need us.*
- unintentional ironic utterances: e.g. After John's copying answers from Mary in the exam, without his noticing it, Mary says, in a different context, *I would never be involved in any cheating.* In this case, the speaker has not any access to certain elements of the situation; and as a result, neither can she be aware of certain consequences which her words have for anybody who has been acquainted with that situation.
- cases where a literal meaning which has a negative appearance is intended to convey some positive attitudes, such as appreciation, gratitude, etc. For instance, a woman can tell her husband, *You're so naughty!* after receiving a present from him.

Nevertheless, Sperber and Wilson (1998) will claim that irony is necessarily echoic, and will come to explain all those instances in terms of echo. To do so, they assume that the notion of echo should be conceived broadly enough, in terms that must obviously go beyond mere linguistic repetition. For them, echo is best associated with the expression, either explicit or implicit, of a certain attitude, and in any case, it must contribute to the relevance of the utterance for the hearer in a definite context. Furthermore, they establish a difference between what can always be echoed—general norms and desires—and what can be echoed only if attributed to specific individuals. The latter may go against generally assumed standards, and as a result can only be echoed or uttered with an ironic interpretation under an appropriate contextual environment, where the ambiguity can be inferred. It may be questioned whether their qualitative approaches to irony and echo are not somehow contradictory, especially as regards their point that irony must be necessarily echoic: one may expect borderline cases, even more so considering that Sperber and Wilson themselves state that irony is not a discrete opposition—ironic *versus* non-ironic—but a gradual one, in which utterances may be *more or less* echoic, depending on the context in which they occur, the accessibility of these contexts to the communicators, and the choice of contexts which they may make, especially taking into account their broad approach to the notion of echo.

One of the main problems of Sperber and Wilson at this stage of development of their theory may have been to adequately establish the focus of their theory, that is, either to restrict it to verbal irony, or also deal with other cases of irony as well. But the problem is that, just as their theory of communication should aim to explain every form, their theory of irony should also be comprehensive enough to account for all possible instances, or at least, for ostensive forms of irony and communication, which do not necessarily equate with their verbal manifestations. It is perhaps in these authors' reflection on whether irony is or not a natural figure—by this meaning that if this is so, it should involve just one interpretive mechanism—that their general theory of irony becomes more inconsistent. After having claimed—as shown above—that irony is *necessarily* echoic, now Sperber and Wilson hold the view that echoic irony applies only to verbal irony: "We have suggested that the echoic nature of verbal irony divides it from a range of *non-echoic cases* (situational irony, dramatic irony, romantic irony, irony of fate) which it resembles in some respects" (Sperber & Wilson 1998: 290, my italics).

In the view of some authors (Varela Bravo, personal communication)[12] some of the most recent and important criticisms of Sperber and Wilson's notion of echoic irony come from those who have approached the study of irony in literary texts. As a matter of fact, the conclusions reached by Sperber and Wilson seem to come from analyses relying upon the study of speech and conversation. Perhaps this can also mean that further studies of irony in literary and written texts in general are necessary with a view to deepening and broadening the scope, methods of analysis and conclusions of the relevance approach to irony. In this sense, it is probably significant that some of the most representative instances of what Sperber and Wilson classify as "non-echoic irony" are to be found in literary texts, especially dramatic irony and irony of fate; perhaps the only exception could be the case of anticipatory irony, which can be found more easily both in literary and non-literary texts. Obviously, this requires much substantial work and comparative studies between literary and non-literary texts, which would go beyond the aims and scope of the present work. The point is not to deny that Sperber and Wilson's view that the difference between literary and non-literary language may be an adequate way to deal with this issue. In contrast to formalist approaches, relevance theoreticians claim that:

> [...] the same cognitive processes are involved in understanding all utterances. This distinguishes our view from the classical (Aristotelian) view of figurative language where figurative utterances crucially involve a departure from a norm, and brings us close to the more recent theories of literary meaning where the distinction between

the metaphorical and the literal does not exist (Blakemore 1992: 51-52).

Nevertheless, this should not exclude the study of both non-literary and literary texts: one may predict that even though they are not different in kind, yet there may be different mechanisms and perhaps quantitative differences between them. Conclusions will only be reached when detailed analyses of both have been carried out.

2.3 How can non-echoic cases of irony be accounted for?[13]

It is in their reply to these authors that Sperber and Wilson show certain views on whether irony is necessarily echoic or not that may be further worked upon. As a matter of fact, they start by claiming that irony must be echoic: "[...] We would like to defend the view that verbal irony is necessarily echoic" (Sperber & Wilson 1998: 283), but in their final comments on the subject they state that two kinds of irony may be distinguished, namely *ostensive* and *non-ostensive*: "We have suggested that the echoic nature of verbal irony divides it from a range of *non-echoic cases* (situational irony, dramatic irony, romantic irony, irony of fate) which it resembles in some respects" (Sperber & Wilson 1998: 290, my italics).

It may be noticed, however, that at the beginning reference has been made exclusively to *verbal* irony, and hence the types of irony which they finally associate with the non-echoic are basically non-verbal.

Here a further distinction is introduced: irony may be either *ostensive* or *non-ostensive*. This, however, is not defined any further:

> We would agree with Hamamoto (and have argued in Sperber & Wilson 1990: 152-53) that there is a common theme to all types of irony, ostensive and non-ostensive (situational, dramatic, romantic, Socratic, etc): they all involve the perception of a discrepancy between a representation and the state of affairs it purports to represent (Sperber & Wilson 1998: 291).

Neither is it specified whether echoic irony and ostensive irony are one and the same thing, although it may be inferred that they are regarded as being so, and the same applies to the relationship to be established between non-echoic and non-ostensive irony. If there is a feature which seems to characterise the contrast drawn by Sperber and Wilson between *ostensive* and *non-ostensive irony* it is the role of the *intention* made manifest in the irony expressed—which seems to apply only for ostensive irony. This will be tested next in the analysis of some types of non-ostensive irony. I want to concentrate on three cases of irony which they regard as non-echoic. These are: anticipatory irony, dramatic irony and situational irony:

- in cases of *anticipatory irony*, the reader may make certain predictions, or, in any case, the unfolding of the different actions will refer back (allude or echo) what had been expressed before: for instance, on reading *La Celestina* the reader may go back to the hints or indices which had been foretold by the different characters, and then check the assumptions that had been entertained. Here, then, the speaker makes some assumptions which will be verified in the future, and she did not have any evidence that this was going to happen, so she could not possibly have intended them to happen. She might have feared that what was said might come true, but she had no way to act upon the unfolding of events.
- in cases of *dramatic irony*, the reader, spectator or external addressee happens to know more than the characters involved. In relevance terms, he enjoys a much wider cognitive environment than that of the characters or participants involved. The assumptions he may make will be confirmed only as the action unfolds, thus leading to a feeling of satisfaction.
- in cases of *situational irony*, which Muecke defines as "'a condition of affairs' or 'outcome of events' which [...] is seen and felt to be ironic" (1969: 42), no ironist is involved. Therefore there is no intention to communicate something ostensively, and accordingly, there is no intention, either.

It appears, then, that ostensive and non-ostensive irony are similar in that they express a discrepancy between a state of affairs and a possible representation of it. They differ in the role played by intention.

The classification of irony into *ostensive* and *non-ostensive* can be said to rely upon the distinction made in Sperber and Wilson's work *Relevance* between *ostensive* and *non-ostensive communication*. In ostensive communication the speaker makes certain information manifest (in the sense described below) to an audience.[14]

But in the distinction drawn between ostensive and non-ostensive communication, Sperber and Wilson refer to a *continuum* of cases which might also apply to irony: "There are not two distinct and well-defined classes, but a continuum of cases of ostension ranging from 'showing,' where strong direct evidence for the basic layer of information is provided, to 'saying that,' where all evidence is indirect" (Sperber & Wilson 1995: 53). Further research could be carried out into this distinction.

In the quotation above, Sperber and Wilson seem to equate verbal irony with ostensive irony, for all the classes of irony regarded as non-echoic are non-verbal. They seem to imply this also in the following: "Although verbal irony has no clear-cut boundaries (because ironical attitudes shade off into others), the echoic mechanism itself defines a class of utterances which *is* a natural kind" (1998: 292). But ostensive-inferential communication and verbal communication do not necessarily equate. Both verbal and non-verbal communication can be used by the speaker to convey both an informative and a communicative intention to the addressee.

They even claim that "the search for a unified pragmatic theory which would cover both intentional and unintentional communication is a mistake" (Sperber & Wilson 1998: 291), which can be justified on the basis of the main tenets of the Gricean pragmatic tradition to which relevance theoreticians belong.

The analysis of the instances of non-echoic irony, mainly, dramatic irony, situational irony, or anticipatory irony, which are also present in every work of literature, tends to show that in these varieties two levels of communication may be found: on the one hand, the communication which takes place at the level of the participants or characters in the story; on the other hand, the communication which is established between the author of the text and the external audience, namely, the reader. It can be easily assumed that using varieties of non-ostensive irony also implies a certain communicative intention, if only at the level of the interchange established between the author and his audience, which may remain implicit, but still it is there for the reader to infer. Such intention would be only *weakly communicated*, in the sense used by relevance theoreticians.[15] Sperber and Wilson themselves admit that "non-verbal communication tends to be relatively weak" (1995: 60).

The question remains whether these two levels of communication can also be applied to other forms of irony, and even to those which Sperber and Wilson refer to as ostensive, and also, and mainly, to verbal irony. Perhaps the application of the distinction between *weak and strong communication* can shed some light on the analysis of the different kinds of irony: in verbal irony, and maybe in ostensive irony at large, as long as the speaker's ironic intention remains usually implicit (otherwise the whole effect will be spoilt) it is only weakly implicated, but is probably stronger than in those instances of non-ostensive irony, or perhaps, rather, in *less* ostensive forms of communication, where either consciously or unconsciously the author has an addressee in mind (what is called the *internal reader*), and it can therefore be predicted that such instances of irony will not be accessible or ostensive to all external readers or addressees.

This section has attempted to show that the final conclusions reached by Sperber and Wilson on the analysis of irony should not mean bringing the study of non-verbal irony to a standstill. What seems to be the case is that those forms which they classify as non-ostensive may imply several levels or layers of communication, and their meaning may not be ostensive to all addressees, but will be to some of them. In every ironic communicative act there may be two different kinds of addressees, that is, on the one hand, those who have access to the context envisaged by the speaker, and on the other hand, those who fail to do so. This being so, in those forms of delayed communication, and particularly in those in which there may be two levels of communication, as happens in literary texts, a further element which adds complexity has to be taken into account: irony may be manifest not to all participants, but only to some of them. Therefore, I think that the question as a whole should be reformulated: rather than classifying irony into ostensive and non-ostensive forms, one might start the other way round: given any piece of irony (be it verbal, situational, romantic, of fate, anticipatory, etc) who is it supposed, or in some cases intended, to be ostensively ironic for? If this has any practical application, it could be the following: whenever any form of irony is found, the way it is related to the context (as Sperber and Wilson themselves have always claimed) has to be searched for, which implies the exploration of the different participants, both at an internal and external level. If somebody or even something is ironic, the irony is surely meaningful, no matter in which direction that meaning is to be sought.

2.4 What role is the context supposed to play? how can the relevance proposals about context be applied to the explanation of irony and the roles played by the participants?

The role of context in communication has been a recurrent concern for pragmatic and discourse analysis approaches. The idea that context is a cognitive entity which will be modified in the course of the communicative interaction lies at the core of the relevance notions of *cognitive environment* and *mutual cognitive environment.*

Already in their 1981 paper on irony, Sperber and Wilson remarked that context has an important role to play in the interpretation of ironical utterances, for it is in context that the clues to guide towards an ironical interpretation are to be found: "the choice between literal and ironical interpretation must be based on information external to the utterance—contextual knowledge and other background assumptions—rather than the form or content of the utterance itself" (Sperber

& Wilson 1981: 301). However, it may be concluded that up to the present moment, some of the key features that Sperber and Wilson confer on context have not been applied to the interpretation of irony. For Deirdre Wilson, context is formed by "the set of assumptions brought to bear in arriving at the intended interpretation," which may be derived from a variety of sources, such as the following: "from the preceding text, or from observation of the speaker and what is going on in the immediate environment [...] from cultural or scientific knowledge, common-sense assumptions, and, more generally, any item of shared or idiosyncratic information that the hearer has access to at the time" (Wilson 41). This shows that the context has a cognitive nature, and is likely to be modified in the course of the communicative interaction.

In a similar way, Katharina Barbe (1995) has studied the relationship to be found between irony and the context where it is produced, and has concluded in favour of a certain relationship between irony, the speaker's communicative intention, and the context in which the ironic utterance occurs. She has defined the context of irony as follows:

> The context of the irony is the setting of the occurrence. This includes the participants, their relationships, and the cultural context as realized by participants' norms and presuppositions, which in turn indicate potential areas of conflicts. Participant idiosyncrasies, social situations, and cultural surroundings [...] all influence the immediate (local) context (Barbe 1995: 77).

As can be inferred from this quotation, the context of irony is defined in cognitive terms by this author, in the sense that it is in context that presuppositions have to be worked out, for instance. But at the same time this cognitive aspect of context does not contradict or deny the fact that communication is above all a social, interpersonal process.

Two important properties related to the relevance approach to context are *context choice* and *context accessibility* or *accessibility of assumptions.* In *Relevance* Sperber and Wilson (1995) debate on whether context is supposed to be *given* or *chosen.* For them, the determination of context means that "some particular subset of the individual's assumptions is selected" (1995: 132). If context is taken to be chosen, this implies that "context formation is open to choices and revisions throughout the comprehension process" (1995: 137). Indeed, were the context given throughout all the communicative interaction, it would be difficult to point to any possible improvement in the participants' knowledge of the world. It can be said that the relevance notions of *manifestness* and of *choice of contexts* aim to overcome the problems created by the concept of *mutual knowledge.* This notion had been put forward by Clark and Carlson, for whom communication presupposes that speakers "share certain knowledge, beliefs and assumptions" (1982a: 1). For these authors, mutual knowledge is based on the factors of "physical co-presence, linguistic co-presence and community membership" (1982a: 6). Sperber and Wilson had criticised mutual knowledge on the grounds that it is the result of communication rather than a precondition for it (1982: 62).

It might also be stated that even though for communication to be successful some factors must be shared, at least many of these seem to have to do with mutual knowledge of the *code* in which the message is expressed, as well as of the cultural allusions that may be necessary for the addressee to grasp the meaning intended. But as Sperber and Wilson show, the code is not the whole thing in communication. With regard to the content of the communication itself, it is certainly true that it has to make some reference to the knowledge, assumptions, beliefs, etc, held by the participants, but unless their "horizon" is somehow enlarged or modified, there is no point in carrying on with a communicative process, which necessarily has to include references to the knowledge maintained by the participants, either shared or not, and to the new chunks of information that become incorporated into the individual's knowledge of the world, taken in its broadest sense.

Moreover, in a general sense, the notion of *mutual knowledge* should not be interpreted as a polarity concept, but rather, as a matter of degree: that is, information is not *either* known or unknown, and in any case, this status is bound to be modified in the course of the communicative interchange. In fact, Clark and Carlson themselves had taken a step back in the characterisation of mutual knowledge and its role in communication, tending to consider that it is not always necessary: "Most uses of language are founded on mutual beliefs or mutual suppositions, which are not nearly as demanding as mutual knowledge" (Clark & Carlson 1982b: 57). Furthermore, in *Relevance* Sperber and Wilson propose the notion of *mutual manifestness*, which is weaker than mutual knowledge and meant to compensate for its shortcomings:

> Instead of taking the code model for granted and concluding that mutual knowledge must therefore exist, we prefer to look at what kind of assumptions people are actually in a position to make about each other's assumptions, and then see what this implies for an account of communication (Sperber & Wilson 1995: 45).

In short, what is mutually manifest is not what is mutually known by addresser and addressee, but is both a subset of the former, actualised in the communicative process, and the information which each participant gathers or learns in the course of it. It could be said that whereas the notion of *mutual knowledge* is a static concept, in contrast, the concept of *mutual manifestness* is not only weaker, but also can be regarded as *dynamic*, in the sense that it reflects the unpredictability characteristic of communication. Perhaps the most important weakness of the notion of mutual knowledge lies in that it is not enough that participants share certain knowledge; that set of background assumptions must also be accessible (in the sense described below) to them in the process of ongoing communication.

The notion of *accessibility* has also been discussed and defined in the framework of relevance theory. For Sperber and Wilson, it is "the organisation of the individual's encyclopaedic memory, and the mental activity in which he is engaged, [which] limit the class of potential contexts from which an actual context can be chosen at any given time" (1995: 138). According to relevance theoreticians, context is a psychological construct, which is extended in the process of communication as participants receive new items and chunks of information. For this reason not all this information will be equally accessible and at the same time. It may be assumed that when communicating a certain message the speaker sets it in a certain context, which, if adequately accessed and selected by the addressee, will give way to his adequate processing of information, and communication will be successful. Otherwise misunderstandings will arise: as predicted by Blakemore, "misunderstandings occur when there is a mismatch between the context envisaged by the speaker and the one selected by the hearer" (1992: 31).

The application of the two notions just dealt with can result in the definition of the roles of the different participants in ironic communication. Katharina Barbe has referred to the different roles of participants in ironic communication. Three types are commonly distinguished: the speaker or ironist, the victim or hearer, and the (evaluating) audience (Barbe 1995: 80). The two relevance notions of *context choice* and *context accessibility* may be applied to the roles played by participants in ironic communication in the following way: the basic difference between the victim and the evaluating audience is that whereas the latter can infer the meaning intended by the speaker, the former would fail to do so, and would remain at the literal level, that is, at the level of the codification/decodification of the message. In terms of the notions of context choice and context accessibility, as defined above, it turns out that the addressee who can rightly infer the ironic meaning intended by the speaker, which may have remained implicit, has access to the context envisaged by the speaker, or in other words, has chosen the context which tends to match with her interpretation. Those participants who fail to grasp the ironic interpretation intended by the speaker would not infer it, would remain at just the literal level, and the context actually selected by them would not match with that pointed to by the speaker.

More recently, Yus Ramos (1997-98, 2000a) has referred to what he terms as the *criterion of optimal accessibility to irony.* He seeks an answer for the question of whether ironic utterances take longer to process than their literal counterparts. The *criterion of optimal accessibility to irony* is as follows:

> The processing effort required for the interpretation of the intended ironic meaning of an utterance decreases in proportion to the increase in the number (and quality) of incompatibilities (detected by the addressee) between the information supplied by the inferential integration of simultaneously activated contextual sources (leading or leading plus supportive) and the information provided by the proposition expressed by the utterance (Yus Ramos 2000a: 12).

What Yus does concretely is to locate those factors which may exert certain influence in the balance between efforts and effects which constitutes the central tenet of Sperber and Wilson's definition of relevance. The basic assumption is once more that the context plays a crucial role in the interpretation of any utterance—and thus also of irony—and that if the information provided by the utterance clashes with the contextual assumptions—or what he terms *contextual sources*—to a greater or lesser extent, then the addressee may have more or less contextual evidence for inferring that the speaker aims to be interpreted ironically. Even though the basic charm of irony is to fail to announce itself, these contextual sources may indeed be useful to make it more accessible. Those clues are the following: encyclopaedic, factual information; the mutually manifest physical context or environment; the speaker's non-verbal behaviour; the addressee's background knowledge of the addresser's biographical data; mutual knowledge; previous utterances in the conversation; and linguistic cues.

As a tentative hypothesis, to be developed in another study, it could be asked whether all those clues can apply not only in instances of ostensive irony, but also in cases of non-ostensive irony.

The question of the processing cost of figurative language and its literal counterpart has also been dealt with, not only in relation to ironic utterances, but with regard to the processing of figurative language as a whole, by authors such as Rachel Giora (1997). In her view, both kinds of language are governed by "a general principle of salience," which is a matter of degree, and according to which "salient meanings [...] are processed first" (Giora 1997: 183). The most salient meaning may be either "literal" or "figurative." In fact, she claims that "a rich context neutralizes the difference between comprehension of literal and nonliteral language" (Giora 1997: 187). Concerning the process of understanding ironic utterances and their relationship with their literal counterparts, she concludes that "the salient, contextually incompatible (literal) meaning of irony is not suppressed when the ironic meaning emerges" (Giora 1998: 89). The graded salience hypothesis seems to coincide with Sperber and Wilson's views in that, in contrast to the Gricean model, the processing of figurative meanings does not necessarily have to rely upon their literal counterparts, which are neither more predictable nor easier to understand. Thus, Sperber and Wilson themselves have claimed that literal, loose talk and metaphorical talk "differ not in kind but only in degree of looseness, and [...] they are understood in essentially the same way" (1985/86: 153). This shows that the relationship between the configuration and processing of both literal and figurative language, as well as that between everyday speech and literary language, is a subject for further exploration.

Conclusion

The present paper has attempted to provide an account of the main trends in the analysis of irony from the relevance perspective. It has been shown that the approach taken to communication as an inferential process by this theory makes it a suitable tool for the analysis of a communicative phenomenon characterised by its great versatility. Through more than two decades (1978-2000) so far, certain topics have been found recurrent, which shows that the theory is consistent. Yet the analysis of certain instances which have been left unexplained so far (those cases which Sperber and Wilson 1998 refer to as non-ostensive) shows that the theory needs to be further developed, so as to deal with both conversation samples and literary instances of irony. Other fruitful studies could be carried out concerning the relationship between relevance and other aspects, due to the versatility of irony commented above, which makes it a proper field for interdisciplinarity. The broadening of the contrastive classification between ostensive and non-ostensive cases may be a fruitful path to be followed by future investigations, via both the intrinsic study of each and the contrastive analysis of both. Even though some tentative proposals have been made in this paper for dealing with some cases of non-ostensive or non-echoic varieties of irony, much substantial research and analysis remains to be done before more definite conclusions may be reached.

Notes

1. See, for instance, Muecke's comment: "The principal obstacle in the way of a simple definition of irony is the fact that irony is not a simple phenomenon" (1970: 8).
2. This is how Sperber and Wilson reject the notion of figurative meaning, a tenet which they also apply to the interpretation of ironical utterances: "The choice between literal and ironical interpretation must be based on information external to the utterance—contextual knowledge and background assumptions—rather than the form or content of the utterance itself" (1981: 301). Similarly, for Fish the literal reading of a text is no less an interpretation than any figurative meaning: "Literal meaning, rather than being independent of perspective, is a product of perspective (it is the meaning that, given a perspective, will immediately emerge); it is itself an interpretation and cannot therefore be the indisputable ground on which subsequent interpretations rest" (1989: 185).
3. In general, this paper will make use of the convention by which the speaker or addressee is referred to by "she," and the addressee by the form "he," with their corresponding adjectives and pronouns, regardless of their real sexes, unless quotations or other references are expressed otherwise.
4. The paper "Irony and the Use-Mention Distinction" by Sperber and Wilson (1981) is generally taken to be the English version of a paper published jointly by these authors in the 1978 monographic volume of *Poétique* devoted to irony. Here, references will correspond to the 1981 English paper.
5. "La mention qui intervient dans l'ironie n'est évidemment pas du même type que celle qu'illustre le discours rapporté" (Récanati 1981: 219; quoted in Perrin 1996: 136); "The mention which occurs in irony is obviously not of the same type as that exemplified by reported speech" (editorial translation).
6. Thus, Lapp notes: "Neben der spezifischen Wertungsfunktion ironischer Rede in bezug auf ihren *Gegenstand* können sich ironische Äusserungen auch wertend *auf sich selbst* beziehen. Durch diese

Selbstwertung der Äusserung auf metasprachlicher Ebene hat der Sprecher z.B. die Möglichkeit, sich vom Inhalt der Äusserung zu distanzieren, sie gewissermassen zu 'entschärfen'" (1992: 81); "In addition to the specific function of assessment of ironic discourse related to its opposite, ironic utterances can also be related to assess themselves. By means of this self-assessment of the utterance at a metalinguistic level the speaker has the possibility of, for instance, distancing herself from the content of the utterance, so as 'to take the edge off,' so to speak" (editorial translation).

7. Concretely, they have pointed out the following: "Communication is an asymmetrical process anyhow [...]. It is left to the communicator to make correct assumptions about the codes and contextual information that the audience will have accessible and be likely to use in the comprehension process. The responsibility for avoiding misunderstandings also lies with the speaker, so that all the hearer has to do is go ahead and use whatever code and contextual information come most easily to hand" (1995: 43). This shows that, at least at this stage, for Sperber and Wilson it is the speaker that is made practically the one and only responsible actant for the process and results to be attained in any communicative event.

8. Some of the ideas introduced in this section were also discussed in the paper "Some questions raised by an afterthought of Sperber and Wilson's on irony," delivered at the XVIII National Conference of AESLA (Spanish Association of Applied Linguistics), held in Barcelona (4-6 May 2000).

9. The notion of *manifestness* is linked by Sperber and Wilson to the property of a given fact or phenomenon of being perceptible or inferable: "a fact is *manifest* to an individual at a given time if and only if he is capable at that time of representing it mentally and accepting its representation as true or probably true" (1995: 39). This notion is also important in the definition of the *cognitive environment*, which refers precisely to "the set of facts that are manifest" to an individual (1995: 39). The cognitive environment becomes *shared* between two or more individuals in the process of any communicative interaction.

10. The distinction between *descriptive resemblance* and *interpretive resemblance* is drawn by Sperber and Wilson to allude to the ways in which utterances represent the things they refer to. On the one hand, the propositional form of an utterance may represent a certain state of affairs if what it states is true of that state of affairs. In that case, the propositional form *describes* the state of affairs referred to, and between both there is a relationship of *descriptive resemblance.* On the other hand, if there is a relationship of resemblance between the

propositional forms of two different representations, then the relationship between both is of *interpretive resemblance*.

11. Concretely, they point out the following: "We propose, then, to analyse indirect speech reports, echoic utterances and irony not *as literal interpretations (mentions)* of an attributed thought or utterance, but simply as interpretations, literal or non-literal, of an attributed thought or utterance. The change corrects an over-restrictive feature of our earlier account" (1992: 66, editorial italics).
12. I thank Prof. Eduardo José Varela Bravo for some valuable and interesting comments which he made about the paper which I presented at the conference of AEDEAN (the Spanish Association of Anglo-North American Studies) held in León in December 1999 ("A revision of the latest relevance proposals on irony").
13. This section is part of my ongoing research, and is central to my doctoral dissertation (in progress). An earlier version was developed in the paper entitled "Echoic and non-echoic irony: are there any recurrent traits between both?" presented at the AEDEAN Conference, held in Ciudad Real in December, 2000. I also want to thank Prof. Deirdre Wilson for her invaluable discussion of this topic at the seminar on metarepresentation held in Vitoria (Spain) from 15 to 18 May 2000, organised by Prof. Begoña Vicente Cruz of the University of the Basque Country.
14. cf. note 10 above.
15. The distinction between strong and weak communication is explained by Sperber and Wilson as follows: "In the case of strong communication, the communicator can have fairly precise expectations about some of the thoughts that the audience will actually entertain. With weaker forms of communication, the communicator may merely expect to steer the thoughts of the audience in a certain direction" (1995: 60).

Works Cited

Aristotle. 1991 (384-322 BC). *Nicomachean Ethics.* Trans. W.D. Ross. *World's Greatest Classic Books* (CD-ROM, Corel, 1995; Electronically Enhanced Text, 1991, World Library, Inc).

Austin, J. 1962. *How to Do Things with Words.* Oxford: Oxford UP.

Barbe, K. 1995. *Irony in Context.* Amsterdam/ Philadelphia: John Benjamins Publishing Co.

Blakemore, D. 1992. *Understanding Utterances.* London: Blackwell.

Brown, P. and S. Levinson. 1978. *Politeness.* Cambridge: Cambridge UP.

Cicero. 1952 (55-45 B.C). *De Oratore.* Ed. and trans. E.W. Sutton. London: Heinemann.

Clark, H.H. and T. Carlson. 1982a. "Speech Acts and Hearers' Beliefs." *Mutual Knowledge.* Ed. N.V. Smith London: Academic Press. 1-36.

——. 1982b. "Critics' Beliefs about Hearers' Beliefs: A Rejoinder to Johnson-Laird, Sperber and Wilks." *Mutual Knowledge.* Ed. N.V. Smith. London: Academic Press. 53-59.

——. and R. J. Gerrig. 1984. "On the Pretense Theory of Irony." *Journal of Experimental Psychology: General* 113: 121-26.

Curcó Cobos, C. 1997. "Irony and Verbal Humour. The Pragmatics of Humorous Interpretations: A Relevance Theoretic Approach." Diss. University College of London. 321-50.

Ducrot, O. 1984. "Esquisse d'une théorie polyphonique de l'énonciation." *Le Dire et le dit.* Paris: Minuit. 177-233.

Fish, S. 1989. *Doing what comes naturally.* Durham, N.C.: Duke UP.

Giora, R. 1997. "Understanding figurative and literal language: The graded saliency hypothesis." *Cognitive Linguistics* 8: 183-206.

——. 1998. "When is Relevance? On the Role of Salience in Utterance Interpretation." *Revista Alicantina de Estudios Ingleses* 11: 85-94.

Grice, P. 1971 (1957). "Meaning." *Semantics.* Ed. D.D. Steinberg and L.A. Jakobovits. Cambridge: Cambridge UP. 53-59.

——. 1978. "Further notes on logic and conversation." *Syntax and Semantics.* Vol. IX. Ed. P. Cole. New York: Academic Press. 113-27.

Hamamoto, H. 1998. Irony from a cognitive perspective. *Relevance Theory. Applications and Implications.* Ed. R. Carston and S. Uchida. Amsterdam/ Philadelphia: John Benjamins Publishing Co. 257-70.

Haverkate, H. 1990. "A speech act analysis of irony." *Journal of Pragmatics* 14: 77-109.

Hickey, L. 1994. "I don't care what you meant: I heard what you said." *Miscelánea* 15: 319-29.

Jorgensen, J., G. Miller and D. Sperber. 1984. "Test of the mention theory of irony." *Journal of Experimental Psychology: General* 113: 112-20.

Lapp, E. 1992. *Linguistik der Ironie.* Tübingen: Günter Narr.

Leech, G. 1983. *Principles of Pragmatics.* New York: Longman.

Levinson, S.C. 1983. *Pragmatics.* Cambridge: Cambridge UP.

Littman, D.C. and J.L. Mey. 1991. "The nature of irony: toward a computational model of irony." *Journal of Pragmatics* 15: 131-51.

Lyons, J. 1977. *Semantics.* Cambridge: Cambridge UP.

Mariscal Chicano, J.M. 1994. "¿Quién finge la ironía pertinente?." *Pragmalingüística* 2: 319-56.

Martin, R. 1992. "Irony and universe of belief." *Lingua* 87: 77-90.

Muecke, D.C. 1969. *The Compass of Irony.* London: Methuen.

——. 1970. *Irony.* London: Methuen.

Perrin, L. 1996. *L'ironie. Mise en Trope. Du Sens des Énoncés Hyperboliques et Ironiques.* Paris: Éditions Kimé.

Pilkington, A. 1989. "Poetic effects: a relevance perspective." *UCL Working Papers In Linguistics* 1: 119-36.

——. 1992. "Poetic effects." *Lingua* 87: 29-51.

——. 1994. "Poetic Thoughts and Poetic Effects: A Relevance Theory Account of the Literary Use of Rhetorical Tropes and Schemes." Diss. University College of London.

Plato, 1956 (428-347 B.C.). *The Republic.* In *Great Dialogues of Plato.* Trans. W.H.D. Rouse. New York: New American Library.

Récanati, F. 1981. *Les Énoncés performatifs.* Paris: Minuit.

Seto, K. 1998. "On non-echoic irony." *Relevance Theory. Applications and Implications.* Ed. R. Carston and S. Uchida. Amsterdam/ Philadelphia: John Benjamins Publishing Co. 239-55.

Sperber, D. 1982. "Comments on Clark & Carlson's Paper." *Mutual Knowledge.* Ed. N.V. Smith. London: Academic Press. 46-51.

——. 1984. "Verbal Irony: Pretense or Echoic Mention?" *Journal of Experimental Psychology: General* 113: 130-36.

——. and D. Wilson. 1978. "Les ironies comme mentions." *Poétique* 36: 399-412.

——. and D. Wilson. 1981. "Irony and the Use-Mention Distinction." *Radical Pragmatics.* Ed. P. Cole. New York: Academic Press. 295-318.

——. and D. Wilson. 1982. "Mutual Knowledge and Relevance in Theories of Comprehension." *Mutual Knowledge.* Ed. N.V. Smith. London: Academic Press. 61-85.

——. and D. Wilson. 1985/86. "Loose Talk." *Proceedings of the Aristotelian Society* LXXXVI: 153-71.

——. and D. Wilson. 1995 (1986). *Relevance: Communication and Cognition.* Oxford: Blackwell.

——. and D. Wilson. 1998. "Irony and relevance: A reply to Seto, Hamamoto and Yamanashi." *Relevance Theory. Applications and Implications.* Ed. R. Carston and S. Uchida. Amsterdam/Philadelphia: John Benjamins Publishing Co. 283-93.

Williams, J. 1984. "Does Mention (or Pretense) Exhaust the Concept of Irony?" *Journal of Experimental Psychology: General* 113: 127-29.

Wilson, D. 1994. "Relevance and Understanding." *Language and Understanding.* Ed. G. Brown et al. Oxford: Oxford UP. 35-58.

——. and D. Sperber. 1992. "On verbal irony." *Lingua* 87: 53-76.

Yamanashi, M. 1998. "Some issues in the treatment of irony and related tropes." *Relevance Theory. Applications and Implications.* Ed. R. Carston and S. Uchida. Amsterdam / Philadelphia: John Benjamins Publishing Co. 271-81.

Yus Ramos, F. 1997-98. "Irony: context accessibility and processing effort." *Pragmalingüística* 5-6, 391-410.

——. 1999. Forthcoming. "Misunderstandings and explicit/implicit communication." *Pragmatics* 9.

——. 2000a. Forthcoming. "On reaching the intended ironic interpretation." *International Journal of Communication* 10.

——. 2000b. Forthcoming. "Literal/non-literal and the processing of verbal irony." *Pragmalingüística* 8.

5

Towards an Inclusive, Multi-functional Sociolinguistic Theory of Stylistics of Fiction

PRAKASH CHANDRA PRADHAN

Teaching fiction in English is a very significant component both at Honours and Postgraduate levels in the majority of the universities in India. Teachers in English literature mostly follow traditional methods of teaching for this art form. By that, they discuss plot/theme/characterization/style, following some of the traditional critics. As a result, their approach is neither analytical in relation to the features of language nor comprehensive in relation to the theme. Such an approach is rather partial and imprecise. A good piece of fictional text is rich in meaning and it has a range of interesting stylistic/sociolinguistic features. As such the teacher needs to be well equipped with special skills in sociolinguistics/stylistics for teaching this art form to the advanced students in the higher stage in a comprehensive manner. For this purpose, the teacher should have a proper knowledge of the inclusive multifunctional sociolinguistic theory of stylistics, as formulated at the end of this paper.

I

For understanding fictional texts, close study and analysis of language is essential. For such an analysis, insights from different areas of study are indispensable. In this respect linguistic philosophy, pragmatics, semantics, sociolinguistics and discourse may be mentioned. Hence such an approach is inclusive rather than exclusive. A single discipline with its precision and systematicity is not matched to capture the multiplicity of meanings and styles in literature. However, each of these disciplines goes a long way with their multiple principles to help us understand a text in its true spirit. Each piece of art needs a close study to exploit the resources of language which are charged with deep meanings.

Stylistics establishes a link between linguistics and literary criticism. It helps us to study the language closely before we make a statement regarding the various meanings of a literary piece of work. The pattern of vocabulary and syntax, the various metaphorical and symbolic modes, the devices used for organization of the text and different modes of presentation of thought are a wide range of stylistic devices manipulated by a novelist to create visionary worlds and memorable characters in his novels. These stylistic clues lead us to understand the meaning in these novels in a more subtle manner. Because of its inscrutable abstract nature, literature poses some forceful resistance to being subjected to crude scientific analysis. In spite of that, close study of language will yield many fruitful areas of meaning which had hitherto escaped our notice. Admittedly, stylistics has yet to establish itself as a fully comprehensive discipline with all-embracing tools to dig out all the hidden treasure in literature. A better and deeper understanding of literature can be made through an interactive approach of contemporary stylistics, theory and criticism. In the recent past stylistics was more criticized than fully appreciated. However, stylistics has grown through sustenance. Critics like Lodge (1966) who thought that stylistics would never be a comprehensive discipline have revised their previous statements. Lodge considers that language is a means to attain artistic creation.

Though a literary critic, David Lodge, in his book *The Language of Fiction,* has made a significant statement in relation to the novelist's business with language: "The novelist's medium is language: Whatever he does, qua novelist, he does in and through language" ("Preface" 1966: IX). He acknowledges the importance of language in studying literary texts. It is true that we come into contact with the fictional world through the language of novels. But a novel, being a fictional work, has a more abstract level of existence than the expression in language. Besides some knowledge about language, the reader must have some pre-existing knowledge about the world—its socio-economic and cultural set-up. He should not be merely happy to "look in language; rather he should look through language" (Leech and Short 38). It now seems that Lodge's statement, though influential and convincing, is still inadequate. Hence stylistics should not be content with analyzing only language. In this connection, Leech and Short make the motives of stylistics very much clear:

> One major concern of stylistics is to check or validate intuitions by detailed analysis [...] language is an immensely complex, rich and variable instrument—it is virtually the medium in which man exists, defining for him his relations to his fellow human beings, his culture, even his own identity [...] so literary expression is an enhancement, or a creative liberation of the resources of the language which we use from day to day. Correspondingly, stylistics builds on linguistics and in return, stylistics challenges our linguistic frameworks, reveals them. In this sense, stylistics is an advance of discovery for both the critic and the linguist (5-6).

What Leech and Short discuss here is quite clear: language is a complex system; language use in context is very important; and stylistics sees beyond language. Though Lodge's statement has some lapses, it was still a historic statement for the study of fiction. Critics at that time indulged in making vague, intuitive and generalized statements without analyzing the resources of language. But in fiction, a close study of language is the "initial assault" that may lead us to new areas of meaning. There was not much theory on fictional prose at that time, and so it could then be affirmed that "literary theory and criticism concerned with the novel are much inferior in both quantity and quality to theory and criticism of poetry" (Wellek and Warren 21).

This statement of New Criticism makes it quite clear that there are as if two types of theories: one is for prose and the other is for poetry. Because of the enormous number of fictional texts, much study could not have been done during those days. Moreover, in poetry aesthetic effect cannot be separated from the "creative manipulation of the linguistic code," whereas in prose "it tends to reside more in other factors such as character, theme, argument which are expressed through, rather than inherent in language" (Leech and Short 2). It seems that a close study of fictional texts is a challenging one; but that does not mean we cannot undertake such a study. A theory of fiction needs to be developed to suit studying the multidimensional aspects of a novel. Hence, we may argue that a theory of stylistics of fiction is not impossible. Lodge, though in a different context, has made a very important argument in relation to close analysis of novels: "The fictional world of a novel is a verbal world determined at every point by the words in which it is represented. Therefore, there can be no essential difference between the criticism of poetry and the criticism of prose fiction" (1966: 46). What Lodge wants to plead is that the tools of the New Critics for close analysis of language in poetry have been devised and they have yielded some essential insights into the creative process of poetry. However, there is a lack of interest in studying the language of fiction from a critic's point of view, undermining the significance of the inclusive multilevel stylistic approach that we have followed. In that book he has argued that the "novelist's medium is language rather than life" (1966: 17). But we would rather plead that a novelist, by way of manipulating the resources of language to create his fictional world, also manipulates the medium of life which can be considered at the level of extra-linguistic features. Another statement that Lodge makes in 1966 in the same book exposes his inability to understand the wider perspective of stylistics that we have achieved today:

> [...] stylistics can never become a fully comprehensive method of literary criticism [...] for both stylistician and critic, the interest and meaning of any linguistic element is determined by its context. But for the latter the context is, in the first place, individual text considered as a whole, while for the former it is the language considered as a whole (1966: 56).

But this view expressed by Lodge is not acceptable to us because stylistics is not merely concerned with the formal patterns of text: it also takes the situations of discourse into consideration. This helps us relating the textual features to the overall socio-cultural meanings expressed through discourse. In this sense, stylistics has led us to take different value-systems of the society and dialogical implications into consideration while we interpret pieces of literature. In this context the views of Roger Fowler seems to be more convincing and valid:

> Whatever is created by the individual writer, it is not the whole being of the text, because nothing is possible without the pre-existing discourse: and that is rooted in social, economic, political and ideological conditions which go far beyond consciousness and control of the writing subject, "the author" (1986: 168).

It is now clear from this that a text is not a matter of linguistic styles only. Merely understanding the features in the language of fiction will lead us nowhere. Hence, we discuss the styles of discourse in addition to linguistic styles in order to validate our opinions on particular texts. The creativity of fiction is based on the author's critical consciousness of the resources of discourse and the practical skill to manipulate the resources of language to certain aesthetic effect. And in order to understand the text, we must develop the consciousness of a linguistic critic.

II

By making our position clear, we fully reject the "objective model" of literary form advocated by the New Critics, and their close linguistic analysis of the text. The statistical stylistic analysis of the text based on vocabulary and syntax is also not acceptable to us. Mere "linguistic competence" (the notion evolved by Chomsky), is not helpful either, because a knowledge of syntax, dictionary meanings, phonology and orthography is not sufficient to understand literary texts. From our experience, we have noted that non-linguistic knowledge about the world is highly essential for comprehending the complicated processes of creation which have been produced by the interaction of language and knowledge about the world. Jonathan Culler

(*Structuralist Poetics* 1975) has argued that "literary competence," i.e. knowledge of the nature of literature and the properties of literary texts, is helpful for understanding literary texts. But the properties of literary texts vary from age to age. It even varies from community to community in their production of literary texts. The reader should have a knowledge of all such variations of the properties of literary texts. Hence, we may define literary competence in terms of knowledge about modes of discourse. Doing so, we may argue that literary competence is a sociolinguistic competence to understand literary texts. For this view, we also get the support of the linguistic critic Roger Fowler, who argues: "Linguistic competence does not include the many extra factors which come into play in concrete use of language; the sociolinguistic ability to match an appropriate style to a context, pragmatic processes in the interpretation of discourse, and so on" (1986: 174).

Fowler argues that the literary critic is merely concerned with reproducing the dominant values and problematic beliefs within a historically specific society as represented in literature. On the other hand, the linguistic critic goes a step further by coming to a reflective understanding of the values of a time and a culture (1986: 178). In this sense linguistic criticism establishes a link between the significance of linguistic analysis of a language use and the aesthetic effect of a language use. As such the critic should be a repertoire of linguistic competence, literary competence, and sociolinguistic competence: "No one becomes a critic simply by learning linguistic analysis; scholarship and sensitivity, wide reading, and membership of a literary culture are called for. But then no one becomes a critic simply by reading; analytic technique is essential and linguistics answers this need best of all techniques" (Fowler 1986: 180). It is now quite clear that analytical techniques of linguistics are very much essential to understanding the aesthetic effect of a literary text. And for that reason, the stylistician should approach literary texts from the perspective of an inclusive multi-level theory of stylistics. The business of a stylistician is "to relate the critic's concern of aesthetic appreciation to the linguist's concern of linguistic description" (Leech and Short 13). In other words, linguistic observation and literary insight are interactive and complementary to each other, and they work in a cyclic process to bring out stimulation to the process of literary interpretation while moving from linguistic observation to the modification of literary insight and literary insight stimulating further linguistic observation. This motion is like the "cycle of theory formulation and theory testing" (Leech 1977). In this context we may argue that literary appreciation and linguistic observation go together where aesthetic function is sought through the analysis of linguistic evidence. This model of stylistics pleads for an inclusive multi-functional theory that can be applied to literary texts for proper understanding.

This theory is also complementary to the sociolinguistic approach to the study of literature. The main thrust of this is based on the multi-functional nature of a piece of utterance. Language performs a large number of different functions, namely referential, directive, emotive, social and so on. Those who have pleaded the numerous roles of language for communicating various types of messages differ on the point of the number of various functions of language. For example, I.A. Richards in his book *Practical Criticism* (1929: 181) distinguishes four types of function and four types of meaning: sense, feeling, tone and intuition. Jakobson distinguishes six functions in language, namely referential, emotive, conative, phatic, poetic and metalinguistic (1961). Each of these functions corresponds to one essential aspect of the discourse situation. Jakobson's theory of language is more systematic than Richards.' In 1973, Halliday acknowledged three major functions: ideational, interpersonal and textual. In Richards' view, "the function" of "feeling" tends to dominate that of "sense," while Jakobson argues that "special poetic function" dominates other functions in poetry. However, Halliday believes all linguistic choices are meaningful and these choices are stylistic. This view of Halliday is an advanced statement which answers some of the flaws of both monistic and dualistic approaches to the study of text.

Any artistic piece of work has to be written in a particular style only. Monism rejects the form-meaning dichotomy. In this way monism gets the support of the New Critics such as Wimsatt (1941) and others. The methods of New Criticism have suited poetry. However, Lodge tries to extend the New Critical method to the language of prose fiction (1966). Lodge believes that for fictional prose criticism is "language criticism." We find some basis in Lodge's thesis that "language is a continuum" as it is used in poetry and prose. This thesis, if accepted, leads us to an accommodation between dualism and monism. As such the more enlightening approach would be "stylistic pluralism" which affirms the multi-level, multi-functional nature of language. This approach avoids the weaknesses of both monism and dualism. In such an approach we can show how choices of language are interrelated to one another within a network of functional choices. A writer's choices of linguistic items can be seen against the background of relations of contrast and dependence between one choice and another. But this is not possible in the case of the monist because monism tends to view "a text as an undifferentiated whole, so that examination of linguistic choices cannot be made except on some ad hoc principle [...] the monist [...] if he follows the logic of his position, would not be able to discuss language at all" (Leech and Short 33). One can discuss meaning by repeating the same words in which it is expressed and one can discuss form by saying that it appropriately expresses its own meaning. On the other hand, the dualist cannot make points on the sociolinguistic dimensions and world-views which are of utmost importance in fictional text. Hence, we would prefer to take the insights of monism, dualism, and pluralism and develop a model which can be based on sociolinguistic aspects and multifunctional approach to the practical study of texts. We may make certain points which may refer to what we mean by sociolinguistic multi-functional approach of style to literary texts.

III

Firstly, this model is concerned with both styles of language and styles of discourse. Secondly, this sort of stylistics mediates between linguistics and criticism, reinforcing and enriching the strength of both. This approach will look through language rather than looking at it. Since "linguistic competence" and "literary competence" are not enough on the part of a reader for understanding the text fully, the reader-critic is to have "sociolinguistic competence" to place himself in a better position while interpreting the literary texts. Next, such a study is concerned with establishing linkage as to why a particular linguistic pattern is used to bring out a certain aesthetic effect. In other words, it is more concerned with *why* and *how* rather than with *what.* This approach will start with analysis of resources of language such as lexis, syntax and phonology; and then it will lead us through the analysis of figurative language, cohesion and coherence to styles of discourse for exploration of socio-cultural meanings in a particular text. In other words, such an approach will relate the linguistic features of text and the extra-linguistic features of discourse during the course of interpretation. It will also depend upon the semantic and pragmatic aspects of language use.

The resources of language are an essential part of a text. Employing an inclusive multi-functional sociolinguistic model, it is possible on the part of a teacher who teaches fiction at the postgraduate level/honours level to bring out the meaning and tone of the fictional texts more clearly to the surface in order to make his students understand and appreciate the texts better. In my view an intuitive-impressionistic analysis is rather vague and unsystematic. On the other hand, analysis and interpretation of novels applying the "inclusive multifunctional sociolinguistic model" would be most convincing to the advanced students of English literature because such an interpretation is more precise and systematic.

Works Cited

Berger, Peter and Thomas Luckman. *The Social Construction of Reality.* Harmondsworth: Penguin, 1972.

Bissert, Noelle. *Education, Class, Language and Ideology.* London: Routledge and Kegan Paul, 1979.

Burton, D. *Dialogue and Discourse.* London: Routledge and Kegan Paul, 1980.

Carter, Ronald and Paul Simpson, eds. *Language, Discourse and Literature: An Introductory Reader in Discourse Stylistics.* London: Urwin Hyman, 1989.

Chomsky, Noam. *Syntactic Structures.* The Hague: Mouton, 1957.

Coulthard, Malcolm. *An Introduction to Discourse Analysis.* London: Longman, 1977.

Culler, Jonathan. *Structuralist Poetics.* Ithaca, New York: Cornell UP, 1975.

——. "Literary competence." *Essays in Modern Stylistics.* Ed. Donald C. Freeman: London and New York: Methuen, 1981. 24-41.

Van Dijk, T.A. *Discourse and Literature.* Amsterdam/Philadelphia: John Benjamins Publishing Company, 1985.

Dittmar, Norbert. *Sociolinguistics.* Trans. Peter Sand. Pierre A.M. Seuren and Kevin Whitley. London: Edward Arnold, 1976.

Edwards, John. *Language, Society and Identity.* Andre Deutsch: Basil Blackwell, 1985.

Fish, Stanley E. "What is Stylistics and Why are they Saying Such Terrible Things about It?" *Essays in Modern Stylistics.* Ed. Donald C. Freeman. London and New York: Methuen, 1981. 53-78.

Fowler, Roger. *Literature as Social Discourse.* London: Batsford Academic Educational Ltd., 1981.

——. *Linguistic Criticism.* Oxford: Oxford UP, 1986.

Giglioli, P.P., ed. *Language and Social Context.* Harmondsworth: Penguin, 1972.

Gumpertz, John J. and Dell Hymes, eds. *Directions in Sociolinguistics.* New York: Holt, Rinehart, and Winston, 1972.

Halliday, M.A.K. *Explorations in the Functional Language.* London: Edward Arnold, 1973.

——. "Language Structure and Language Functions." *New Horizons in Linguistics.* Ed. John Lyons. Harmondsworth: Penguin, 1970. 140-65.

Holloway, John. *Narrative and Structure: Exploratory Essays.* Cambridge: Cambridge UP, 1979.

Hudson, R.A. *Sociolinguistics.* Cambridge: Cambridge UP, 1980.

Jakobson, Roman. "Closing Statement: Linguistics and Poetics." *Style in Language.* Ed. T.A. Sebeok. Cambridge, Mass.: MIT Press, 1960. 350-77.

Leech, G.N. *A Linguistic Guide to English Poetry.* London: Longman, 1969.

——. *Explorations in Semantics and Pragmatics.* Amsterdam: John Benjamins, 1980.

Lodge, David. *The Language of Fiction: Essays in Verbal Analysis of the English Novel.* London: Routledge and Kegan Paul, 1966.

——. *After Bakhtin: Essays in Fiction and Criticism.* London and New York: Routledge and Kegan Paul, 1980.

——., ed. *20th Century Literary Criticism: A Reader.* London/New York: Longman, 1972.

Ohman, Richard. "Speech, Action and Style." *Literary Style: A symposium.* Ed. S. Chatman. New York and London: Oxford UP, 1971. 240-54.

Palmer, F.R. *Semantics.* 2nd ed. 1976. Cambridge: Cambridge UP, 1981.

Pratt, Mary Louis. *Towards a Speech Act Theory of Literary Discourse.* Bloomington: Indiana UP, 1977.

Prince, Gerald. *Narratology: The Form and Functions of Narrative.* Berlin/ New York/Amsterdam: Mouton, 1982.

Quirk, Randolph and Sidney Greenbaum. *A University Grammar of English.* 1973. ELBS 1979. Essex: Longman, 1987.

Richards, I.A. *Practical Criticism.* New York: Kegan Paul & Co., 1929.

Ricoeur, Paul. *Interpretation Theory: Discourse and the Surplus of Meaning.* Fort Worth, Texas. The Texas University Press, 1976.

Robins, R.H. *General Linguistics: An Introductory Survey.* 3rd ed. London: Longman, 1980.

Stubbs, M. *Discourse Analysis: The Sociolinguistic Analysis of Natural Language.* Oxford: Blackwell, 1983.

Todorov, Tzvetan. "Structuralism in Literature." *Approaches to Poetics: Selected Papers from the English Institute.* Ed. S. Chatman, New York: Columbia UP, 1973. 153-68.

——. *Introduction to Poetics.* Trans. Richard Howard. Sussex/Manchester: The Harvester Press, 1981.

Toolan, Michael J. *The Stylistics of Fiction: A Literary Linguistic Approach.* London and New York: Routledge and Kegan Paul, 1990.

Trudgill, Peter. *Sociolinguistics: An Introduction to Language and Society.* 1971. Harmondsworth: Penguin, 1971.

Turner, G.W. *Stylistics.* 1973. Harmondsworth: Penguin 1974.

Ulmann, S. *Meaning and Style.* Oxford: Blackwell, 1973.

Wallace, Karl, R. *Understanding Discourse: The Speech Act and Rhetorical Action.* Baton Rouge: Louisiana State UP, 1970.

Wellek, René and Austin Warren. *Theory of Literature.* 1949. 3rd ed. Harmondsworth: Penguin, 1963.

Widdowson, H.G. *Stylistics and the Teaching of Literature.* London: Longman, 1975.

Wimsatt, W.K. *The Verbal Icon.* Lexington, Ky: U of Kentucky P, 1972.

Wisman, Frederick, ed. *The Principles of Linguistic Philosophy.* 1959. Trans and ed. R. Harries. 1959. London: Macmillan, 1965.

Wright, Austin M. *The Formal Principles in the Novel.* Ithaca and London: Cornell UP, 1982.

✪✪✪

6

LANGUAGE OF DRAMA: A CONSIDERATION

N.V. RAVEENDRAN

Conversation in drama is a complex linguistic as well as paralinguistic activity, the study of which requires a detailed examination of the social, linguistic, and pragmatic aspects of speech acts. The effectiveness of dramatic dialogue depends upon the competence of the agents and patients on stage with respect to the above factors on the one hand, and the competence of the audience to assimilate the interaction on stage in terms of what it sees and overhears on the other. This paper attempts only to outline how a complex art form like drama can be looked at from the point of view of dialogic interaction on the stage; this is different from the case of the literary art forms like poetry or the novel where the printed page is the field of observation. I begin with an attempt to identify drama among other literary art forms, and then proceed gradually to examine the aspects of conversation in general and dramatic dialogue in particular.

I

Drama might have evolved from the play-acting of children, or from the rituals of primitive religions. The term 'drama' derives from a Greek word meaning 'things done.' In India, this art form was described as the imitation of the terrestrial (human) or extra-terrestrial (superhuman) life, and was placed under the general term 'roopaka,' which was subdivided into different categories like Nataka, Prakarana, Bhana, Prahasana and so on (Chaitanya 1977: 247). Whatever be the name ascribed to it, it is imitative action in which the interplay of literary and theatrical art is discernible, producing the unique dramatic experience.

It is paradoxical that drama is at once a literary art and a representational art. As a piece of literary art, a play is a fiction made out of words. It has a plot, characters, and dialogue. But it is a special kind of fiction—a fiction acted out rather than narrated. Unlike in the play, in poetry and fiction it is through the words of a narrator who stands in between the reader and the characters that the details are made known. But in the play nothing stands in between the audience and the total make-up of the dramatic world. Characters appear and events happen without any intermediate comment or explanation. Drama, then, offers a direct representation of its reality, and in this sense it is a representational art.

Plays are written to be performed, except for a few 'closet dramas' that were written to be read. But it is true that most often for drama lovers, the dramatic experience is in practice confined to the plays in print rather than in performance. For a study of drama in printed form one has to be unusually resourceful, because dramatists, when they write the script, are influenced by the physical characteristics of the stage for which they are writing.

On the performative aspect of drama J.L. Styan (1965: 4) comments: "As we sit in the theatre we willingly adjust our eyes and ears to receive a multiple barrage of impressions from the instant the curtain rises, each impression having been carefully prepared and transmitted at the right moment." This shows that the very nature of drama offers resistance to the style study of it, unlike in the case of poetry or novel. The audience gets the message not only from the dialogue, but also from gestures and movements. Styan (1965: 4) observes further: "A gesture, or a sudden cessation of a gesture, the movement of one actor away from or towards another, a pace upstage, will hold our complete attention and tell us what we have to know." Some of the mime may indicate ordinary life, when the style of the play is different from everyday life as in the case of ballets, or dance. Even the mask an actor wears may tell something about the character represented. The costume, its colour and the make-up will explain the character. In dance dramas like Kathakali, the whole of the communication is through signs (mudras), costume, decorative paintings on the actor's face, eye movements, movements on stage, and verse (non-choric) sung off-stage. The interpretation relies mostly on the spectator's prior knowledge of the story, the signs (mudras) and movements of the actor and his costume, similar to those of the ritualistic plays of olden times. In modern dramas even the degree of brightness or shadow surrounding an actor will assist in forming or intensifying an impression. Amidst all these there is the voice of the actor: the multiphasic speech varying from causal grunts to the heightened artificiality of rhetorical poetry and lyrical song. So, to G.B. Tennyson (1967: 3), drama is "literature that walks and talks before our eyes."

Drama is, therefore, the most complicated of art forms, during the performance of which most of the components of stage presentation will be at work. It incorporates ingredients which belong to painting and sculpture, dance and music, poetry and novel. "Visual and aural, mimetic and verbal are all the facets of the one art of drama: reading a play, we dare not ignore the fact" (Styan 1965: 5).

From another point of view, drama is a form of literature: an art made out of words. It should be understood, then in relation not only to the theatre, but also to literary forms like essay, story and poem. One knows that in literature words are used either to create plots and characters, or to express ideas and feelings. Words contain ideas which are communicated either through direct address to the reader as in a rhetorical situation, or overheard by him, as in a poetic situation. In other words, to transfer to the reader ideas and feelings, plots and characters are constructed. The manner adopted may be rhetorical in the case of essay or story, and poetic in the case of poetry. Scholes and Klaus (1971) distinguish the nature of story, essay, poetry and play in the following way:

1. **Story**: uses words (narration) to develop a view of characters and situation through the report of storyteller to reader—its essential quality is narration.

2. **Essay**: uses words to establish ideas addressed directly by the essayist to the reader.
3. **Poem**: uses words to express feelings addressed by a speaker talking or thinking to himself rather than to the reader. Its essential quality, then, is meditation.
4. **Play**: uses words to create action through the dialogue of characters talking to one another rather than to the reader. The essential quality of drama is interaction.

A novel or a poem is the words of which it consists. A play script, however, is less than a play, and a production is more than a play script. In reading a novel the reader takes in one impression at a time, but in the theatre, the audience receives many. The playwright depends upon actors to mediate between words and audience. Because drama is a complex interaction of words and action, full meaning can only come from performance. Since the act of reading a play is not enough, an understanding of the ways in which movement, character, space, action and reaction function dramatically is essential for a full experience of a play. It has to be understood in terms of its dramatic meaning as well as its thematic and narrative meaning.

There are exceptions to this conception when the dramatist happens to be a subtle artist—ripe with poetic greatness—capable of creating illusions with words that may equal manifestations on the stage. While one reads the lines picturing a determined Macbeth moving towards Duncan's chamber, with dagger in his hand, imagination soars up creating an illusory world. Now the reader can see Macbeth moving, see the pulled up sinews of his face and his determined look, and can hear his whisper. But this happens only when the playwright "combines the power of words [...] and the power of dramatic technique to make possible the achievement of that extraordinary power" (Perrine 1974: 912).

At the macro level, character, dialogue and plot, and, at the micro level, succession and juxtaposition of scenes, orchestration of the dialogue, implied action, positioning of characters, costume, stage settings and the subtext, constitute the elements of drama. Character, dialogue and plot together make possible the imitative world of every play, for characters are like (not identical to) people, and dialogue and plot are like things people say and do.

The plot is a highly specialized form of experience. Unlike the everyday conversational event, every event in drama is a carefully designed pattern and process. The plot is a wholly interconnected system of events deliberately selected and arranged in order to fulfil a complex set of dramatic purposes and theatrical conditions. Thus plot is an extremely artificial element, which is intended to engage the interest of the audience over hours, embodied and interpreted by the scenario. As for the characters, the dramatic and theatrical necessities determine their nature. They are not identical representations of everyday men and women. The contexts, modes, and other elements contribute to the differences between real life and drama. In the classical Greek theatre, for example, characters were visually defined by the fixed expression on their facial masks. Clearly it would have been impossible to respond to these characters as if they were complex human personalities. Thus plot and characters are not identical to events and people in the real world; they are only imitations of reality made by the dramatist. What the audience visualizes and overhears is, therefore, mimesis.

Scholes and Klaus (1971: 56) observe that dramatic dialogue is a highly specialized form of conversation designed to deal with the diverse needs created by the various contexts and modes of drama. It can hardly be expected to sound like the usual patterns of speech. In ordinary conversation people adjust their style to meet the needs of those with whom they are talking, reinforcing with a wide range of facial expressions, bodily gestures, and vocal inflections, many of which are unconscious actions. The speaker will try to rephrase his thoughts if he feels that the listener—interlocutor—is not able to understand what he says. In all the circumstances in a speech situation, the individual speaker will rapidly adjust his words in accordance with the thoughts of those with whom he is talking.

Drama cannot afford to reproduce conversation with precision and exactitude. Time is a factor that restricts conversation on stage. The characters have to express ideas and feelings within the time allotted to them, unlike in the leisurely ordinary conversation. The theatrical performance demands that the conversation should be audible not only to the interlocutor, but also to the audience in the theatre. Consequently, the continuity of dialogue must be very clearly maintained at every point. On the basis of what it hears, the audience must be able to infer the nature of each character and the past as well as the present circumstances in which the various characters are involved. In older poetic dramas the artificial verse rhythm, as in the use of rhymed couplets recited by characters, represented the formalness of the language used by the aristocrats and their sophisticated mannerisms. The elegance, and to a certain extent wit, of such characters were intensified with well-rhymed verse. "Dialogue, then, is an extraordinarily significant form of conversation, for it is the means by which every play implies the total make-up of its imaginative world" (Scholes and Klaus 1971: 56).

Dialogue must fulfil the needs not only of the audience but also of the actors. It is the script from which the actors take their cues. This means that dialogue must imply the whole range of expressions, gestures, inflections, and movements required in performance. Because it has to serve so many purposes all at once, dialogue remains artificial when compared to everyday exchange. Thus in reading any segment of dialogue, one should always keep in mind the numerous purposes.

Any play depends to an important degree upon the people for whom it is written and their reasons for going to the theatre; and the way the play is written for acting and speaking depends upon the theatre in which it is to be performed. These two factors of audience and playhouse are not really separable of course, and much of the fascination of the study of drama comes from the imaginative excitement caused by the interplay of the various factors already discussed.

II

Though dramatic dialogue differs from everyday conversation, it is always difficult, or rather impossible, to identify a set of intrinsic properties specific to dramatic discourse as distinct from everyday or literary uses of language. The semantic, rhetorical, and pragmatic principles of dramatic dialogue remain substantially unexplored, maintains Elam (1980: 135). So before one looks into those unexplored aspects of stage conversation, it would be of some use to have a look at those already explored facets of everyday dialogic intercourse.

In 1955, before the study of conversation had really begun in the modernist manner, J.L. Austin proposed six postulates to be observed to make a correct utterance. The first postulate demands the existence of an accepted conventional procedure having certain conventional effects, to be observed while one speaks. The second states that the persons and circumstances involved must be legitimate and relevant. The third is to the effect that all participants in conversation should participate actively and properly. The fourth necessitates their complete participation. The fifth requires the person who begins the conversation to share the thoughts and feelings of the group as such. The last brings to the fore the need for a subsequent conversation by the participants (Austin 1965: 15).

Fowler (1986: 104) says that the most important approach to speech as action is the theory of 'speech acts' or 'illocutionary' acts, as originally proposed by Austin and developed by J.R. Searle. The basic insight is that language use has an extra dimension which has been somewhat neglected by logicians and linguists: a performative dimension. The linguist is interested in how language encodes meanings, and in such semantic properties as well-formedness, ambiguity, contradiction, tautology, etc; the logician, in the conditions for the truth or falsehood of the propositions expressed in languages, and in logical relationships between propositions in terms of truth-criteria.

Studies conducted by enthusiasts gradually led to the formation of different groups with different insights. The 'ethnomethodologists' like Sacks, and 'pragmatists' like Grice analyse conversational interaction from diverse viewpoints. The 'ethnomethodologists' are principally concerned with the kind of rules which regulate the taking-up of the running topic by the speakers, and also the shift from speaker to speaker. The points at which the transition occurs are called places of transition relevance, which takes place at possible completion points of sentences, clauses or phrases, in other words, syntactic constituents. (For a detailed examination see Sacks, Schegloff and Jefferson, 1972). The pragmatist Grice in his 'Cooperative Principle' of conversation (1975: 45-46) has four maxims, namely: 'Quality' 'Quantity,' Manner' and 'Relation' (the relevance of the maxims in the study of dramatic dialogue will be considered later in this paper). This implies that language has a pragmatic function also. Utterances are used to perform actions as well as communicate propositions, true or false. Fowler (1986: 104) maintains that this principle is easy to grasp in connection with certain utterances containing performative verbs such as 'promise,' 'declare,' 'name,' 'baptize,' 'request,' 'order' and 'guarantee.'

It was in his William James Lectures (1967) that H.P. Grice set out his enquiry into the general conditions that apply to conversation. The same appeared in print in Cole and Morgan (1975). Grice's theory is in fact an account of how utterances are interpreted. It attempts to provide a framework into which every aspect of interpretation of an utterance can be fitted. Following Grice, conversation is now "conceived as a cooperative venture governed by maxims of truthfulness, relevance, informative, and manner." Grice draws a major distinction between what is actually said and what is tacitly implicated, suggesting that every aspect of interpretation can be assigned by linguistic rule, while what is implicated is largely determined by social and other maxims. The implicatures are subclassified into various types, the most important being the conversational implicatures, governed by the conversational maxims.

Grice maintains that irony, metaphor, meiosis (understatement), and hyperbole can be analysed in terms of conversational implicatures. They all result from the violation of the same maxim: "Do not say what you believe to be false." The salient feature of a figurative utterance, as Grice sees it, is that it is false. The hearer concludes that the speaker must have been attempting to get across some closely related propositions which does not violate the maxim of truthfulness: in the case of irony, for example, it might be the opposite of what is said, and in the case of metaphor it might be a comparison, so that the metaphor is re-interpreted as implicating a simile.

Ananda Vardhana uses the Sanskrit term 'dhvani' to mean almost what is meant by Grice's 'implicature.' But here one need not violate any maxim to effect 'dhvani' —the desired effect will be achieved with or without the breaking of the maxim "Do not say what you believe to be false." For example, in the *Dhvanyaloka* example, the woman out to meet her paramour in the bush near the ferry point tells a pedestrian: "The path is quite safe; only moments a ago a lion crept into his den in the bush near the ferry point." The woman is clearly implicating a warning the intention of which is to avoid nuisance. But in the case of a highly contextual utterance by a mother to a daughter, "My dear it is getting dark," the mother implicates a series of actions to be done by her daughter like bringing back the cow, taking clothes left for drying, lighting the oil lamp and the usual chants at twilight (Marar 1979: 32). She does not break any of the maxims. Yet, many things other than what is uttered are understood.

Grice's approach, with all its plus points, is not foolproof. It raises a number of new problems (for a consideration of these, see Wilson and Sperber, 1981). But as a theory it can provide a lot of help in any attempt to study conversational interaction, and so in the following section I shall attempt to show how this and other theories can help us understand dramatic dialogue.

III

In a drama the performers and spectators are in a real world, but the performance represents another world. The world constructed during the performance is spatio-temporal, different from the living world of the theatre. The characters, whether they are fully individuated (to take T.S. Eliot's *Murder in the Cathedral* as an example, 'Thomas') or only partly individuated (in the same play, 'Knights,' 'Priests,' 'Tempters,' etc), form part of the dramatic world from the above point of view. The characters have actanial roles (dramatis personae) such as the villain, the donor, the helper, the sought-for person and her father, the dispatcher, the hero or the false hero. They are participants in the communicative events, the dialogic interaction. Dialogic exchange of information-bearing utterances—the discourse level of drama—is the most immediately present to the spectator or auditor (Elam 1980: 136).

The participants (actants or dramatic characters) should possess a set of projected qualities and capacities to engage themselves in communicative events on the stage. Keir Elam lists them as:

1. A supposed *linguistic competence,* i.e. mastery of the rules (phonological, morphological, syntactic, lexical, etc) of the language in question.
2. A broader *communicative or semiotic competence* incorporating "the psychological, cultural, and social rules which discipline the use of speech in social settings." This includes such factors as knowledge of the pragmatic rules of linguistic interaction (the rules of conversation), the ability to use language for given communicative ends, the capacity of producing appropriate utterances adapted to their context, awareness of social and deictic roles, and mastery of non-linguistic semiotic systems that are not necessarily involved in the communicative exchange.
3. A background knowledge of the persona, objects and events referred to and an ability to locate them in the dramatic world.
4. An explicit or implicit social status giving the speak authority to make certain utterances ("Off with his head!") in an appropriate way, and determining the listener's duty or right to receive such utterances.
5. A set of intentions or purposes as speaker, in making the utterances.
6. The ability on the part of the speaker to assume the role of listener and vice versa.
7. The capacity to create 'non-actual' worlds referred to in

the course of dialogue, expressing a set of supposed desires, wishes, hypothesis, beliefs, fantasies, etc.

8. A location in an 'actual' spatio-temporal context.

The character-to-character communication takes place in the dramatic context in: (a) the dramatic world at large at the macro-context; and (b) a particular communicative point at the micro-context. Along with the macro-context there are two distinct components: (a) the situation in which a given exchange takes place, which means the set of persons and objects present and their physical circumstances; (b) the supposed time and place of their encounter. The communicative context is usually known as the context of utterance, comprising the relationship set up between speaker, listener and discourse in the immediate space and time. The context-of-utterance can be represented as: speaker, listener, time of utterance ('now'), location of utterance ('here'), and utterance. The dramatic discourse is always tied up with the speaker, the listener, and the immediate spatio-temporal coordinates, but it is at the same time dynamic to the extent that the participants and the time and location of utterance indicated undergo continual change.

Language gains an active and dialogic function from deixis. The role of deixis in creating an interpersonal dialectic within the time and location of discourse is studied by Elam (1980: 138) in his examination of the opening dialogue in George Bernard Shaw's *Heartbreak House.* An important aspect noticed here is that drama consists first and foremost in an 'I' addressing 'you' (dialogue) here and now (space-time).

Deixis allows the dramatic context to be referred to as an 'actual' and dynamic world already in progress. Deictic reference presupposes the existence of a speaker referred to as 'I,' a listener addressed as 'you,' and a physically present object indicated as 'this.' It resides in 'shifters' (empty signs) insofar as it does not, in itself, specify its object, but simply points, ostensively, to the already constituted contextual elements. An indexical expression such as 'Will you give me that, please?' remains ambiguous unless uttered in a context where 'shifters' like *you, me,* and *that* have evident referents. A mode of discourse like the dramatic, which is dense in such indexical expressions, is disambiguated—acquires clean sense—only when it is appropriately contextualised. It is, in other words, 'incomplete' until the appropriate contextual elements (speaker, addressee, time, location) are duly provided.

Demonstratives like 'this,' 'that,' etc in the dramatic dialogue can be shown clearly with the help of gestures. At times the demonstrative 'that' is clear in expressions such as 'Look at that beautiful blonde.' But in the hands of some great playwright stage directions for gestures get inscribed in the dialogue itself. This is what happens when Polonius says: "Take this from these if this be otherwise.' It is absolutely clear that Polonius is pointing to his own head and shoulders.

The language of drama calls for the intervention of the actor's body in the completion of its meanings. In the words of J.L. Styan (1971: 2), "the words as spoken are inseparable from the movements of the actors who speak them." 'I' and 'you' are the main active role in dramatic conversation, and within the 'I'/'you' relationship, it is the first person that is dominant. That means dramatic dialogue is egocentric: the speaking subject defines everything.

Spatial deixis (words showing the dramatic space) takes priority over the temporal. It is above all on the physical 'here' (space) represented by the stage and its means that the utterance must converge. The general semantic process which may be called 'spatialization of time' is especially powerful in a mode of discourse which must relate the several temporal levels at work to the immediate presence of the speaker within a strictly defined space.

The speech event is, in its own right, the chief form of interaction in drama. The dialogue exchange constitutes dramatic action. The 'action dynamic' of the play is carried, above all, by the intersubjective force of discourse. This conception of the function of dialogue stands apart from traditional dramatic criticism, where action is taken to be limited to 'external' events such as murders, battles, the physical comings and goings of characters and so on. In order to emphasize the importance of dialogue, examination of the types of acts performed through language becomes necessary.

Searle (1969: 12) maintains that speech-act theory is mainly concerned with 'rule-governed behaviour.' It aims to bring speech events under a general theory of action. It is this 'language as action theory' that is to be approached in order to understand the action functions of discourse in drama (Elam [1980: 157]). Dramatic discourse is a network of illocutions and perlocutions, or, in other words, linguistic interaction, which is less descriptive than performative. Utterances fall into three general categories: the proposition-bearing statements called constantive utterances, the 'performative' utterances which are not subject to the notions of truthfulness or falsehood, and the 'executive' use of language, i.e., the use of verb phrases comprising the first person singular pronoun and simple present indicative verbs (e.g. "I promise to pay the bearer Rs. 5," or "I declare this bridge open for traffic"). In the delivery of a single utterance three types of act may be performed:

(a) Locutionary act: the basic of producing a meaningful utterance in the speaker's language, in accordance with the syntactic, phonological, morphological and all other relevant factors of speech.

(b) Illocutionary act: the very purpose of making an utterance; saying something, asking questions, ordering someone to do something, promising, asserting the truth of a proposition, etc. Here the speaker's intention to reveal his thoughts to others is meant. It is illocution that constitutes the speech act proper.

(c) Perlocutionary act: Performed by means of saying something, such as persuading someone to do something, convincing one's interlocutor, moving him to anger, and so on. The effect created on the interlocutor is called the perlocutionary effect.

These classes of act are different levels of pragmatic make-up of an utterance. For example, in saying to the participant in a dialogue: "Give me five rupees, please," one performs the utterance act of producing an acceptable English sentence, the propositional act of referring to oneself and five rupees, the illocutionary act of requesting the five rupees—and, with luck, bringing five rupees—and the perlocutionary act of persuading the listener to give one a five-rupee note. For effectiveness of an utterance, or in other words "to make a statement felicitously," a speaker "must, among other things, utter a declarative sentence [...] (he) must be the right person to make the statement [...] (he) must not mumble [...] or break in the middle. (He) must believe what (he) say(s) [...]. And (he) must ground (his) future conduct or speech in a contrary understanding of the state of the world" (Ohmann 1971: 247).

A perlocutionary act must always precede an illocution; not all illocutionary acts will have perlocutionary effect ("Hello, my name is T.S. Eliot"). Thus in language there exists a kind of social, interpersonal, executive power, and it is that pragmatic aspect of 'doing things with words' which is dominant in drama. Ohmann (1973: 83) observes of dramatic dialogue: "the action rides on a train of illocutions [...] movement of the characters and changes in relation to one another within the play appears most clearly in their illocutionary acts." He proceeds further (1983: 89) to make an explicit observation: "Thus conflict is enacted, not in an idealized clash of positions or beliefs whatever that would be. Illocutionary acts move the play along."

Speech acts in drama involve agents (speakers), patients (listeners) intentions (illocutionary), and purposes (perlocutionary), together with an act type, a modality (they can be oral, written or even gestural) and a setting (communicative situation). Now the question is, who performs the illocution: the dramatist or the actor who utters his words? Who, in other words, is really speaking? It will seem to the spectator that the actor is really involved. But what the actor actually performs is the basic utterance act of articulating or *saying* the lines in a comprehensible fashion. He has no illocutionary intentions in saying them. The illocutionary act belongs only to the dramatic context, defined according to the interpersonal relations obtaining in it. It is the audience's task to interpret the physical sayings on stage as higher-order speech events in the dramatic world.

Participants in speech events are engaged in a form of interaction, which means that they share not only a common language and more or less similar logical and epistemological principles but also an agreed end, that is, the achievement of an effective and coherent exchange. As H.P. Grice (1975: 45) observes, the successful conduct of linguistic interaction is possible only on the basis of a joint commitment to the communicative objective: "Our talk exchanges do not normally consist of a succession of disconnected remarks, and would not be rational if they did. They are, characteristically, to some degree at least, cooperative efforts; and each participant recognizes in them to some extent a common purpose or set of purposes, or at least the mutually accepted direction." Grice (1975: 45) formulates this as a global conversational rule, which he names the conversational principle: "Make your conversational contribution such as is required, at the stage of which it occurs, by the accepted purpose or direction of the talk exchange." What he argues is that the exchange is regulated by indispensable principles of decorum allowing coherence and continuity. These principles are stated as maxims implicitly governing the participants' contributions.

1. *The maxim of quantity*: (a) the contribution should be informative as is required for the purpose of exchange; (b) the contribution should not be more informative than required.
2. *The maxim of quality*, expressible as the supermaxim: "Try to make the contribution one that is true": (a) the speaker should not say what he knows to be false; (b) he should not say that for which he lacks evidence (this in Searle (1969: 60) is the sincerity condition, one among the three principal kinds of conditions which must be met in order to fulfil a perfect speech act. This means that the speaker must genuinely want, for example, the requested information; he must feel sincere gratitude when he gives thanks; he must believe that his advice is of authentic benefit to the listener, and so on).
3. *The maxim of relation*, i.e.: "Be relevant."
4. *The maxim of manner*, expressible as a supermaxim, "Be perspicuous": (a) the speaker should avoid obscurity; (b) he should avoid ambiguity; (c) he should avoid unnecessary prolixity; (d) he should be orderly.

Grice goes on to show how the speaker may exploit the maxims in order to mean more than he says—it is on the basis of these conversational rules that 'unspoken' meanings are often understood. For example, if the writer of a novel asks a critic to read his work, and the critic after reading it comments on the quality of its binding and layout, the 'unspoken' meaning will be very clear to an observer. The critic according to Grice 'implicates' the unspoken meaning—thus creating conversational implicature.

Implicatures may come out of the conscious or unconscious breaking or exploiting of the maxims. If the patient is an active participant he will easily understand the implicature. The deliberate abuse of the maxim of relation, for example, generates an implicature in a given situation in which speaker A tells speaker B that he has not seen the latter's wife for long, to which there is no reply except a comment from a comment from another participant C on the quality of the tie A is wearing. From this apparently irrelevant comment A will infer that his remark is for some reason out of place. The maxim of manner, "Be perspicuous" can be exploited to communicate something which a third participant, a child, for example, must not understand, if the persons of dialogue are the parents of the child talking about scx.

Similar implicatures are put to use in the dramatic dialogue also. The conversational maxims, naturally, must be modified, according to the dialogic, monologic, and rhetorical conventions at work. The requirement under the fourth maxim, 'Avoid prolixity' (avoid circumlocution), for instance, is scarcely applicable in the case of Elizabethan or modern poetic dramas. The dramatic speaker must produce utterances which are informative, 'true' with respect to the dramatic world, comprehensible and relevant to the occasion. On such occasions the audience may be able to read between the lines (understand the implicature).

Roger Fowler (1986) maintains that the dramatists deploy sequencing, speech acts, and implicatures to create the verbal illusion of interaction. For a sample analysis, he takes the opening exchange in John Osborne's *Look Back in Anger* (1956), where three characters dominate action. The three characters—Jimmy Porter, his wife Alison, and their friend Cliff—speak in very distinct tones. Much of the dialogue consists of verbal harassment of Alison and Cliff by Jimmy. It is Jimmy who controls what is spoken about, and, to a large extent, the other two try to escape ironic comments. Through the conversation Jimmy is seen asserting a series of judgements and prejudices which begin to build an impression of a character. He begins with a rhetorical question, uses metaphors to suggest that his friend is ignorant, and for plain abuse uses sentences within the rules of conversation. The exchange, therefore, is full of implicatures and rhetorical attacks.

Having outlined various linguistic and pragmatic aspects that constitute conversation, and the applicability of the rules based on them in categorizing and interpreting conversation on stage, I conclude this paper with a passing reference to the rhetoric of drama—to the figures referred to as *metalogisms* by certain linguists. These are logical and referential figures, as opposed to syntactic and semantic ones: they include irony, understatement, paradox, antithesis and hyperbole. They are context-bound devices to the extent that they depend on the audience's ability to measure the gap, as it were, between reference and referents. Metalogisms are 'pragmatic' figures which have a central place in the rhetoric of drama, as it is in drama that one can see the most appropriate situation for them to be effective. The rhetorical analysis of plays has been limited to a literary approach which typically encompasses poetics in general, and the study of imagery and tropes in particular. But in dramatic dialogue 'figurative' acts have an upper hand over imagery and tropes. The metalogistic figure of antithesis is perhaps the most common in dramatic interaction. In poetry it often has the effect of creating a logical or conceptual balance, but in drama it typically carries the conflicting propositional, illocutionary and ethical comments of the speakers.

Works Cited

Austin, J.L. *How to Do Things with Words.* New York: OUP, 1965.

Chaitanya, Krishna. *A New History of Sanskrit Literature.* New Delhi: Manohar, 1977.

Elam, Keir. *The Semiotics of Theatre and Drama.* London and New York: Methuen, 1980.

Fowler, Roger. *Linguistic Criticism.* Oxford: OUP, 1986

Grice, H.P. "Logic and Conversation." *Syntax and Semantics Vol. 3. Speech Acts.* Ed. Cole and Morgan. New York: Academic Press, 1975. 41-58.

Marar, K. *Pathinanchupanyasam* (Fifteen Essays). Kottayam: NBS, 1979

Ohmann, Richard. "Speech, Action, and Style." *Literary Style: A Symposium.* Ed. Seymour Chatman. New York: OUP, 1971. 241-54.

——. "Literature as Act." *Approaches to Poetics.* Ed. Seymour Chatman. New York: Columbia, 1973. 81-107.

Porter, Joseph A. "Pragmatics for Criticism: Two Generations of Speech Act Theory." *Poetics* 15.3 (1986).

Perrine, Laurence. *Literature: Structure Sound and Sense.* New York: Harcourt Brace Jovanovich, 1974.

Sacks, H., E. Schegloff, and G. Jefferson. "Simplest Systematics for the Organisation of Turn-taking for Conversation." *Language* 50 (1974).

Scholes, Robert and Carl H. Klaus. *Elements of Drama.* New York: OUP, 1971.

Searle, John R. *Speech Acts: An Essay in the Philosophy of Language,* Cambridge: OUP, 1969.

Styan, J.L. *The Dramatic Experience.* Cambridge: OUP, 1965.

——. *Shakespeare's Stagecraft.* Cambridge: OUP, 1971.

Tennyson, G.B. *An Introduction to Drama.* New York: Holt, Rinehart and Winston, 1967.

Wilson, Deirdre, and Dan Sperber. "On Grice's Theory of Conversation." *Conversation and Discourse.* Ed. Paul Werth. London: Croom Helm, 1981. 155-78.

✪✪✪

7

The Symbolism of Literature

GANGADHAR GADGIL

The nature of the symbolism of literature is inevitably determined by what literature seeks to express. Therefore the problem really boils down to the nature of the content of creative literature. What does literature express? Does it make the same type of statements about life and reality as are made in political or moral philosophy? Does it try to interpret and evaluate and reality from a moral and political view? If the answers to these questions are in the affirmative, moral and political considerations will inevitably come in when evaluating literature.

Many authors are deeply interested in the political and social problems of their times. Some are profoundly committed to certain moral and political ideas and values. Quite a few have declared that they write only to express their deep-rooted convictions; and it cannot be said that what they have written is not genuine literature.

Great literature often raises profound and disturbing moral issues. We find that an author's moral ideas or view of life influence his style, and his mode of presentation and characterization. Graham Greene's mode of presentation and characterization cannot be dissociated from his preoccupation or obsession with a certain moral predicament. The same can be said about Sartre and many others. Moral and political ideas seem to permeate literature and shape it.

After all the authors write about men and women about the

world in which they live. Language is their vehicle of expression. Words embody ideas. It would therefore seem futile to say that a literary work does not interpret reality or express a view of life which is based on moral and political ideas.

Nor, it seems, is it possible for a reader to remain unaffected by the view of life expressed in a literary work. As T.S. Eliot puts it: "Though we may read literature merely for pleasure, or 'entertainment' or 'aesthetic enjoyment,' this reading never affects simply a sort of special sense; it affects us as entire human beings; it affects our moral and religious existence."

The case for recognizing the relevance of moral and political considerations in evaluating creative literature thus seems to be incontrovertible.

Yet such a recognition seems to go against my experience both as a reader and a writer. When I read a novel, I do not find it necessary to accept the author's moral and political ideas in order to enjoy it. I do not commit myself to the view of life embodied in the *Mahabharat,* when I say that it is a great literary work. I do not have to reject Dostoevsky, when I accept T.S. Eliot as a great writer. I am no doubt profoundly affected by the moral and political issues raised in *Nineteen Eighty-Four.* But is not for understanding these issues that I read that novel. The novel disturbs me and sets me thinking. But my agitated thinking is not an attempt to resolve the issues. They are there and to try to resolve them seems to come in the way of fully experiencing and enjoying that novel. The issues are incidental to something different and, if I may say so something deeper. A novel is something unique and any attempt to generalize from its theme and content seems to be a violation of its integrity. The moral and political ideas it expresses are like sparks that fly off a rotating wheel. You cannot collect them and store them and use them. Once they fly off they are dead and reduced to ashes. A novel or a poem does not answer any questions or resolve any issues. Great artists have been tempted to try to resolve issues in their novels. But whenever they have tried to do so, they have failed. Any such attempt seems to go against the very formative principle in terms of which a literary work takes shape.

It is no doubt true that a writer has certain moral and political ideas and convictions. He has a certain view of life which finds expression in his literary work. But it seems to me far more important that what he writes is a novel or a poem. He uses for self-expression a certain kind of symbolism and he cannot do in a novel or short story something that the nature of his symbolism does not permit him to do.

I have said at the beginning that the problem boils down to the nature of the content of literary work. The nature of the content can be best understood through a study of the nature of the symbolism used.

A creative writer uses more or less the same words which are used in ordinary speech or in a scientific treatise. The words are strung together in sentences which have the same grammatical structure. Yet anyone who reads creative literature is aware that a writer uses language in a unique manner and to serve a unique purpose.

Broadly it can be said that a creative writer uses language to express an emotional experience. A word symbolizes not merely a conception or an idea but an emotional response that is associated with the conception or the idea. In so far as it symbolizes an emotional response or experience, it defines it. It indicates the form, the structure, the blend as well as the intensity of the emotional experience. If the meaning of the term "idea" is widened so as to include all types of mental responses associated with it, then a word as used by a creative writer symbolizes an idea which is different from and yet related to the logical conception or idea symbolized by that word. There is no one unique emotional response associated with a word. In fact, a writer, insofar as he creates something unique and new, gives a new "meaning" to a word. He uses it to symbolize a different emotional happening. This is done by bringing together a number of words in a unique combination.

The combination of words has usually a grammatical structure. In fact a creative writer needs it to convey his "meaning." Yet he is always to some extent at war with grammar. He finds the grammatical structure of a sentence inadequate to convey his meaning. He therefore uses various devices to overcome this inadequacy. One of them is the introduction of rhythm in his sentences. Another is the use of imagery. An image fuses together the meanings of a group of words instead of merely linking them up. A poem or a novel has a structure of its own which is superimposed on the grammatical structure. This structure corresponds to the structure of the emotional experience it symbolizes.

An emotional experience does not exclude sensuous intellectual and moral ingredients in the complex and rather amorphous whole that is experience. Thoughts and emotions influence and shape each other. Feelings do not belong to a non-rational world which is discontinuous with the rational world of thought. Rationality consists in the recognition and discovery of forms as well as their interconnections and as such it is inherent in us. Our sensations organize themselves into forms which we perceive. Our feelings too have definite forms which becomes progressively articulated. Feelings thus are not irrational. They are the ingredients of rationality. They somehow participate in knowledge and understanding. Feelings and systematic logical thought are thus two interconnected ingredients of human rationality. There is no inherent contradiction between the two; and therefore there is nothing incongruous in thoughts being the ingredients of the emotional experience that is expressed in literature.

But thoughts expressed in creative literature do not exist exclusively as thoughts. They exist as ingredients of emotional experience. Their function is not to interpret reality or to justify certain values. It is to define or to make meaningful the emotional experience of which they are the constituent elements. When Macbeth says that life is a tale told by an idiot signifying nothing, we are not called upon to examine or accept that statement as a valid generalization about life and reality. It defines and makes it possible to clearly visualize Macbeth's intense emotional experience.

The nature of the symbolism used in creative literature makes it impossible to look upon its thought content in any other manner. To generalize is the essential nature of logical reasoning. An interpretation of reality has to be in the very nature of things a generalization, which is logically worked out. A system of moral or political ideas can be formulated only by a chain of logical reasoning. But what a literary work symbolizes is a particular emotional experience. It is concerned with something that is individual and unique. Its structure is shaped by the structure of that specific emotional experience. It therefore cannot generalize. It cannot arrive at or express logical conclusions as logical conclusions.

It is sometimes argued that observation and reasoning are not the only methods of arriving at truth. Truth, it is said, can be discovered intuitively. It can be revealed to a man in a flash of insight. This argument has been too often refuted to need any elaborate discussion. Intuition plays as great a part in the field of science as in the field of creative literature. It suggests the existence of a new and hitherto unsuspected hypothesis or idea. It brings various constituent elements of experience into a new relationship. But intuition is not always dependable; and whether the hypothesis suggested by intuition is valid or not has to be decided by the methods of observation and reasoning. A truth intuitively realized has therefore to be put in a logical form. It cannot take a "poetic" form and stand apart from scientific statements.

That a creative writer is not engaged in establishing any generalizations about society or moral values is conceded by a reader the moment he realizes that he is reading a novel or a poem. "Once upon a time" is how all stories begin, and nobody cares to verify the veracity of the writer's statements. If the writer says that a princess had wings, the statement is accepted. A reader does not expect from a creative writer the kind of cogency he expects from a moral philosopher or a political scientist. He expects from him a different kind of cogency. The princess can have wings but a sentence cannot have a wrong rhythm. A writer cannot use a wrong image. If there is a piece of reasoning in a novel, it has to have a logical consistency only to the extent to which it is demanded by the emotional context in which it is made.

Great writers have always been intensely interested in ideas and thoughts. They have been interested in interpretations of reality and moral evaluation of social institutions and individual behaviour. Yet their interest in ideas is not of the same order as that of a moral philosopher. In Tolstoy's *War and Peace* or in the *Mahabharat* we come across different interpretations of reality and moral standpoints, expressed or suggested at different points. Sometimes they are brought to bear upon the same situation. These interpretations have a life of their own and they wander through these books at their own will and enrich their "meaning." As a reader one does not find it necessary to accept any one of them and to reject the others. One does not find it disturbing that the different and very often conflicting interpretations should be present in the same book. They are in some peculiar way insubstantial like shadows and do not collide.

There are of course other and lesser writers who at least apparently express only one view of life in their creative works. Thomas Hardy is one of them. But this consistency on the part of the writer does not make the reader commit himself to the author's views of life. On the other hand it impoverishes the meaning of the author's work. Creative literature does not demand commitment to the views or thoughts expressed in it. In fact it demands that the reader's interest in ideas and thoughts should be secondary. It should be incidental to his interest in the form or meaning of emotional experience.

This assertion is apparently contraindicated by historical experience. All major systems of belief have found expression in creative literature and works of art. It cannot be denied that the *Mahabharat* and the *Ramayana* have for hundreds of years led people to accept the system of beliefs that is Hinduism. Christianity has similarly found creative literature a convenient instrument for the propagation of faith. At the same time all religions and creeds have been extremely suspicious or intolerant of creative literature that expresses belief which they do not accept.

There is a reason for this. All systems of belief require that their adherents should have not only certain convictions and logically formulated views, but also certain emotional attitudes. These emotional attitudes have to be clearly formulated and defined in the context of various situations and predicaments.

This is done by creative literature and other forms of art. On the other hand there are certain emotional attitudes which are dangerous to a system of beliefs. It is necessary that adherents to that system of beliefs should not be exposed to these emotional attitudes. Literary expression of these emotional attitudes is therefore discouraged.

At the same time all systems of beliefs have recognized that creative literature is not a dependable means of formulating and expressing beliefs. The beliefs have been logically formulated in philosophical works and all problems of interpretation and application of the system of beliefs have been always solved by a reference to these logical formulations of beliefs. The primacy of the logical formulation of a belief over its expression in a literary work has always been recognized. It has been always demanded that a belief as expressed in creative literature should conform to the belief as formulated in logical terms. A Gothic church is not regarded as adequate for ensuring adherence to the system of beliefs that constitute Christianity; a sermon has to be preached in the Gothic church.

The correlation between creative literature and a system of beliefs has always been recognized to be tenuous, and history has confirmed this. Many systems of beliefs have died a natural death in the course of history. They are no longer accepted. Yet the literary works which are supposed to express these systems of beliefs still continue to be accepted as great works of art. They have a meaning which is still valid and valuable to us.

Emotional experiences and beliefs are no doubt interrelated. They are both ingredients of the rationality of man. But it is not possible to express their relationship in terms of simple equations which are always valid. A particular emotional experience can suggest a belief. But it can also suggest other beliefs, and in any case it does not necessarily lead to or require the acceptance of particular belief.

Totalitarian systems always find themselves on the horns of a dilemma when dealing with creative literature. On the one hand they need it to strengthen the adherence to the system of beliefs on which they are based. On the other hand they are highly suspicious of it. For behind any work of creative literature there is a spirit of free inquiry. Creative literature inquires into the multiple forms of emotional experiences. Such a spirit of free inquiry is dangerous in two ways. It may lead to the formulation or symbolization of emotional experiences which are dangerous—which suggest awkward questions and dangerous possibilities. Secondly, free inquiry in one field of mental life is bound to stimulate free inquiry in another field, viz., the field of thought.

A totalitarian system tries to solve this dilemma by requiring that all creative literature must conform completely to the accepted system of beliefs. But no such complete conformity is possible. For the very nature of creative literature makes such conformity impossible. A totalitarian system therefore has to make do with pseudo-literature. It can conform because it is organized on a logical or pseudo-logical basis. It is organized on the same basis on which the accepted system of beliefs is organized. It is therefore safe. But it is not adequate because it is not literature. It cannot vibrantly create the emotional attitudes that are necessary to strengthen the adherence to the accepted system of beliefs.

SECTION II

8

Language, Identity and African Literary Theory

ANTHONIA C. KALU

Introduction

African identity remains a significant analytical focus for African literature in European languages. Research in this area spans several disciplines: the sociological, cultural, linguistic, political, religious, educational, economic, among others (Clark, 1968; Irele, 1981; Egejuru, 1978; Achebe, 1975; Amuta, 1989; Ogbaa, 1992). Most works are descriptive while others define and/or analyze the impact of European language use on African identity (wa Thiong'o, 1972 & 1986; Peterson and Rutherford, 1990; Ngara, 1985; Gorman, 1968; Jeyifo, 1990; Anozie, 1981; Obiechina, 1990). Although solutions remain elusive through analysis in traditional disciplines, creative writers and other artists continue to delineate the nature and depth of the crisis. The use of European languages to explore African identity results in increased effort to match scholarly inquiry with artistic vision. This, in turn, deepens the problem and creates deeper crisis. In her discussion about autobiography and memoir, Toni Morrison (1990) explores the differences between (a) fiction and fact and, (b) truth and fact. She asserts that while facts can exist without human intelligence, truth cannot. Morrison's appraisal of this relationship has obvious implications for fiction—the reordering of facts while retaining truth—biography and literary criticism.

> "[...] the scholarship of the biographer and the literary critic seems to us only trustworthy when the events of fiction can be traced to some public verifiable fact. It's the research of "Oh, yes, this is where she got it from" school, which gets its own credibility from excavating the credibility of the sources of the imagination, not the nature of the imagination [...]. [Truth] may be more excessive [than imagination], it may be more interesting, but the important thing is that it is random—and fiction is not random" (303).

The African creative writer's work is accepted as having the capacity to "be traced to some public verifiable fact" because she codes with local speech, confronting the colonizers' "already said" with local images and color. S/he is free in a way the literary critic is not because she cannot remove the "facts" from their milieu; she can only rearrange them for clarity. On the other hand, the critic records creative freedoms taken by finding (again?) existing frameworks. The problem of authenticity inherent in these two modes of exploration is at the root of the language and identity question. Eventually, it is a question of authority and power. Within the world of technological inventions, analysis provides the mechanic with the tools for necessary repair work on new and old technologies but urges inventors to engage on the level of improvement or change. However, in the humanities and social sciences, especially in the literatures of marginalized cultures, analysis has the tendency (power?) to subjugate local creativity to European knowledge bases. And, when authority invalidates, crisis ensues.

For African literature in European languages, the dynamics of scholarly inquiry generally ignores Africa-centered scholarship but admits the creative writer's portrayals of African experience. And, as Morrison says, "when the events of [African] fiction can be traced to some publicly verifiable fact [...], literary analysis of Africa-centered fiction is acceptable. Current difficulties which tie language to identity exist because the Africanist and African Americanist are yet to work with the creative writer "[...] to find and expose [the] truth about the interior life of people who didn't write it [...] [using] [...] the approach that's most productive [...] the recollection that moves from the image to the text. Not from the text to the image" (Morrison 1990, 303).

Teaching or analyzing African literary works without full recourse to their African backgrounds necessitates the use of analytical frames that reflect host department norms.[1] The predictions of such frames necessarily reflect those of the host culture. The point here is: Cohesion between the African creative writer's vision and the African literary critic's use of productive analytical tools will result in a perceptual shift, facilitating the (re)construction of paradigms for the initiation of policies for relevant African development programs. In this work, I will examine selected analytical tools from European and African knowledge bases and conclude with examples of the proposed paradigmatic shift using selected African fictional works.[2]

Western Epistemology, Theory and the Relevance of African Languages

In *Forms of Explanation: Rethinking the Questions in Social Theory* (1981), Alan Garfinkel explores the relationship between, individual characteristics and societal structure. is focus on society, economic stratification and individual social achievement are useful for exploring the alternative analytical strategy and research program suggested here. Garfinkel concludes that explanations are in conflict with the questions they answer when those questions are formulated such that their answers "[...] do[es] not explain this, [...] cannot answer that, [...] suppress[es] this, [...] confuse[s] that" (133). He shows that plausible answers proceed from questions that take structural presuppositions into consideration. Using counterfactuals, Garfinkel argues that:

> [...] every explanation has presuppositions which serve to limit the alternatives to the phenomenon being explained[...]. [And that] in some cases the presuppositions take a special form. Recall [for instance] the discussion of the class being graded on a curve. There was exactly one A to be given out to the class, and it turned out that Mary was the one who got it. Now it is possible to ask

> Why did Mary get an A?
> and get an answer like
> She wrote a good final.
>
> Yet this answer is misleading. [...] for if we asked, counterfactually, what would have been the case if everyone had written a good final, the answer is not that everyone would have gotten an A. The fact that if everyone had written a good final, not everyone would have gotten an A, means that there are structural presuppositions at work in framing the question (108). (My emphasis)

Using counterfactuals to examine structural presuppositions is significant to expanding existing analytical methods in African literary criticism. A broader-based research program demanding reexamination of current frames of reference will advance the search for relevant answers to the language and identity question in African literature. First, two significant frames of reference will be reviewed.

In his *Methodology of Scientific Research Programmes* (1978), Imre Lakatos explores Popper's "'logic of scientific discovery' ('or methodology,' or 'system of appraisals,' or 'demarcation criterion,' or 'definition of science')" (140), and finds that "... for Popper, the logic of discovery or 'methodology' consists merely of a set of (tentative and far from mechanical) rules for the appraisal of ready articulated theories" (140). He adds,

> [...] scientific theories are not based on, established or "probabilified" by, "facts" but rather eliminated by them. For Popper, progress consists of an incessant, ruthless, revolutionary confrontation of bold, speculative theories and repeatable observations, and subsequent fast elimination of the defeated theories: "The method of trial and error is a method of eliminating false theories by observation statements." "Conjecture [are] boldly put forward for trial, to be eliminated if they clash with observations." Thus the history of science is seen as a series of duels between theory and experiment, duels in which only experiments score decisive victories [...]. Popper realizes, of course, that we always test large systems of

> theories rather than isolated ones. [...] he suggests that we should guess—and, indeed, agree—which part of such a system is responsible for the refutation (that is, which part is to be regarded as false), perhaps helped by independent tests of some portions of the system (140, 141). (My emphasis)

Lakatos' discussion of Popper illuminates a number of presuppositions that confound research in African literary studies and the search for compelling research methods. Popper and Lakatos argue that "theories are not based on, established or "probabilified" by, "facts" but are eliminated by them." Western scientific method is progressive because its research agenda is predicated on the idea that all forms of knowledge within a given culture stem from the same epistemological base. Consequently, research in the scientific community focuses on the "appraisal of ready articulated theories" within a recognizable system. Analyses, theory and research emanate from a framework supportive of relevant realities. Familiar references include Plato, Aristotle, Galileo, Shakespeare, Einstein, the Bible, history, the arts, science, education, business theory and practice, politics and political economy. While references span disciplines and historical figures, all cohere on a substructure traceable to a common linguistic or cultural ancestor. Consequently, for the African scholar using European languages there is no real exit into African discursive modes embedded in African experience and framed in African languages. Efforts to apply African dialectics in the research process result in citation or description of African usage in texts.

For African scholarship, then, the question becomes: Do African experience and culture allow for the existence of communities with the prerogative to "'guess' and/or 'agree' [on]—which part of [...] [the African] [...] system [...]'" to refute, appraise or enhance? How are such communities constituted? What are the requirements for full membership and participation? W.E.B. DuBois' (1903) discussion of double consciousness in the United States suggests that the African American scholar has limited access to such a community. Also, according to Frederick Douglass' and other autobiographical accounts[3] from early America, when people of African descent are involved, family and kinship must be discounted. Debates over the place of African American literature in the American literary tradition depicts the currency of this dilemma. On the continent, emergence from colonial domination denies the African the right to use national origin as plausible explanation for membership. Consequently, the decision to use Western languages and research methods excludes the application of African ways of knowing in the formulation of authentic research programs about the African experience.

The conflict between language and identity defies full examination because Africanists' responses have yet to elicit compelling analyses of the African experience. For instance, in *The African Assertion* (1968) Austin Shelton claims:

> [...] there were several constant factors in the growth of African nationalism. The first and most important because the others depended on it, was that the missionary brought a new form of education—European education—which within the period of a few generations developed in Africans a broad knowledge about European ways and a new awareness of African history, and consequently an increased desire for freedom from European rule. The most important element in this education was the use of the vehicular language, which enabled the African to communicate very effectively with other peoples not only in Africa but throughout the world. [...] growth of a common language, which enabled people to communicate across tribal barriers (14,18).

Seen as structural and communication barriers, African languages are excluded early as tools for African development programs. A colonialist view of African development and progress, this exclusion is perpetuated in the rudimentary nature of African languages instruction of African children in western-style school systems across Africa.

In the African Diaspora, particularly the United States, the Ebonics debate attracts attention without significant action as educators and politicians struggle with (ignore?) issues of authenticity and utility of a language spoken by a significant number of school-age African American children. Within the African intellectual community, the extent of the language/ identity dilemma is seen in Ngara's (1985) exploration of La Guma's *In the Fog of the Season's End*:

> La Guma is South African "Coloured" and, unlike Ngugi or Achebe, has the advantage of using English as a mother tongue. He is familiar with the idiom of Coloured, Afrikaaners and, evidently, African speakers of English [...] (89-90).

Ngara continues with the following observation:

> La Guma is obviously not concerned with language variation as a reflection of the idiosyncrasies of individual speakers! [...]. The author is right in attributing a formal style of speech to Elias Tekwane because the majority of good African speakers of English learn the language in the formal situation of the classroom and from books, and do not use the colloquial style of Coloureds or Black Americans (92). (My emphasis)

The assumption that although he learns from books, the "good African speaker of English" is progressive and an achiever whose speech represents how Standard English is spoken needs more careful examination. Significant here is how colloquial English fits into English life and experience. How, for instance, is Standard English derived? Do non-African speakers of Standard English speak colloquial forms? How do "African" colloquialisms fit into English experience and culture?

The second set of assumptions use the divide-and-conquer technique. Ngara's analysis asserts the following: (a) colloquial usage is non-progressive; (b) although La Guma has the "advantage" over Ngugi and Achebe, his advantage is not useful because his propensity for colloquialism prevents its productive utilization. This is a subset of the argument against the utilization of family relationships referred to above. The divisiveness inherent in the discussion of colloquialism requires no further examination. Coloureds and Black Americans are implicated through non-inclusion (not exclusion!) in the group designated "good speakers of English." It is important to note that, by implication, African languages belong to this last group; they, too, cannot contend as carriers of meaning. Therefore, their non-inclusion as authentic research tools by "good speakers" of European languages is their fault! In light of the above, the colonialist's claims about the "vehicular" function of the English language for the African speaker is not supported by current efforts to develop African literary theory.

Abiola Irele's (1981) investigation of the language question also notes a number of problems across the continent and Diaspora. Focusing on the "situation of the African writer," he concludes,

> [...] His problem lies in the fact that however intimate his relationship to the European language, there is always the pressure upon him, in addition to the normal artistic creation, to bridge that distance between the African world and the European language. The point at issue here is not whether an African can successfully write in English or French—we have enough evidence that that particular issue is resolved—but whether in the present circumstances, the work that he produces can have meaning for his African audience [...]. The serious study of African literature—the insertion of this literature in a stream of cultural development determined by the educational and institutional framework of the whole national community—is hampered by the language problem (55). (My emphasis)

Prevailing research on the language and identity question revise or extend some of the explanations in the above quotation. Irele and others who present this line of argument provide the foundation for the exploration of the methodological roots of "[...] the point at issue [...]" (Irele, 55). Their observations and suggestions answer the question: What is the role of the African writer/scholar/critic?

Both Ngara and Irele assume explanatory postures which identify African literature as a problem-child of European languages. They also agree that despite its problematic relationship with European languages, African literature serves the multi-purpose duty of facilitating cultural development, (re)education, re-institutionalization of new African communities and other progress-enhancing projects "[...] across tribal barriers" (Shelton, 18). Although both seem to agree with Shelton that the English language does not constitute a linguistic barrier, they maintain that it poses basic problems for Africa and Africans. The African scholar who uses European language(s) is a constructor of bridges not a propounder of innovative thought. The point here is that the African world is perceived as "already-known" through the pronouncement of African languages as non-contenders in the search for truth. The perception that Africa has nothing new to offer denies the African scholar full access to recognizable "agreed-upon" systems, including African systems. Unlike colloquial and standard English, African and European worlds are seen as having incompatible knowledge bases embedded in divergent systems.

With reference to the Popperian dialogue above, the African scholar has no prerogative to "guess" or "agree" on which refutations will result in the rejection of any theory with the potential to initiate changes to any system. Further, since bridges are constructed between known entities, and Africans have the responsibility "[...] to bridge that distance between the African world and the European language," African efforts to construct theories (not the theories themselves!) also become "facts" which, according to Popper, eliminate theories. This aspect of the discussion is the most frustrating for the African scholar/critic embarked on the project of bridging. Rather than discovery and innovation, explication remains the most acceptable avenue for Africanist participation in contemporary knowledge-seeking communities. Further, exceptions which allow the incorporation of innovators into the dominant research/knowledge community also disallow reentry into relevant African communities.[4] Thus the African's crisis of identity is a fabrication of western assumption that as "facts" Africa, Europe and the Americas contain "facts" which Africans may not (re)discover.

Knowledge-Seeking Communities, Language and Society

In his discussion of the makeup of scientific communities, their functions and roles Thomas Kuhn (1986) illuminates some of the assumptions that give rise to this circumstance by looking at exemplars and rules. He asserts,

> [...] the members of a scientific community see themselves and are seen by others as those uniquely responsible for the pursuit of a set of shared goals, including the training of their successors. Within such groups communication is relatively full and professional judgment unanimous [...]. Communities in this sense exist of course, at numerous levels. The most global is the community of all natural scientists. At an only slightly lower level the main scientific professional groups are communities: physicists, chemists, astronomers, zoologists, and the like. For these major groupings, community membership is readily established except at the fringes [...]. It is only at the next lower level that empirical problems emerge [...]. Typically [more isolation] may yield communities of perhaps one hundred members, occasionally significantly fewer. Usually individual scientists, particularly the ablest, will belong to several such groups either simultaneously or in succession.
>
> Communities of this sort are the units that this book has presented as the producers and validators of scientific knowledge. Paradigms are shared by the members of such groups (146-47). (My emphasis)

Requirements for community membership are linked with stratification criteria, identifying the scientific communities' assumptions and research goals. Comparing the structures and functions of traditional African communities with Kuhn's scientific communities illuminates the African language and identity issue. The resulting gestalt facilitates a perceptual shift which requires consistent reversals of familiar modes of discourse and the application of the concept of symbolic generalizations such that the African viewpoint/experience becomes primary. Ngugi wa Thiong'o (1972) explores early efforts that redirected traditional African views of the world, initiating the installation of colonialism and an alien African self.

> Thus acceptance of the Christian Church meant outright rejection of all the African customs. It meant rejection of

> those values and rituals that held us together: it meant adopting what in effect was a debased middle-class mode of living and behaviour (sic). The European missionary had attacked the primitive rites of our people, had condemned our beautiful African dances, the images of our gods, recoiling from their suggestion of satanic sensuality. The early African convert did the same, often with even greater zeal, for he had to prove how Christian he was through this rejection of his past and roots (32). (My emphasis)

Rather than mere citation of the explanatory posture of the above passage, the object here is the examination of the communities wa Thiong'o refers to and their functions. Clearly, the missionary works from a conceptual base is similar to Kuhn's scientists'. Both have the responsibility to train their successors. For both groups of successors, admission to the group depends on the ability to prove their understanding of prevailing concepts through the application of a "[...] logic of discovery or "methodology" consist(ing) merely of a set of [...] rules for the appraisal of ready articulated theories" (Lakatos, 140). Also, according to Popper, for progress to occur "[...] only experiments (must) score decisive victories [...]" (Lakatos, 141) over theories and "facts" must eliminate speculative but repeatable observations.

For wa Thiong'o's African convert, the presumed absence of African "facts" and the "suggestion of satanic sensuality" encourages the convert to boldly put portions of the African system forward for trial and eventual refutation by the missionary's "facts." The difficulty here is that as a non-member of any African community of knowledge seekers, the missionary has neither the experience nor the tools to determine what constitutes "facts" within African ways of knowing. Consequently, acceptance of the missionary-as-trainer/African-as-successor schema results in identity crisis for the African. But, within the colonial structure, the missionary, already occupying the highest position within the hierarchy of the new knowledge-seeking communities, retains current status or, like Kuhn's able scientist, gains acclaim through the solution of "[...] empirical problems [that] emerge" (Kuhn, 146).

Although the above method facilitates the repositioning process, it does not fully clarify the conflict between the question of African identity and its explanations. The assumptions that mask this conflict are discernible through investigation of the process of knowledge acquisition. Corresponding appraisal within a familiar African knowledge-seeking community—the community of elders—is illuminating. Kuhn's discussion of how students use symbolic generalizations to learn illustrates the dynamics of the knowledge acquisition process in the sciences. The science student learns to solve more problems through finding correlations and family resemblances. Eventually, a learning strategy is developed within which the scientist "[...] is tempted to identify stimuli one-to-one with sensations [...]" (Kuhn 158).

Significant to this work are some of the assumptions generated when this concept is transported to African environments. As Kuhn points out, an individual using such a strategy for the acquisition and assessment of knowledge begins to expect people from different societies to behave alike, i.e., as if they see/should see the same things as himself. This assumption jettisons the idea of universalizing claims through using "[...] trial and error [as] a method of eliminating false theories by *observation statements*" (Kuhn 140). Consequently, invalidated African knowledge results in conflicts between questions and explanations for the African scholar/researcher.

Though similar, in some ways, to those of the west, African ways of knowing are essentially different in derivation and implementation. I am not here suggesting that only African-born Africanists have access to African ways of knowing. The non-European born western-trained scholar/critic is proof that individuals from different societies can acquire ways of knowing unfamiliar to their birth cultures. However, while the acquisition of new symbolic generalizations requires suspension of disbelief by the learner, it also suggests the expansion of boundaries. Although successful implementation of its predictions requires in-depth knowledge of spatial and temporal modes and their significance within the host culture, its acquisition does not mandate relinquishing existing viable cultural cognitive modes (learning how to drive does not mandate losing knowledge of how to ride a bicycle, for instance). Clearly, the requirement that "[...] conjectures [...] boldly put forward for trial, [...] be eliminated if they clash with observations [...]" (Kuhn 140) was not a part of the colonialist agenda but African traditions and norms remain important for the discussion of African ways of knowing.

The colonists' universalizing strategy excluded learning constructs that enabled full use of African ways of knowing. Since universals evoke family resemblances to initiate discovery and practice, the colonists used that capacity for conversion and domination, stopping short at full consideration of Africans or African experience and culture. Though essential to universalistic assumptions and stated as part of the language-based refocusing of the African, African development was hampered early by European social practice through the negation of intellectual and political deployment of universals. Consequently, Africa and Africans continue to experience economic and political stagnation and related dilemmas that obstruct individual and national progress.

In African literary studies, this situation results in applications of the European knowledge-base such that (a) inter-textual analysis (especially between African and non-African works) and other bridging concepts are over-explored; (b) efforts to explore African dynamics result in discussions of "[...] tired, basic topics [...] like "oral elements in the writings" of a few well-known authors" (Stephen Arnold quoted in Zabus, 1990:21); (c) emphasis on western mechanisms and processes of erasure obstructs comprehension of those things which the West perceives as eliminable in the African continuum. Consequently, the African remains unknown, becoming instead a "[...] present day proverbalizer [who is] textually bound to be a logos-eater [...]" (Zabus, 27). The intricate relationship between identity and language requires objective exploration and validation of how the African re-creates the African self with words. This entails examination of the analytical strategies that Africans use to delineate and implement African life and experience. The alternative research paradigms called for here will sustain meaningful existence and continuation.

Achebe's works have popularized one of the systems for Igbo self re-creation—the community of elders that authorize the structure of the community, the requirements for group membership, conditions for retention of membership, patterns that encourage participation and methods which encourage such patterns. The community of elders exists in recognizable forms all over Africa and the African Diaspora. In most African and African Diaspora literature, it manifests as a group that represents strongly-held beliefs and practices. Among African Americans, the community of elders is found in the Black Church. For the Igbo, the community of elders is a significant facilitator in the communication process. This difference is evident in the Igbo concept of the existence of things in pairs—*Ihe di abuo-abuo*. Or, as Achebe says, "Wherever Something stands, Something Else will stand beside It" (Achebe 1975, 94). Within this duality every possible idea has a complement and every complementary pair generates its own complement. The possibility for endless replication is infinite, embedding change, development and progress as essential in Igbo thought. Further, while every pair of complements is balanced in itself, equilibrium and harmony are maintained within the whole. The most frequently referenced system of complementary opposites is the pair made up of the world of the living and that of the ancestors. About this pair, Achebe says,

> This "spiritland" where dead ancestors recreate a life comparable to their earthly existence is not only parallel to the human world but is also physically contiguous with it for there is constant coming and going between them in the endless traffic of life, death and reincarnation. The masked spirits who often grace human rituals and ceremonies with their presence are representative visitors from this underworld and are said to emerge from their subterranean home through ant-holes. At least, this is the story as told to the uninitiated. To those who know, however, the masked "spirits" are only symbolic ancestors (1975: 95).

Equilibrium and harmony are maintained by "*those who know*," i.e., members of the knowledge-seeking community of elders. The totality of what they know is what I refer to here as Igbo (African) ways of knowing. I am not using the term "epistemology" here because its definition which is tied to that of the word "know" makes it less encompassing and locks this discussion about methodological shifts into familiar, authenticated western-based definitions. I find "ways of knowing" more pliable because it allows for a broad-based discussion of what is know-able and the structures in which such knowledge becomes relevant.

For example, Okonkwo's story (Achebe 1958) provides insights into Umuofia's requirements for membership and retention into the community of individuals who demonstrate potential to contribute positively to the advancement of Umuofia life and experience. Okonkwo's initiation into this group is predicated on a number of related concepts expressed (in Okonkwo's case) as "When a child washed his hands, he could eat with kings" (12). Comprehensive and effective application of this statement depends on the verity of other statements about hand-washing such as "If the left hand washes the right hand, the right hand will wash the left hand" or related statements "Let the eagle perch and let the hawk perch. He who says, no, to the other, may his wings break," which depict degrees of derivation and implementation of cleanliness, uprightness, justice, morality, thrift and the incorporation of upward mobility in the society. Once an individual is initiated, ability to maintain harmony and equilibrium among related concepts predicts retention of membership. This is why it was said of Okonkwo, "Looking at a king's mouth, one would think he never sucked at his mother's breast" (28). Okonkwo's inability to see the relationships between his success and recognizable learning strategies ("sucked at his mother's breast") remains a constant source of concern for other elders. Viewed in this light, Okonkwo's failure assumes a meaning more relevant to Umuofia's approaches to knowledge construction. It becomes possible to see why his frequent misinterpretations lead him to actions that do not fit Umuofia thought.

> In a flash Okonkwo drew his machete [...]. The waiting backcloth jumped into tumultuous life and the meeting was stopped. Okonkwo looked at the dead man. He knew that Umuofia would not go to war [...] (188).

The people of Umuofia, waiting for him to apply his understanding of the symbolic generalization that illuminates the discourse between life and the negotiations for living (a complementary pair), are agitated when he eliminates life, causing irreversible imbalance. Despite his merit-based initiation into the community of knowledge-bearing elders, Okonkwo consistently misunderstands the community's symbolic location in the expanse of the complementary pair: "the world of the living/the world of the ancestors." Achebe draws attention to the ubiquity of this way of knowing after Okonkwo's death.

> There was a small bush behind Okonkwo's compound. The only opening into the bush from the compound was a round hole in the red-earth wall through which fowls went in and out in their endless search for food. The hole would not let a man through. It was to this bush that Obierika led the Commissioner and his men. They skirted round the compound, keeping close to the wall (190).

Although Okonkwo's compound is built to allow for interaction with the bush, the hole in the red earth wall does not allow human intruders in either direction. The bush is one of the closer examples of the unknown universe in the inhabited world of the living. In other parts of the Igbo village, this boundary is delineated not by a wall but by a constructed ridge or fence, the planting of one or more sacred trees, shrubs, or groves. Whatever the structure, the boundary is symbolic and movement between the two worlds is controlled (skirted) using social norms and taboos thereby making un-mediated crossings like suicides an abomination.

Consequently, for Umuofia, Okonkwo's suicide is not the act of a tragic hero. Obierika, Okonkwo's best friend, who has watched his struggles to understand his responsibilities as an elder says, "That man was one of the greatest men in Umuofia. You drove him to kill himself; now he will be buried like a dog [...]." But Obierika's response is that of an individual who has lost a friend; it is subjective and deals with the present. In addition to Obierika's comment, Achebe uses the voice of an un-named man to delineate the external manifestations of Igbo tradition for this situation. The lack of a name, a convention in African oral narratives, under girds an objective, distant, inscrutable knowledge base: "It is against our custom," said one of the men. "It is an abomination for a man to take his own life. It is an offense against the Earth, and a man who commits it will not be buried by his clansmen [...]. We shall make sacrifices to cleanse the desecrated land" (188).

Given Igbo perception of human potential in the negotiation between the world of the living and that of the ancestors, i.e., the known and the unknown, Okonkwo's death cannot be seen as heroic. His propensity to eliminating life with the knife, the gun or the rope is a reflection of his inability to perceive the vital ties that bind[5] the people to their world. Okonkwo's suicide is a final negation of this negotiation potential because it puts a knife on the thing that holds the people together, disjoining them from life at the individual, community and ancestral levels. Like the death of Ogbuefi Ezeudu, the death of a man of Okonkwo's stature, should be cause to celebrate this relationship between the worlds of living and the ancestors. Celebrating this continuity reaffirms life. Okonkwo's suicide negates both his life and the complementary relationship he bears to the group of elders. Consequently, his suicide's perceived threat to the community's capacity to uphold life and the living renders his "[...] body [...] evil, and only strangers may touch it" (190).

Although, at the time of Okonkwo's death, Umuofia is already familiar with the idea of "[...] the white man whose power you know so well [and who can] order[ed] [...] meeting[s] to stop" (188), their knowledge of this new power does not stop the meeting. The question becomes: What constitutes the end of dialogue (the meeting in progress) in Umuofia (colonized Africa)? In pre-colonial Umuofia, productive dialogue and the knowledge-seeking process are under constant scrutiny. Presumption of group continuity maintains the process; abbreviation and unmediated excision work against it. Thus

Achebe's use of the un-named man's voice to speak Umuofia's mind during a crisis of the magnitude discussed above is pertinent to Igbo knowledge-seeking process.

After the meeting is stopped, some men re-convene in Okonkwo's compound and the District Commissioner "[...] find[s] a small crowd of men sitting wearily in the *obi* [...]" (189). He notes that, "[...] one of the most infuriating habits of these people is their love of superfluous words [...]" (189). He decides to give Okonkwo's story some attention in "[...] a reasonable paragraph [...]" in his book because "[...] there was so much else to include, and *one must be firm in cutting out details*" (191). Although his strategy, stated in the title of his book-in-progress, *The Pacification of the Primitive Tribes of the Lower Niger,* involves the stultification of Umuofia's language and rhetorical modes, his instruction to the messengers to take Okonkwo's body to the court after *they* cut it down from the tree fits the colonist's process of looking for family resemblances. The familiar surroundings of the western-style court allows the Commissioner to continue to act from his own knowledge base and speak his language. Unfamiliar with the Commissioner's knowledge base, the people of Umuofia cannot mediate his abbreviation of their story—the stultification of their identity in his world.

In order to accomplish his pacification project, the Commissioner has to find a segment of Umuofia that contains a convincing portion of Umuofia's knowledge-seeking community. The small band of men make up this portion. After Okonkwo's response to a dialogue in progress and Umuofia's query, "Why did he do it?" (188), this group's recourse to ancestral wisdom becomes a matter of form and application. Thus, the unidentified man's voice is that of the "[...] waiting backcloth [that] jump[s] into tumultuous life [...]" (188) when Okonkwo kills the court messenger. The question is: In what way is this man unidentifiable? Given that the little band of men and the Commissioner listen to and act on the information he provides, only a non-trivial answer to this question will suffice.

Clearly, the man is only unidentifiable within the context of the new dialogue under construction. The "[...] little band of

[Umuofia] men" (also unidentified) know him, and the knowledge base that mandates his participation. In the evolving dialogue between Igbo ways of knowing and the western-style novel, the relationship between the little band of men, the unnamed man and the ancestral knowledge-base becomes an authentic avenue for the retrieval of the Igbo (African) self. The form of the novel and that of the Commissioner's book do not allow his naming in a way that makes sense to the understanding of the rest of the story.[6] Since his lack of a name in this scene expands the relationship he bears to Umuofia, further illumination of his presence and contribution in a time of crisis must be based on Umuofia (Igbo) ways of knowing. His contribution shows an understanding of the Igbo concept of duality in existence: *Wherever Something stands, Something Else will stand beside It.* This man, if he understands the English language will not speak it because his operation within Umuofia knowledge-base demands Umuofia's preservation. An essential element in the discussion about the communication in progress (in the novel), language use and identity, his name does not need to be specified because its relevance depends on context. Obviously, the language and identity question requires, for its illumination, the assumption that the language of the individual whose identity is in crisis be used on its own terms; an assumption that African-born creative writers make early in their works. The vehicular nature of European and African languages in the new duality must be explored in order to actualize the forms of knowledge they convey if their users are to remain self-sustaining.

Achebe deploys this assumption to the extent that Igbo "speaks" to English and vice versa in his works. Given the constraints of the novel, background and setting, characters, dialogues, etc., are (re-)conceptualized to maintain authenticity. Obviously, changing the language of the new discourse will not be helpful because the system is already jeopardized (remember Okonkwo's son, Nwoye?) Rather, a conscious re-structuring of the parameters of relevant discourses is required such that every component and participant within evolving pairs of complements are recognized and fully utilized.

To this end, traditional Igbo communities use available artistic forms to initiate constant and detailed discussion of events and ideas thus mediating between perceived relationships and their outcomes within (Achebe, 1989: 51-54). Traditional Africa's use of art to sustain and preserve language and culture is a stylistic device that contemporary African writers have only indirectly explored. The prevalence of this technique in most African societies before and after western intervention is evidenced, for instance, in the existence of aspects of this mode of discourse in African-American signifyin(g).[7]

The Artist as Custodian of African Knowledge Bases: Achebe and Nwapa

A brief exploration of some traditional Igbo linguistics postures in the works of Achebe and Nwapa shows that their use of the English language announces Africa's need for conscious re-structuring and self-redefinition after colonization and independence. Both authors successfully insert the English language into the fabric of Igbo verbal arts, revealing a new duality in Igbo ways of knowing. Achebe and Nwapa use the English language in ways that make it part of the culture which the colonizer sought to abbreviate or discredit. Unlike the colonizers, both writers' re-structuring of the new discourse focuses attention on English and Igbo ways of knowing. Their innovative postures facilitate communication between traditional and contemporary frameworks. The result is a new dispensation; a new medium of action whose change agents are rooted in two enduring traditions.[8] Continuity is maintained across Igbo (African) experience by the use of dialogue driven by core relational statements in the culture. Consequently, emphasis on external manifestations of the new duality reflects unmediated examination of its new texts and results in crisis.

For instance, when Ezeulu sends Oduche to the new religion (Achebe, 1964: 50-51) with the charge, "I want one of my sons to join these people and be my eyes there [...]" (51) he is situating Oduche for simultaneity in ideological and linguistic posturing. Oduche must understand the new religion so well that Ezeulu's perception of it at the time of Oduche's recounting of his experiences should enable Ezeulu to straddle both cultures.

Ezeulu, the Keeper of Umuaro's god of war and defence, must "see" clearly the relationships between the old and the new. Explicitly, Oduche's role is to formulate a new construct that will extend the existing paradigm such that Umuaro's greatness is complemented, not deleted, by that of the new dispensation.

In *Anthills of the Savannah,* the characters delineate the extent of the struggle necessary to implement Ezeulu's charge to Oduche. Chris and Ikem both earn their living transmitting information in the new dispensation, Beatrice is a Senior Assistant Secretary with a first-class honors in English. Early chapter titles introduce Christopher Oriko and Ikem Osodi, identifying them as "First Witness" and "Second Witness," respectively. This double naming is characteristic of praise-naming in most African cultures and extends the Oduche/Ezeulu project. According to tradition, their names reflect duties and achievements as the new *ozo*—men of title—in the contemporary society. But, productive contemporary dialogue requires conscious reappraisal of the points of interaction from which the new dispensation emanates. Initially, that is not true of Beatrice Nwanyibuife Okoh who grows up in a Christian household in Kangan and earns a first class honors degree in English from the English Queen Mary College. Brought up in the new dispensation, Beatrice has a sense of being "[...] two people living inside one skin [...]" (81). Always on her own, she sees no reason to "[...] ask the world to interrupt its business for no other reason than to find out what one insignificant female did or did not do [...]" (77).

While Beatrice seems to believe that self-erasure is "[...] a little matter of personal pride [...]" (77), Nwapa's Efuru (1966) goes to the marketplace twice in one day to accept public affirmation and acceptance and the responsibilities that accrue from mature womanhood in Ogwuta tradition. Unlike Beatrice, Efuru claims what is due her and does not apologize for being female as the "coming out" ceremony initiates her into her people's objective world. For instance, while Beatrice is mystified about having enemies after attaining a university degree from England, Efuru's lessons on the same issue are quickly learned during her ceremonial visits to the market. Although named

Efuru (the lost) she is also called Nwaononaku—the one that dwells in wealth—an Igbo expression about wealth that encompasses various levels of reality and existence. Also, while Beatrice works in isolation and cannot translate either her names or her educational achievement in a foreign land into self-affirmative cognates in the new dispensation, Efuru's sense of dwelling in wealth is portrayed in the support the elders (represented by her father, Ajanupu, and Adizua's mother, Ossai) give her even when she defies custom to marry a man who is "not known." In her marriages, Efuru's conscious appropriation of the alternative that requires defiance and independence calls attention to traditional frameworks about marriage and in-law relationships. For the elders, this action is the first indication that Efuru has the potential[9] to "[...] see new and different things when looking with familiar instruments in places where they (the elders) have looked before" (Kuhn, 91). Thus the elders agree to the re-negotiations and, much later, when it is obvious that she is not biologically prolific, her father guides her to a viable conclusion within another traditionally established alternative.

Efuru's worship of *Uhamiri,* the woman of the lake, keeps her secure in her self, enabling her to continue to question and explore Ogwuta ways of knowing despite continuous gossip about her childlessness. Rather than comprising "[...] competing discourse (in the Bakhtinian sense) of economic independence and maternal satisfaction [...]" (Andrade, 100), Efuru's story portrays Ogwuta women's efforts to come to terms with their perceived reality. Their efforts, like Efuru's, are complemented by the community's purposeful implementation of harmony and equilibrium in otherwise disabling situations. To that extent, Ossai and Ajanupu take her into their family and Ajanupu defends her when her second husband, Gilbert, maltreats her. Though motherless, she develops a strong sense of well-being in the wholesome acceptance of Ossai and Ajanupu, her female in-laws.

Efuru's relationships with these two women implicitly address two Igbo postures relevant to female psychic health. The first is the traditionally acknowledged and sanctioned usable power of the female community, an African tradition that seems laden with contradictions and still defies anthropological and western feminist analysis of the "oppressed" African woman.[10] The second is the Igbo convention that enables the extension of one's kinship group through in-law relationships which are largely managed and nurtured by women. The latter situation is crucial in the negotiation of processes with the potential for change in status. Although perceptibly managed by men, the extended family system is activated through female links.

Achebe's Beatrice does not have knowledge of this advantage. Born into a household set in the middle of a Christian Mission compound (a colony within colonized territory), she lacks the sense of self within Igbo traditions which Efuru takes for granted. Her childhood memories revolve around a household kept in check by the whip and garnished with morning and evening prayers. However, even from the western-based prayer rituals, she remotely recognizes the power of the Igbo language through the echoes of meaning she gleans from the phrase *uwa t'uwa*—world without end. For Beatrice, the power of this Igbo phrase which occurs at the end of some prayers lies not in its meaning but in "[...] its capacity for infinite replication [...]" (77). Although *uwa t'uwa* provides Beatrice a door between familiar and unknown worlds, her first attempt to appropriate its possibilities is obviated by the whip wielded by her father, a teacher of the new dispensation. Working alone within the redefined parameters of the new Igbo family Beatrice observes, "[...] my father and my mother had their own world, my three sisters had theirs and I was alone in mine [...]" (79). Even her foreign name is abbreviated to "[...] either B or BB [...]" (76). For Beatrice the phrase "Nwaononaku" (one who dwells in wealth) which complements Efuru's given name is an abstraction.

Dispossessed and transplanted, Beatrice's re-entry into her birth culture is obstructed by the demands on her to make meaning of Bassa which, like her childhood home in the Mission, is poised between two un-reconciled worlds. As she moves from school to school and finally to a foreign university and academic excellence, Beatrice must find meaning for herself in the emerging dispensation. For example, she deciphers a meaning of woman different from what Efuru is taught through observing basic postures like the establishment of an Anglican mission compound of her childhood in which "The female teachers lived in the *smallest building of all*, a three-room thatched house set, *for protection I suppose*, between the pastor and the catechist" (77). The new arrangement of houses at the mission not only rejects the structure of Okonkwo's compound discussed earlier, it also hems Kangan (African) women into a new "logic of discovery," which denies them the option to "dwell in (the) wealth" whose production and maintenance, until now, has been predicated on their full participation and implicit freedom.

The endless possibilities which Beatrice, the irrepressible priestess ("[...] sometimes I feel like Chielo in the novel, the priestess and prophetess of the Hills and the Caves [...]") recognizes in *uwa t'uwa* enable her to continuously reject the boundaries imposed by her Mission upbringing and adult life in Bassa. Gleaned from a foreign prayer in translation, *Uwa t'uwa* becomes the link to her unrealized power as the Daughter of Idemili; her all-inclusive heritage. Unlike Efuru, Beatrice lacks ancestral or communal guidance. Alone, she suffers the humiliation and betrayal accruing from the new dispensation's perception of her as Nwanyibuife—a female is *also* something—a disposable addition to His Excellency's party held at Abichi in honor of a visiting reporter from the U.S. Unlike Oduche, Ikem or Chris, Nwanyibuife is not a witness and Beatrice is a misfit. Consequently, the language she develops to talk about herself is individualistic and defensive.

Similarly, Nwapa's Efuru appears initially lost to everything and everybody. Not only does she defy tradition, she seems a negation of Ogwuta concepts of mature womanhood. However, everyone that comes in contact with her is involved in the efforts to retain her participation in the community. Her father waits for her to re-negotiate the discussion about her marriage which enables him to establish relationships with his in-laws. The women in her home of marriage claim the responsibility of affirming her womanhood; and, her father guides her to the worship of the woman of the lake. On a general level, the needy seek her mediation and help. Though on the surface Efuru is the cause of a great deal of gossip, each situation ends in her emotional and/or spiritual fulfillment.

The community's acceptance of Efuru's potential for seeing beneath the surface is evident in the women's talk about her. For instance, when they are at the end of their financial tether, Nwabata says to Nwosu, "'What can a woman do?' you say everyday. In the end, a woman does something [...] I will not go to Efuru either. She is a woman like myself, and therefore I will find it more difficult to go down on my bended knees and beg for more money when we have not paid the debts we owe her" (166). Also, when Omirima the gossip, is reminded by Amede that, "Some [women] bring in riches also," Omirima is quick to redirect the conversation by asserting, "Yes, you are right, but that is not what I am saying at the moment [...]" (160). In different ways both women implicitly defer to the community's support of Efuru's womanhood despite her inability to be biologically prolific. In the above examples, this deference is made through denial. Nwabata does not want further confrontation with Efuru while Omirima refuses to discuss her. Both women implicitly recognize and accept society's endorsement of Efuru's right to appropriate alternative modes of self-definition and expression.

Since a primary motivation in the implementation of duality in existence is re-generation and the facilitation of relevant relationships, the process does not exclude negative references about the subject. What is required is that participants in such dialogues remain aware of parameters significant to the total discourse. Nwapa's exploration of this apparent inconsistency is portrayed in Efuru's ability to bear one child. Within Igbo ways of knowing, she reflects the tendency (not the demand) in women to create. When this creative tendency is threatened or absent, communal support through traditionally established outlets like *Uhamiri* redirect individual efforts toward self fulfillment. Cultural stability and progress are ensured when language, culture and the self are consciously reconciled by the individual and community.

Conscious reconciliation between the various aspects of existence is the responsibility of the Igbo artist and philosopher.[11]

Nwapa and Achebe assume this responsibility in their works. Their re-deployment of the relationships between Igbo language and culture reveals the endless possibilities of the concept of duality in Igbo thought. The authority with which they write is conferred by the Igbo world-view whose contemporary figurations straddle two enduring cultures but whose basic meanings do not depart from Igbo thought. Like the traditional chief priests/priestesses whose roles and functions necessitated their mediation of the world of the living and that of the ancestors, the familiar and the unknown, contemporary African writers continue to reappraise African thought, relating it to the new, provocative Western presence in every *obi*, village square and shrine. And, like the ritual and religious objects of the traditional sages, the protagonists in contemporary works remain tools for the exploration of stability, change, progress and their complements. Through the questions they ask, the contemporary writers' works become reminiscent of the divination processes of their predecessors, forcing us to pay attention.

As a worshipper of *Uhamiri* for example, Efuru becomes one of the representatives of the beautiful woman of the lake who lives at the bottom of the lake but controls activities in and around it. However, her real power is understood by the knowledge-seeking community of elders who have the ability to see below the surface. Representing *Uhamiri* in her role of retrieval, Efuru mediates between the people and Difu, the western-trained medical doctor. Her bridging function between the people and Difu and the new dispensation is facilitated by the completeness of her immersion in Ogwuta ways of knowing. Viewed in this light, the answer to Efuru's question, "Why then did the women worship her?" about *Uhamiri* becomes obvious. The woman of the lake is worshipped because worshipping her[12] provides a new tool that will facilitate development of new ways of seeing for Ogwuta (Igbo and African) women who otherwise will be hemmed into stagnating frames of reference should they prove unable to use or conform to prevailing norms. Rather than "[...] hav(ing) everything [Efuru] needs [...]" (Andrade, 100), alternatives like *Uhamiri* announce the flexibility of the boundaries of existing paradigms such that Ogwuta woman can

"[...] adopt new instruments and look in new places [...] [so that] familiar objects are seen in a different light and are joined by new ones as well [...]." And, significantly, "[...] there is no geographical transplantation; outside the laboratory everyday affairs usually continue as before" (Kuhn, 91). Since *Uhamiri* is perceived as existing at the bottom of the lake, i.e., outside the location of Ogwuta's normal cultural practice, this second alternative to existing paradigms allows for exploration of options from the outside. Unlike Kuhn's scientists, the Ogwuta woman with access to *Uhamiri* is not confined to the laboratory, i.e., the normal physical boundaries available for research and exploration. A tool that frees her from her physical obligations as a wife on certain days of the week *Uhamiri* also allows cognition and confrontation of possibilities in both worlds; she is re-positioned for the construction of a new paradigm and a new self.

In Achebe's Bassa, Beatrice achieves this re-positioning through Elewa who is closer to the people's way of knowing. During the naming ceremony of Elewa's baby-girl, every warring group that has resulted from the changing order in Bassa is represented: the living and the dead, men and women, civilians and soldiers, Christians and Moslems, the educated and the uneducated, and people from the major ethnic groups of Kangan. The elders arrive late but they approve the young people's audacious re-interpretation of tradition. Their approval is based on their understanding of the total expanse of duality. In the world of the living, Nwanyibuife—Woman-is-Something—is an expression of one of the complements: woman/man, young people/elders. The young people give a traditionally male name to the baby-girl, "[...] We shall call this child AMAECHINA: May-the-path-never-close [...]" (206). Traditionally referring to the path between the living and the dead, the name refers to the maintenance of the balance between creativity and progress. Achebe, the modern priest/artist suggests reevaluation of the communication strategies fashioned out of the common experience of the near-loss of a way of knowing embodied in Sam, Chris, Ikem, Beatrice and Elewa.[13]

By having Beatrice name Elewa's and Ikem's daughter,

Achebe's continuing discourse about re-positioning is instructive. The naming ceremony allows Beatrice to assume her role as a Daughter of Idemili, the priestess whose re-positioning is sanctioned by the community and empowered in both worlds. Consequently, Beatrice is able to rename, i.e., re-create the parameters of the new dispensation. Her yearning to understand core relationships in issues of continuity and continuance is realized. Using her re-appropriated power as Daughter of Idemili to support her status as *educated Igbo woman,* she re-negotiates her power over language by assigning the male name Amaechina to the girl-child thereby calling attention to the re-positioning that the African scholar/critic (Beatrice with her honors degree in English) must make. In the absence of ancestral guidance, she uses Igbo words to re-initiate communication as a self-(re)-creative process and to ensure linkages between the traditional and the postcolonial state in crisis.

Conclusion

Although things did fall apart, Achebe's Beatrice Nwanyibuife resumes the discussion about self-regeneration as a significant element in Igbo thought. For the African scholar/critic, Efuru, Elewa and Nwanyibuife reinforce the flexible boundaries available to the Igbo (African) woman within traditional African cultures. These characters allow for a re-visioning of the extent to which the African woman can engage her own re-creation/re-positioning process within western knowledge-seeking communities. Ultimately, it is this re-positioning that will allow the Beatrices of Africa to re-enter African communities and cultures from where they can engage, again, shelved discussions about Africa's continuance. Their availability for Africa's reappraisal reduces the tendency to close, without question, Africa's paths to posterity. The successes of African creative writers suggests that if they are joined by African scholars in the urgent work of re-visioning and re-invention, the paths to African knowledge will again conjoin theory with praxis, language with identity.

Notes

1. Examples include Chinua Achebe's *Things Fall Apart* which has been translated into many European languages and which features in US

High School curricular. Yet, many US college students express ignorance of Igbo people and their ways. Bucchi Emecheta's *The Joys of Motherhood* provides a similar example in feminist discourses or Women's Studies classrooms.

2. For full discussion and application of this framework, see: Anthonia Kalu, *Women, Literature and Development in Africa* (Africa World Press. Forthcoming).
3. Despite the society's patriarchal norms and pervasive rumor that Frederick Douglass' master was his father, Frederick was neither claimed by the master nor given legitimate access to other family members or property.
4. Incorporation of pathfinders of African descent using western universalist postures include the acclaim given to people like Dr. Martin Luther King, Jr., Bill Cosby and Oprah Winfrey in the United States and Nelson Mandela and Desmond Tutu in South Africa. This is not to imply that these people are not leaders and achievers. Rather, the western-dominated modes of incorporation make it difficult for people of African descent to claim them in the same way that western communities and knowledge seekers claim historical figures like Aristotle, Shakespeare, Einstein, etc.
5. This phrase is borrowed from Bernard Makhosewe Magubane's title, *Ties That Bind: African American Consciousness of Africa* (New Jersey: Africa World Press, 1987).
6. The point here is that within the novel form, naming this character would disrupt the plot. Since he has no previously recognizable role or function in the story, he has no "right" to utter such profundity. Additionally, because of Obierika's emotional/subjective ties to Okonkwo, his character cannot carry the weight or meaning of this information. Given the setting, etc., the use of an unnamed man in this scene makes sense only in the context of Igbo verbal arts as a credible resource.
7. See for instance: Henry Loius Gates, Jr. *The Signifying Monkey: A theory of Afro-American Literary Criticism* (New York: Oxford UP, 1988).
8. One of the problems that initiators of African development projects face is that the legacy of colonialism in Africa stem from 17th, 18th and 19th Century Europe. European knowledge from this era was presented to Africans as progress. Their incorporation into African ideas about progress make for difficult transitions at the end of the 20th Century when European nations and the United States have moved on to different ways of knowing. In contemporary African literature, this problem is evident in the name choices for characters.

When these names are derived from the European, they usually echo names from the colonial or early post colonial encounters.

9. It is important to note that within Igbo tradition and custom, Efuru's "running away" to Adizua is an avenue that exists for women in this situation. Notice that no one accuses her of committing an abomination against any person or gods. Significant comments about Adizua focus on his poverty and the fact that he is "not known."

10. See for instance: Ifi Amadiume. *Male Daughters, Female Husbands* (London and New Jersey: Zed Books, 1987) 59-62; M. S. O. Olisa, "Political Culture and Stability in Igbo Society," *Conch* 3.2 (September 1971): 24-25; Elizabeth Isichei. *Igbo Worlds* (Philadelphia: Institute for the Study of Human Issues, 1978) 74.

11. Anthonia C. Ogbonaya, "Chinua Achebe and the Igbo World View" (Ph.D. diss., U of Wisconsin, 1984) 101.

12. It is significant to note here that Nwapa's Efuru does not ask why Uhamiri doe not give children. That is a question between Efuru and her *chi* - personal god. Rather, Efuru's question is: Given that "She (Uhamiri) gave women beauty and wealth (i.e., sources and processes for self identification and reclamation) [...] she had never experienced the joy of motherhood. *Why did women worship her*?" (221) Neither Ogwuta people nor Efuru ask Uhamiri for children; she has none to give. She is perceived (and used) as a tool that facilitates the match between the known (lack) and the desired (material wealth and/or psychic health).

13. Achebe began this discussion of near-loss in *Things Fall Apart* (1958). It is signaled by the two names Ikemefuna (May-my-strength-never-be-lost) and Ikem (My strength). Thus the implicit request the young people make in Amaechina's (Ikem's daughter's) name suggests a consciousness of the repositioning that should occur. This dialogue which involves the death of a male child in *Things Fall Apart* and the birth of a female child in *Anthillls of the Savannah* reflects Achebe's consciousness of the strengths of the Igbo language and its capacity for infinite replication and (re-)discovery.

Works Cited

Achebe, Chinua. *A Man of the People*. New York: Anchor Books, 1989.

——. *Anthills of the Savannah*. New York: Doubleday, 1987.

——. *Arrow of God*. London: Heinemann, 1966.

——. *Morning Yet On Creation Day*. London: Heinemann Educational Books, 1981.

——. *No Longer At Ease*. New York: Ivan Doblensky, 1961.

——. *Things Fall Apart*. New York: Fawcett Crest, 1969.

Amuta, Chidi. *The Theory of African Literature: Implications for Practical Criticism.* London & New Jersey: Zed Books, 1989.

Andrade, Susan Z. "Rewriting History, Motherhood, and Rebellion: Naming an African Woman's Literary Tradition." *Research in African Literatures* 21.1 (Spring 1990): 91-110.

Andrews, William, ed. *Frederick Douglass: My Bondage and My Freedom.* Chicago: U of Illinois P, 1987.

Anozie, Sunday. *Structural Models and African Poetics: Toward a Pragmatic Theory of Literature.* London: Routledge & Kegan Paul, 1981.

Clark, J.P. "The Legacy of Caliban." *Black Orpheus* 2.1 (February 1968): 16-40.

DuBois, W.E.B. *The Souls of Black Folk.* New York: New American Library/ Signet, 1969.

Egejuru, Phanuel A. *Black Writers, White Audience.* New York: Exposition Press, 1978.

Garfinkel, Alan. *Forms of Explanation: Rethinking the Questions in Social Theory.* New Haven: Yale UP, 1981.

Gorman, T.P., ed. *Language in Education in Eastern Africa.* Nairobi: Oxford UP, 1970.

Irele, Abiola. *The African Experience in Literature and Ideology.* London: Heinemann, 1981.

——. "The African Imagination." *Research In African Literatures* 21.1 (Spring 1990): 69-78.

Jeyifo, Biodun. "The Nature of Things: Arrested Decolonization and Critical Theory." *Research in African Literature* 21.1 (Spring 1990): 33-46.

Kuhn, Thomas. *The Structure of Scientific Revolutions.* New York: New American Library, 1986.

La Guma, Alex. *In the Fog of the Season's End.* London: Heinemann, 1972.

Lakatos, Imre. *Methodology of Scientific Research Programmes.* Eds. John Worrall and Gregory Currie. Cambridge: Cambridge UP, 1978.

Ngara, Emmanuel. *Art and Ideology in the African Novel: A Study of the Influence of Marxism on African Writing.* London: Heinemann Educational Books, 1985.

Nwapa, Flora. *Efuru.* London: Heinemann Educational Books, 1966.

Obiechina, Emmanuel. *Language and Theme: Essays on African Literature.* Washington, D.C.: Howard UP, 1990.

Ogbaa, Kalu. *Gods, Oracles and Divination.* Trenton: Africa World Press, 1992.

p'Bitek, Okot. *Song of Lawino and Song of Ocol.* London: Heinemann Educational Books, 1972.

Petersen, Kirsten Holst and Anna Rutherford, eds. *Chinua Achebe: A Celebration.* Sydney and Oxford: Dangeroo Press and Heinemann, 1991.

Shelton, Austin, ed. *The African Assertion: A Critical Anthology of African Literature.* New York: The Odyssey Press, 1968.

wa Thiong'o, Ngugi. *Homecoming.* New York: Lawrence Hill and Company, 1972.

——. *Decolonizing the Mind: The Politics of Language in African Literature.* Nairobi: Heinemann, 1986.

Whorf, Benjamin Lee. *Language, Thought and Reality.* Ed. John B. Carroll. Cambridge: The M.I.T. Press, 1988.

Zabus, Chantal. "The Logos-Eaters: The Igbo Ethno Text." *Chinua Achebe: A Celebration.* Ed. Kirsten Holst Petersen and Anna Rutherford. Sydney and Oxford: Dangeroo Press and Heinemann, 1991.

9

The Trajectory of African Critical Discourse in English: An Overview

MALA PANDURANG

Modern African literature in English is a body of work that has emerged out of the colonial encounter between Africa and Europe, and the imposition of literacy in an alien and non-indigenous language on what was a predominantly oral culture. Creative writing in English was thus produced by writers caught in a 'double-bind' situation—writing in an alien tongue but trying to capture and reassert their own unique 'African Sensibility.' What we have therefore is a literature with a strong directive purpose that demands much more than the mere evaluation of individual texts as independent aesthetic products. (The term 'African' is used in the context of this paper as a referent to a specific area of cultural and socio-political experience central to the postcolonial creative act. There is no intention of totalizing all literary production from the continent).

For socio-historical reasons, the growth of modern African literature in English has been intrinsically bound up with the effect of colonialism and neo-colonialism on the African creative consciousness. If creative writing was fired by the determination to give a voice to an identity that had been deliberately negated and to produce a strong counter-hegemonic discourse against the colonial master-narrative, African critical scholarship was born in a similar crisis of identity, and out of the fear of intellectual re-colonization. D.S. Izevbaye explains in *The State of Criticism in African Literature* that the call for African critical concepts was "not just a rejection of established modes of literary study [...] but a rejection of certain entrenched modes of thinking which perpetuate the stock attitude to Africa" (1975: 3). Critics had to demand a voice where one had for so long been rendered voiceless.

A useful tool in facilitating an understanding of the evolution of African critical sensibilities would be a brief review of the historical trajectory of African critical discourse. This paper will not attempt an in-depth critique of theoretical frameworks, nor does it claim to be a comprehensive study of all the trends that have emerged in the past three decades. This essay will however introduce certain issues that have shaped current oppositional discourses on African literature, and it will discuss the political grounding of these debates in the hope that the student of African literature will explore these issues further in order to imbibe a comprehensive critical inwardness. There is also the strong possibility that the debates discussed may open new perspectives of exploring and understanding the creative production of other marginalized groups. (Literature produced in South Africa is a category within itself, and a discussion of critical trends in the South African context merits a separate paper.)

***

The quest for the assertion of a specific 'Black' cultural psyche can be traced back to the reaction of Francophone African writers against the French colonial policy of total cultural assimilation. This movement was also fueled by the ideology of the Black nationalism of Marcus Garvey, and the Pan-Africanism of Du Bois. The Négritude movement of the 1930s played a decisive historical role in the development of a distinctive African aesthetic which attempted to separate itself from the 'universal' Eurocentric evaluation of content and style. Its prominent practitioners (Aimé Césaire, and Leopold Senghor, for example) thus became the early advocates of a nativist position that makes a distinction between 'our literature' and 'their criticism.' Also important in the teething stages was the identification of psychological patterns that could serve as metonyms of the colonized/colonizer relationship, in texts like *Robinson Crusoe* and *The Tempest.*

Octave Mannoni's *Prospero and Caliban. The Psychology of Colonization* (1956) gave impetus to the development of counter-discursive strategies aimed at subverting those images projected in Western literature that supported the colonial claims of a 'white civilizing mission.' However, the most seminal influence on early nationalist literary criticism was undoubtedly Frantz Fanon's *The Wretched of The Earth* (1961). Implicit in Fanon's incisive analysis of the ideological tools used by the colonizers to sustain psychological control over the natives, is the possibility of evolving nationalist strategies of decolonization. Equally important, Fanon's recognition of the vital role that language plays in mental colonization created a vital awareness that language could also be used as a counter-weapon and be made to perform a psychologically affirmative function. If literary responses of the 1950s and early 1960s reflected a strong anti-colonial indignation and a call for cultural emancipation, so did the pioneering criticism that began to emerge from critics like Mphahlele, Achebe, Soyinka, Ngugi, Awonoor and Armah, who were primarily creative writers themselves. Early essays like Achebe's *The Novelist as Teacher,* and *Colonial Criticism* (later published in a collection of essays entitled *Morning Yet on Creation Day* (1975), and the essays of Ngugi wa Thiong'o collated in *Homecoming* (1972), attacked the general tendency to read African literature written in English as a deviant from the main normative body of English literature. These writers were reacting to notions of the 'universal' and to the 'paternalist' comments of critics like Adrian Roscoe, who suggests in *Mother is Gold* (1971) that African fiction should be subjected to the much flaunted tests of Western scholarship, or Eustace Palmer, who similarly asserts in *An Introduction to the African Novel (1972) and The Growth of the African Novel* (1979) that "[...] since we are still concerned with the same genre (*i.e. the novel*), the same criteria (i.e. *Western*) should apply." "To allow different criteria," according to Palmer, "is to provide loopholes for mediocrities" (1972). If many of the early critical discussions were sociologically orientated, this was because of the 'newness' of the literature and also because most of it was being analyzed by Western critics. Gerald Moore's *Seven African Writers* (1962), later revised and expanded into *Twelve African Writers* (1980), is a good example of this kind of early sociological interest.

The emergence of the first generation of university-trained critics by the late 1960s added a new dimension to African critical discourse. Formalist concerns imbibed by these critics from their training in Western universities become clearly evident in the kind of close textual explication that began to appear. The formalist approach of the Ibadan school of criticism (Dan Izevbaye and Eldred Jones, for example) challenged earlier modes rooted in anthropological and social paradigms, and gained in popularity among university academicians. However, by the early 70s the growing frustration with post-independence leadership and the continued dominance of Western cultural hegemonic practices under conditions of what Neil Lazarus describes as "the deadly sinuosity of neo-colonialism" (1990: 85) had important consequences on many postcolonial intellectuals who insisted that one could not exclude extra-literary concerns from any discussion of literary production. What developed as a concomitant among African radical intellectuals was a sense of urgency to move towards the active politicization of critical discourse. Formalist methods were rejected as being apolitical and indifferent to the socio-cultural complexities of literary production, especially in a context where oral and literary modes overlap. Critics who privileged theories of 'reading' over 'hearing' and 'seeing' were accused of being 'Eurocentric.' Roger Berger points out in his essay on *Contemporary Anglophone Literary Theory* (1990) that what emerged was not a division between schools representing divergent methodologies, but rather between groups of critics who could be graded according to their position in relation to what Berger refers to as "the Fanonist threshold" (142). This 'threshold,' he explains, divides critics who accept a certain 'accommodation' with existing Western textual strategies from those who reject 'Eurocentric' methodologies outright for what they claim as an 'Afrocentric' means of understanding the creative production. Objections raised by these two oppositional schools against each other become crucial in the ensuing debates of the late 70s and the 80s and can be read in terms of a struggle between the attitudes of two ideologically opposed camps. In *The Nature of Things: Arrested Decolonization and Critical Theory* (1990) Jeyifo points out that the development of critical scholarship is often discussed a 'subsumption' into two supposedly distinct polarized camps, namely: the 'Africanists,' who demand an objective literary scholarship based on an 'aesthetic formal criteria of evaluation' such as Solomon Iysere, Eldred Jones, and Daniel Izevbaye; and the 'Nationalists' like Ngugi and Chinweizu, who emphasise extra-literary concerns and connect artistic expression with commitment to a new social order. Jeyifo points out that, however, a strict dichotomy does not always hold. Africanists do tend to be politically liberal, while nationalist scholars are not entirely indifferent to questions of form and design. Jeyifo's suggestion that critics must reject the 'false binarism' that keeps the best features of the 'Africanist' and the 'Nationalist' schools apart, and that they can always draw on the works of literary scholars in other discursive spaces, is a very valid one.

Georg Gugelberger in *Marxism and African Literature* (1985) identifies five schools of African criticism that had developed by the 1980s. What is interesting is that these 'schools' are again marked by a strong ideological divide. These categories are discussed below—with a few further explanatory details:

(a) Larsonists

This term came into popular use after Ayi Kwei Armah accused the American critic Charles Larson in *Larsony—or Fiction as Criticism of Fiction* (1977) of producing a kind of criticism which, according to Armah, was nothing but a kind of "fiction about fiction." 'Larsonists' thus became a popular term used by Afrocentric critics to criticize Western critics whose methods of evaluation were primarily based on European normative modes. Indeed, Indian scholars of African literature must indeed guard themselves from being 'Larsonists' as a result of a very limited and restricted reading.

(b) Afro-Eurocentric critics

This category refers to African critics who attempt to apply a European theoretical framework to African writing. Sunday O Anozie's use of structuralist methods in *Structural Models and African Poetics: Towards a Pragmatic Theory of Literature* (1981) is often quoted as a text that instigated a number of debates on the viability of modern Western theoretical practices in the reading of texts produced in a different cultural context. Anthony Appiah in his sharply critical review article of Anozie (*Strictures on Structures: The Prospects for a Structuralist Poetics of African Fiction*) speaks of the need to think twice before getting embedded in European thought patterns. Appiah warns that the rush to apply Western academic theories can lead to an intellectual submissiveness.

(c) Bolekaja Critics

The word 'Bolekaja' (associated with Yoruba bus-conductors known for their aggressiveness) has come to be synonymous with the famous 'troika' of Chinweizu, Jemie and Madubuike, the authors of *Towards the Decolonization of African Literature* (1983). These critics admit to an "unabashedly polemical and pedagogical stance," and they spare no words in their attack against African Eurocentrists. In particular, acrimonious criticism has been directed against Wole Soyinka for the 'obscurantism' of his language. Soyinka's use of borrowed theatrical techniques and his forcing of African drama into a Western mould, they assert, are contradictory to the essential character of oral art.

(d) Ogunists

This term is derived from Ogun, the Yoruba God of creativity. Ogunists include critics like Soyinka who write in the European modernist tradition and defend their mythopoetic/formalist modes in terms of postcolonial syncretism.

(e) Marxist critics

Marxist critics insist that creative work has to be discussed in relation to other products of human culture, and in the context of the economic roots of its production. Critics like Ngugi and Chidi Amuta have shifted from traditional critical modes towards advocating that literature should perform a vital revolutionary function by instigating change from within social structures. In *The Theory of African Literature; Implications for Practical Criticism* (1989), Amuta criticizes any form of Africaneity that has recourse to the past, and questions the utility of a return to any pre-colonial cultural modes as advocated by the Bolekaja critics. There is also an ongoing debate on the inadequacy of European Marxist theory for the critique of cultural practices in the African context.

It is important to take note of a new and exciting field of critical scholarship that is still in stages of growth—that of *feminist discourse* which questions the production and circulation of meaning from the perspective of gender. Right up to the 80s, critics ignored the category of gender, and the voice of the African woman went unnoticed. Gender was subsumed in the discussions of colonial and class oppression. African feminist criticism is now speaking from the margins of both fields, and is in the process of formulating a space and theoretical positions of its own. For example, the essays collected in *Ngambika. Studies of Women in African Literature* (1986) register protest against the patriarchal cast of cultural studies and warn against gross generalizations and any attempts to homogenize conditions of black African women. Women writers like Mariama Ba and Buchi Emecheta create a feminist discourse from within the creative text, and illustrate the position of the African woman from within the dominant power structures both in colonial and postcolonial Africa. It is a measure of the success of feminist discourse that literary works that constitute the canon of African literature in English are now being re-read in terms of how both men and women have been constructed. This new and exciting discourse, still in the process of being formulated at this historical moment, will certainly have an important effect as it increasingly, and effectively, begins to question patriarchal positions, and in doing so subverts traditional discursive practices.

***

In the context of shifting focus from traditional critical modes to radical alternatives, the two most influential texts in the setting-up of an oppositional critique of African literature have, without a doubt, been Chinweizu, Jemie and Madubuike's *Towards the Decolonization of African Literature* (1983) and Ngugi's *Decolonizing the Mind. The Politics of Language in African Literature* (1986). These two texts have provoked innumerable debates, after which African literary scholarship has never been quite the same. *Towards the Decolonization of African Literature* has been attacked for the extreme position that the authors take in discrediting those writers who have taken literary techniques from European precedents. It has also been critiqued for the very reductionist viewpoint that literature produced in Africa is an entirely autonomous entity with its own models and norms, and can therefore be evaluated only by African critics. It is important to be aware of the limitations of any extremist nativist position—the staking of 'territorial rights' is a highly debatable issue. Yet whatever the counter-arguments against the standpoint of the 'troika,' what makes the text a significant landmark in the history of African discourse is that it compels a recognition that what often passes for 'African' literature is in fact Western literature that has been Africanized. *Towards the Decolonization* also asserts that any attempt to turn towards 'orature' demands a parallel need to develop a theory rooted in the dynamics of oral tradition, and to recognize that these forms should be recovered and treated as a legitimate enterprise for 'literary' criticism.

The primary theoretical focus of Ngugi's *Decolonizing the Mind* is the relation of linguistic displacement to cultural displacement, and the intimate relationship between the imposition of an alien, colonial language and mental colonization. The process of 'decolonizing the mind,' Ngugi argues, involves a much more radical movement not only from modes of European cultural production but from the language of the oppressor which carries a culture-specific worldview. Only through such a radical move is it possible to de-isolate the phenomenon of literature and to reduce the existing distance between the writer and 'the people.' Ngugi describes in detail how his successful experience with the Kamirruthu People's theater made him realize the implications of writing in his own native tongue (Gikuyu) in the struggle against the dominant

Kenyan neo-elite class, whom he accuses of being agents of neo-colonization. Ngugi's emphasis is on the political function of the critic and he insists that both the creative artist and the critic must derive direction from a social conscience.

The basic demands of the oppositional critics can be shortlisted as: a questioning of the epistemological criteria of Western scholarship; a reconsideration of the actual relevance of the present sophisticated academics of the establishment; and a ruthless interrogation of the pressures of international capital and neo-colonial forces on cultural formations within the third-world milieu. Adebayo Williams argues in *Towards a Theory of Cultural Production in Africa* (1991) that the political reality of America contrasts sharply with the political reality of Africa and the rest of the third world. He points out that "the triumph of deconstruction in America must be linked to the fact that this mode of critical approach offers a powerful pedagogic weapon that is in harmony with the historical and political reality of American society. With the overpowering of the state by civil society and with the nearly total dominance of market considerations, the individual becomes the measure of all things in such a society" (18). In the context of the third world, however, emphasis on discontinuities and fragmented consciousness can serve no valid purpose. To arrive at a better historical understanding, Williams asserts, "the African theorist must seek to reconnect all dis-connections, to tie together all loose ends." Anthony Appiah warns that the third-world critic must keep his/her bearings "in the shark-infested waters around the semantic island of the postmodern." This is especially true in an quasi-intellectual academic environment where we tend to cite Foucault, Bakhtin or Spivak without any serious engagement with the specific social and cultural dynamics that have gone into the production of the text. Such criticism does not go beyond the superficial. An understanding of the debates that have shaped African discourse over the past three decades can indeed compel the critic from India to (a) rethink the ways in which we tend to hijack 'knowledge' from the West (b) rectify the denial of history (c) actively mediate our own texts (d) and perform, with an acute sensitivity, a responsible role in a world beset by inequality and exploitation.

Works Cited

Achebe, Chinua. *Morning Yet on Creation Day.* London: Heinemann, 1975.

Adebayo Williams. "Towards a Theory of Cultural Production in Africa." *Research in African Literatures* 22. 2 (1991): 5-20.

Amuta, Chidi. *The Theory of African Literature: Implications for Practical Criticism.* London: Zed, 1989.

Armah, Ayi Kwei. "Larsony or Fiction as criticism of Fiction." *New Classic* 4 (1977): 33-45.

Anozie, Sunday O. *Structural Models and African Poetics: Towards a Pragmatic Theory of Literature.* London: Routledge. 1981.

Berger, Roger A. "Contemporary Anglophone Literary Theory." *Research in African Literatures* 21.1 (1990): 141-52.

Chinweizu, Jemie and Madubuike. *Towards the Decolonization of African Literature.* Enugu: Fourth Dimension Press, 1980.

Comas, James. "The Presence of Theory. Theorising the Present." *Research in African Literatures* 21.1 (1990): 5-29.

Davies, Carol and Anne Adams Graves. *Ngambika: Studies of Women in African Literature.* Africa World Press, 1986.

Fanon, Frantz. *The Wretched of The Earth.* New York: Grove Press. 1968.

Gugelberger, Georg M., ed. *Marxism and African Literature.* London: James Currey, 1985.

Izevbaye, D.S. "The State of Criticism in African Literature." *African Literature Today. No 7.* Ed. Eldred Jones. London: Heinemann Educational Books, 1975.

Jeyifo, Biodun. "The Nature of Things: Arrested Decolonization and Critical Theory." *Research in African Literatures* 21.1 (1990): 33-48.

Lazarus, Neil. *Resistance in Post-colonial African Fiction.* New Haven: Yale UP, 1990.

Mannoni, Octave. *Prospero and Caliban. The Psychology of Colonization.* Trans. Pamela Powesland. London: Methuen, 1956.

Moore, Gerald. *Seven African Writers.* London: OUP, 1962.

——. *Twelve African Writers.* Hutchinson, 1980.

Ngugi wa Thiong'o. *Homecoming.* London: Heinemann, 1972.

——. *Decolonizing the Mind. The Politics of Language in African Literature.* London: James Currey, 1986.

Palmer, Eustace. *An Introduction to the African Novel.* London: Heinemann, 1972.

——. *The Growth of the African Novel.* London: Heinemann, 1979.

Roscoe, Adrian. *Mother is Gold. A Study in West African Literature.* London: Cambridge UP, 1971.

Said, Edward. *"Orientalism Reconsidered." Literature, Politics and Theory: Cambridge Papers from the Essex Conference, 1976-1984.* Ed. Francis Barker, et al. London: Methuen, 1986. 210-29.

10

INDIA, INDIAN, INDIANNESS: PROBLEMATISING THE INDIAN ENGLISH NOVELIST'S IDENTITY

SUBHENDU MUND

India, Indian and Indianness are some of the extra-literary tensions demanding attention of the critics and historiographers engaged in the study of the body of literature called Indian Writing in English (IWE hereafter). The problem is more of historiographic concern because a literary critic may not have to go beyond the text. The problematic here is both textual and contextual, and even calls for other disciplines such as politics, historiography, sociology and ethnography for perceptual clarity. Moreover, postcolonial/ postmodern discourses on nation and narration elevate the problem to an unprecedented level of theoretical exercise.

In her influential essay "The Anxiety of Indianness," Meenakshi Mukherjee addresses the issue vis-à-vis the *bhasha* literatures. Why a Marathi novelist is not called an *Indian* writer in Marathi, but one writing in English has to be called an *Indian* writer in English, she wonders. Elaborating "the larger burden of culture, tradition and civilization" (168) which a writer has to bear, she expresses her anxiety over "the issue of Indianness" becoming "a favourite essentializing obsession" not only with the critics and book-reviewers, but even the writers themselves. She focuses on *English* as the centre of the issue:

> [...] the complicating factor being that English is not just any language—it was the language of our colonial rulers and continues even now to be the language of power and

privilege. It is not a language that permeates all social levels or is used in subaltern contexts (168).

K.R. Srinivasa Iyengar, C.D. Narasimhaiah, V.K. Gokak and other nationalist scholars, more preoccupied with the task of giving IWE "a local habitation and a name," nd unaffected by the onslaught of the postcolonial discourses, did not have to worry about issues like India/nation, Indianness/nationness and the sociopolitical definition of the term "Indian." n the 1970s, there was a shift in focus: the critic was more concerned about the writer than the general body of literature. In his *A History of Indian English Literature* (1982), M.K. Naik spelt out the anxiety: "If Henry James found being an American to be 'complex fate,' being an Indian English writer would appear to be a far more complex destiny" (284).

The world (and India) since the late 1980s has been passing through unprecedented proliferation of culture. Globalisation, explosions in information technology, new market economics in book publishing and promotion and other factors have not only effected a lot of social mobility but also new definitions of the changing realities. There has been considerable immigration, which has created a sizeable diaspora of Indians in both developing and developed countries. In fact, diasporic writing has of late been very influential. The Indian English writers, especially the novelists, are being increasingly patronised by big publishing houses, astronomical signing amounts are reportedly being given to Indian novelists implying a very large readership in India and other English-speaking places. Indians, and writers genetically connected to India, are being honoured with coveted literary prizes. The world academia seems to be showing a lot of (unusual) interest in IWE, as is evident from the overwhelming critical responses and theoretical engagements manifest in printed words, electronic media, and, of course, the international seminars, conferences and readings.

In this fast-changing scenario, the postcolonial ambivalence is always raising its disturbing Janus head. While an Indian reader prides over a Rushdie or an Arundhati Roy, not to speak of a Jhumpa Lahiri or a Sir Vidia Naipaul, he/she is also perturbed by the basic issues involved. The English books are respected, but the books in *bhasha* literatures are loved. Much as the reader would like "glocalisation," the "English book" still reminds him/her of a colonial past and the practitioner of the English book could seem to be the relic of what Macaulay prophesied in 1835: "a class of Indians: Indian in blood and colour, but English in taste, in opinions, in morals and in intellect" (*Minute on Indian Education*).

Besides, a historiographer is challenged by the apparently unimportant technicality of classification and categorisation, which help in the organisation of one's materials in a meaningful and logical manner. A historian of literature cannot act autonomously; he/she has to rationalise his/her choice of authors. Let us take the case of Sir Ferozkhan Noon. Noon was born in undivided India, and published his books as an *Indian*, but after the partition chose to become a citizen of Pakistan, and eventually rose to great political heights. In fact, he had published a colourful monograph (*India*: 1941); and a bulky novel (*Scented Dust*: 1942), written in answer to the query of "an American lady," his co-passenger, on his way to England by sea. Noon set out to write a novel which would showcase India to the West: "I have attempted to answer her queries in a language, which is not my own" (Foreword). Similar are the cases of Attia Hossain, Bapsi Sidhwa and many others.

The second category is that of writers of Indian descent who are citizens of other countries. Most of such writers have not lived in India (like Naipaul, David Dabydeen, even Jhumpa Lahiri and many more) for a long enough time to be "Indianised." These writers still get involved with India and her issues, and we, on our part, wish to appropriate them, Jhumpa Lahiri was born in London to Bengali parents, grew up in Rhode Island (USA), studied at Boston University, now lives in America and considers America her "home." Naipaul's relationship with India is much too well known to be elaborated. In spite of his legendary status of being an unsympathetic critic of India, he is reported to have said to C.D. Narasimhaiah, "I am profoundly Indian in my feeling, profoundly Indian in my sensibility [...]" (117).

Then there are the writers who are not Indians in the strict sense but are domiciled in India owing to matrimonial or other reasons. The case of Ruth Prawer Jhabvala is not an isolated example, there are many others also. Sara Banerji, the author of *The Wedding of Jayanthi Mandal* (1987) and other novels, was born in England, spent her childhood in the African bush, and met her future (Indian) husband in London. She spent the first seventeen years after her marriage in South India and supervised tea plantations, but she thereafter lived in Sussex. There are many other writers who are technically "foreigners," but have become "naturalised" in India.

There are some writers who were born in India but not of Indian parents and wrote mostly India-related fiction and poetry, but may not be "Indian" in their attitude. The most obvious instance is that of Rudyard Kipling (1865-1936). The Indian novel in English has an answer to Kipling in Mirza Moorad Alee Beg Gaekwaree, an important novelist of the late nineteenth century. His historical novel *Lalun the Beragun: Or the Battle of Paniput. A Legend of Hindustan*, published in 1884, is a remarkable work in which Beg has not only dramatised his emotional affiliation with Indocentric issues, but also experimented with language and style to Indianise the western form and the English language.

The most conspicuous among these categories, however, is that of the diasporic writers. Since the late 1980s, we have had a steady flow of novels and other forms of writing written by India-born writers living elsewhere. Their literature presents various literary and extra-literary tensions, which obfuscate the extant principles of literary criticism. True, we have had our share of such writers earlier also. Raja Rao, Nirad C. Chaudhuri, even Kamala Markandaya, to name a few, live(d) and write(wrote) from foreign lands. But the recent diaspora seems to have alienated the immigrants from their roots. Critics like Devy have strong reservations on this issue: "Just as it is desirable to leave Naipaul out of our account, it is also desirable to leave out writers like Rushdie, Rohinton Mistry and Bharati Mukherjee out of any consideration of Indian English literature" (IOI).

"Homeland" and "home" seem to have acquired new definitions in the postmodern context. Yet it is true that these writers have not consciously distanced themselves from their place of origin. Salman Rushdie's observation seems to be representative of the immigrant's "profound uncertainties":

> It may be that writers in my position, exiles or emigrants or expatriates, are haunted by some sense of loss, some urge to reclaim, to reclaim, to look back, even at the risk of being mutated into pillars of salt. But if we do look back, we must also do so in the knowledge—which gives rise to profound uncertainties—that our physical alienation from India almost inevitably means that we will not be capable of reclaiming precisely the thing that was lost; that we will, in short, create fictions, not actual cities or villages, but invisible ones, imaginary homelands, Indias of the mind (10).

Bharati Mukerjee, who lived in Canada and now lives in the USA, cannot, like Rushdie, fictionalise her expatriate experience. To her, Indianness is now a metaphor:

> I have joined imaginative forces with an anonymous driven underclass of semi-assimilated Indians with sentimental attachment to a distant homeland, but no real desire for permanent return [...] Instead of seeing my Indianness as a fragile identity to be preserved against obliteration (or, worse, a "visible" disfigurement to be hidden) I see it now as a set of fluid identities to be celebrated [...] Indianness is now a metaphor, a particular way of comprehending the world (3).

While all these categories of writer baffle the Indocentric project of historiography, they also generate a fresh inquiry into the issue of political/national affiliation of a creative writer. Does a creative writer have to identify him/herself with a political hegemony or a geopolitical reality? How does the absence of a national identity affect one's creativity or the reception of the readers? How does one define an Indian? What do we mean by India? What does Indianness signify?

The pioneers of Indian English criticism had essayed to outline the answers to some of these fundamental issues. It may be reiterated that till the middle of the twentieth century, IWE was not much concerned with these questions related to identity.

Notwithstanding its limitations, it did have strategies to identify itself with the "nation." The writer was able to affiliate literature to nationalist discourse, even Gandhian politics, without having to sacrifice aesthetic quality. Since its very inception, IWE had been able to foreground the ideas of the nation and nationalism through the fiction of Kylash Chunder Dutt (*A Journal of Forty-Eight Hours of the Year 1945*: 1835) or through *The Republic of Orissa: A Page from the Annals of the Twentieth Century* (1845) by Shoshee Chunder Dutt (1824-85). Writers of the early period like A. Madhaviah, Sarath Kumar Ghosh, Siddha Mohan Mitra and A.S.P. Ayyar (1899-1963) had already prepared a solid groundwork for works like Raja Rao's *Kanthapura* (1938) to be written. Indian English fiction of the colonial era was considerably successful in projecting the idea of India before the countrymen as well as the world outside. When the foundation stone of Indian English criticism was being laid, the pioneers were not quite affected by apprehensions and uncertainties. Iyengar could be prophetical in his perception of the status and the future of IWE and could easily pronounce:

> There is no doubt that with its own individual vision and voice Indo-Anglian literature will grow—like other languages of contemporary India,—from strength to greater strength; and help to make us a new nation and a new people, a modern nation and a progressive people, wedded to the tasks of national reconstruction and international harmony (*IWE* 58).

With the growth of IWE, and that of the decolonised nation-state with its related tensions, there was natural proliferation in literary form and content. In a span of about fifty years the new India had to receive and assimilate the explosion of science, technology and knowledge of other kinds. Rapid industrialisation, urbanisation and modernisation almost coincided with global movements like the non-aligned movement and the Commonwealth at the political and feminism and pop culture at the social levels. The new nation-state did also have to experience resistance from within its own framework of societal and political structures. There was Partition to begin with, followed by real and shadow wars. After the Nehruvian era of a dream India, Indian politics lacked the certainties of the past. The sporadic movements of the late 1960s and the 1970s, such as merger of princely states, language agitations, reorganisation of provinces, Naxalite movements, and finally the Total Revolution of Jaya Prakash Narayan, resulted in the declaration of internal emergency in 1975 by Prime Minister Indira Gandhi.

The 1980s and after have been a period of postmodern anxiety for India. The advent of Salman Rushdie as an influential novelist in the 1980s opened up new possibilities in interpretations as well as authorial devices in the postmodern/postcolonial contexts. To be precise, Rushdie's emergence preceded even Saidian influence in the Indian academia and literary circles. The efficacy of the novel as the most communicative form in postcolonial literature and the centrality of history in postcolonial narration were foregrounded. The engagement of critics like Homi K. Bhabha, Gayatri Chakravarty Spivak, Aijaz Ahmad, Partha Chatterjee, Ashis Nandy, Ranjit Guha, Meenakshi Mukherjee, Gauri Viswanathan, Arun P. Mukherjee, Harish Trivedi, Vijaya Mishra, G.N. Devy, et al., in the theorisation of the postcolonial discourses brought forth issues like nation and narration, the woman question, subaltern condition, Nativism, Essentialism, etc, to an Indocentric reconsideration. The postcolonial/postmodern condition also proved congenial for linguistic and stylistic innovations.

The postcolonial aura has generated several related studies like Nativism and Essentialism, which strive to shift the focus to the marginalisation of bhasha literatures, indigenous culture and the narrative traditions of India. It is in this context that the fundamental issues concerning Indian identity and Indianness have resurfaced. The "English book" marketed as "Indian" literature to the overseas readers and the "Indian" authors' new status as potential winners of prestigious international prizes are the matters now creating uneasiness in the academic and readership circles. That most of the novelists and poets are unable to locate their work in the geographical or sociological realities of India, that Indian English literature is vaguely pan-Indian, even mostly diasporic, does not affiliate it to the essential

Indian experience. It may of course be argued that literature should not be expected to restrict itself to a well-defined geographical boundary and the present times are more transnational/global/international; and that literature is timeless and the author has his/her autonomy, and so on; but we must remember that all great works of literature are products of specific spatiotemporal dynamics.

Coming back to the issues which this paper aims to address, it may be worthwhile to take the cue from the now famous words of Benedict Anderson: "nation-ness is the most universally legitimate value in the political life of our times" (3). Nationalism has, in the recent times, come to be regarded as a bad influence. In the West, nationalism replaced religious belief in the nineteenth century when the crisis of faith had started concerning the individual and the community. The same nationalism was translated into a motivating agent during the two world wars. Now a cricket match or a mediocre book or a terrorist attack on the WTC towers or the Parliament can create strong nationalist feelings. Nationalism is generally seen as the most insurmountable hindrance to the realisation of the dream theory of "One World." Nationalism is even seen as "bad" or "good," and it is argued that "good nationalism" is healthy for a nation.

Frantz Fanon seems to give the most rational solution to the problem. According to him, "National consciousness, which is not nationalism, is the only thing that will give us an international dimension" (199). The postcolonial creative writer may be expected to identify with the national consciousness and project, what Said calls "an enlightened postnationalism" (277). This national consciousness may be seen as a distinct form of "Indianness" in IWE. This may be read not as a political construct but as basically a cultural formation, because in the postcolonial and postmodern perception, nation-ness or national consciousness cannot be isolated from a comprehensive, all-pervasive hegemony of culture. Such a perception will not need any physical definition or identifying qualities to set at rest the riddle of Indianness, India or Indian.

Indianness is a qualifying mark, which has always obsessed

the essentialists as well as literary theoreticians with its enigmatic ethereal quality. As early as 1918, James H. Cousins had said prescriptively that Indian writers in English should be "Indian" in all aspects except "the language," and, interestingly enough, had laid emphasis on the expression of "self" in their writing:

> [...] if they are compelled to an alternative to writing in their mother-tongue, let it be, not Anglo-Indian but Indo-Anglian; Indian in spirit, Indian in thought, Indian in emotion, Indian in imagery, and English only in words [...]. Let their ideal be their expression of themselves but they must be quite sure that it is their self, not merely faint echoes and shadows from others or from the transient phases of desire (179).

Indians writing in English was a phenomenon which had initially invited curious responses, and statements like "Matthew Arnold in a sari" or "Sita in skirts" are much too well-known. The imperialist historiographers kept insisting on the inclusion of IWE in the "great tradition of English literature" as a reluctantly accepted "literature of dominions," as in *The Cambridge History of English Literature* (1916). But interestingly, even colonial administrator of Lord Curzon's reputation could not overlook the possibility of a new genre of literature, like American literature, written by Indians in English:

> If there is the possibility of literary prognostication with any success, it may be said that there will spring up a class of Indo-English poets in the future who will do for the poetic interpretation of India what Longfellow, Lowell and Walt Whitman have done for America (qtd. in Toru Dutt 7).

Curzon's prophecy, made about a hundred years ago, came true sooner than he might have expected, for the sudden outburst of creative activities in the early decades of the twentieth century, especially in fiction and poetry, made the presence of IWE quite conspicuous. The beginning of the Gandhian mass movements in the 1920s gave it a well-defined shape. Even after decolonisation, its identification with politics and culture at the pan-Indian level prompted nationalist scholars to look upon IWE as the instrument "to promote all-India consciousness" and a "national identity" (*IWE* 699). Even G.N. Devy, who has objections to the term "India," also agrees that IWE has a role:

> as a national literature of India rather than as a regional literature of any desi tradition. Whether Indians like it or not, the fact remains that at the moment it is the only national literature in India (19).

Namwar Singh, a well-known critic of Hindi literature, also believes that it is the Indian writers in English who have accepted the responsibility of writing what can truly be called "Indian literature":

> If truth be told, it is these Indian writers in English alone who are the representative writers of "Indian literature;" the literature of any other Indian language such as Hindi, Bengali or Tamil must remain regional literature (150).

Yet, in other influential quarters, IWE's *Indianness* is still questioned, chiefly due to the language, which is used as its medium - the language, which keeps reminding the readers of the colonial rule. This, and the factors discussed earlier, have been intermittently causing anxiety over issues like nation/ India, nationality/Indian and nationness/Indianness. As Meenakshi Mukherjee has rightly pointed out, IWE is actually burdened with the badge of "Indian" prefixed to this genre of Indian literature, the kind of identification mark which the *bhasha* literature do not have to carry.

Right or wrong, the scholars and historiographers and critics of IWE cannot escape this anxiety. Willy-nilly, they will have to address this Hamletian dilemma and "set things right."

K.R. Srinivasa Ieyngar, the man who had engaged himself to the "cause" of IWE with the zeal of a missionary and the expertise and skill of an accomplished champion, pleaded for the inclusion of IWE in the roll-call of the "other literatures of contemporary India." Yet he was aware that IWE has a dual role to play: local and global/universal. He elaborates his perception of IWE in the "Postscript" to the 1984 revised edition of his IWE (1963). Expressing happiness over the growing popularity of IWE in academia, as well as the preference it had started enjoying in journals, periodicals, seminars and conferences, he says: "one can legitimately entertain a reasonably fair hope for the future." At this point he draws our attention to the ambivalent position of the Indian English writer and the critic on the issue of "Indianness": "They are concerned with the 'Indianness' of IWE, and this is natural enough; and they are equally anxious to measure IWE by the best English (or Anglo-American) standards" (775). He finally advises the writer to "keep in touch (to the extent possible)" with writing in English in other countries, and yet to "try to invest his writing with the distinctive feel and force and soul of Indian sensibility" (776).

Iyengar does not, however, explain what this "sensibility" consists in; but elsewhere he emphasises as "the equality of Indianness" in IWE—"in the choice of subject, in the texture of thought and play of sentiment, in the organisation of the material in terms of 'form' and in the creative use of language" (698). C.D. Narasimhaiah addresses the problem at length vis-à-vis the *bhasha* literatures in his essay "Wanted: The Concept of a National Literature for India." He selects four novels from among the *bhasha* literature and tries to demonstrate how the elusive and enigmatic "Indianness" is manifest in them. These works, he points out, "show a remarkable Indianness" owing mainly to "the manner in which the great Indian tradition is kept alive in each work." Some of the characteristics, according to him, are "continuous references woven into the texture of the work as metaphor, symbol, myth, allusion, analogy from the Ramayana, Mahabharata, Bhagataba, Buddha, Ramanuja, Chaitanya, Sankaradev, the Bhakti poets and the folktales" (181). He shows how R.K. Narayan and other "master artists" "have invariably probed, discovered, and rediscovered the old and revalidated it." He argues that Narayan is a writer who "writes with the Indian world view at the centre which becomes evident in novel after novel" (183).

It is true that IWE may not always be able to pass a rigorous test of Indianness, owing to obvious reasons. The rootedness of *bhasha* literatures may be difficult to find in IWE; the characteristics enumerated by Narasimhaiah and other nationalist scholars may not always be there in the works of

IWE. Critics and scholars who exclude everything but an aesthetic value in a work of art may not accept the nationalist or political prerequisites as essential. Internationalists/transnationalists may see nationalistic predilections of a writer as retrogressive politics. Besides, it is not possible for any honest artist to be committed to an essentially nationalistic hegemony. Moreover, from the practical point of view, no novel or play can truly and collectively represent the multiplicity of Indian life. A Marathi novelist recreates the Marathi milieu, as an Oriya one might exclusively represent the realities of his/her world. Singularly, no *bhasha* literature can or should be expected to represent the whole of India. It is therefore, unreasonable to have such an expectation from IWE, but we do entertain such an expectation. If we expect IWE to represent the nation and manifest Indianness/nationness, then paradoxically, we have a priori accepted that IWE is the *only* literature capable of being the national/pan-Indian literature of this nation-state.

This reminds us of the other three literatures of India—Sanskrit, Urdu and Hindi—which have not been particularly identified with any geopolitical hegemony. The practitioners of these and other *bhasha* literatures live(d) and write(wrote) in many geographically different and unrelated places, even in other countries, but were/are perhaps never questioned about their national or political affiliation. The works in these literatures re more or less appreciated on the basis of literary merit. There should not be any problem in upholding such a perception of IWE also. It can be local, national and global; local because it is located in a real geographic space; national because if not consciously, then unconsciously, it would embody nation-ness; global/transnational because its medium is English and the world-view is broader.

Concepts like nationalism and nation have undergone a subversive influence in the postmodern context of language. The epistemology of postmodernism refuses to confine the concept of nation/nationalism to geographical boundaries or self-consciously held political principles. It prefers to be identified with large cultural systems. Even Benedict Anderson defines nations as "imaginative and cultural artefacts rather than empirical or scientific entities."

All said and done, the aesthetic approach to literature or the plea that Art is for Art's sake now seems to be utopian in today's perception. Literature has, fortunately or unfortunately, come to mean more than that. In the postcolonial discourse literature assumes the role of interpreter of the colonised's experience of subordination, marginalisation, even domesticisation. Said's definition of literature as essentially a part of "the social world" foregrounds the locatedness of the postcolonial text to the realities of human life:

> My position is that texts are worldly, to some extent they are events, and, even when they appear to deny it, they are nevertheless a part of the social world, human life, and of course the historical moments in which they are located and interpreted (*The World, the Text and the Critic* 4).

Thus, disturbing issues like India/nation, Indian/nationality and Indianness/nationness seem to be very pertinent in the context of IWE. Nevertheless, there cannot be any incontrovertible definition of these terms, nor can there be any touchstone theory to identify Indianness in a work of art. One who genuinely feels Indian and sees life as the Indians do may well be called an Indian even though he is born elsewhere or lives in a foreign land. We have accepted Mirza Moorad Alee Beg, Ananda Coomaraswamy and Ruth Prawer Jhabvala. The common reader finds nothing to complain about the national identities of Attia Hossain, V.S. Naipaul, Jhumpa Lahiri or Tehmina Durrani. Coomaraswamy was born to a Simhalese Indian father and an English mother; he did not live in India, nor was he a citizen of this country; "and yet the entire orientation of his thought is so unmistakably Indian," argues M.K. Naik, "that it is impossible not to consider him an *Indian English* writer" (3).

Needless to say, this "orientation" is not difficult to find in literature for a sensitive reader. In spite of the tendency of IWE to homogenisation of realities and essentialising India, and its studied distancing from the specificity of "locale," not to speak of its non-specific, metropolitan or diasporic spatial position, it is sure to construct and re-present the idea of India. This idea of India has no doubt enough room for any number of "insider-outsiders" and "outsider-insiders" provided one feels that one belongs.

Works Cited

Anderson, Benedict. *Imagined Communities: Reflections on the Origin and Spread of Nationalism.* London: Verso, 1983.

Bhabha, Homi K. *Nation and Narration.* London and New York: Routledge, 1990.

Cousins, James H. *The Renaissance in India.* Madras: Ganesh & Co., 1918.

Devy, G.N. *In Another Tongue: Essays on Indian English Literature.* New Delhi: McMillan, 1995.

Fanon, Frantz. *The Wretched of the Earth.* Trans. Constance Farrington. New York: Grove Press, 1966.

Iyengar, K.R. Srinivasa. "Indian Writing in English." *Contemporary Indian Literature.* 1957. New Delhi: Sahitya Akademi, 1981.

——. *Indian Writing in English.* 1962. New Delhi: Sterling Publishers Private Limited, 1984.

Mukherjee, Bharati. "Introduction." *Darkness.* 1985. New Delhi: Penguin, 1990.

Mukherjee, Meenakshi. "The Anxiety of Indianness." *The Perishable Empire.* Delhi: OUP, 2000.

Naik, M.K. *A History of Indian English Literature.* New Delhi: Sahitya Akademi, 1982.

Narasimhaiah, C.D. *The Function of Criticism in India.* Mysore: CIIL, 1986.

Noon, Feroz Khan. *Scented Dust.* Lahore: RSM Gulab Singh & Son, 1942.

Said, Edward. *Orientalism.* London: Routledge, 1978.

——. *The World, the Text and the Critic.* Cambridge, Mass.: Harvard UP, 1983.

Singh, Namwar. "Decolonising the Indian Mind." Trans. Harish Trivedi. *Indian Literature* 151 (Sept.-Oct. 1992).

Toru Dutt: *A Sketch of Her Life and An Appreciation of Her Works.* Madras: G.A. Natesan & Co., 1917.

✪✪✪

11

Psychoanalysis and Indian Writing in English: Promises and Possibilities

RAJESHWAR MITTAPALLI

Sigmund Freud, the father of psychoanalysis, acknowledged that poets and philosophers discovered the unconscious long before he did. For that reason he advised aspiring analysts to study literature as part of their training. Meredith Anne Skura goes a step further and argues: "the poets have discovered" not just the unconscious but "*psychoanalysis* before Freud did, and that at its subtlest and most wideranging [...]. It is not the mere presence or expression of primitive and unconsciously apprehended elements but the attempt to come to terms with them and to work them into the texture of conscious experience that makes the poets the predecessors of Freud."[1] Peter Brooks views the literary critic's job too to be not very different from that of the psychoanalyst: "I believe that the persistence against all the odds, of psychoanalytic perspectives in literary study must ultimately derive from the conviction that the materials on which psychoanalysts and literary critics exercise their powers of analysis are in some basic sense the same: that the structure of literature is in some sense the structure of mind."[2]

Indeed psychoanalysis and literature have always been viewed as two very closely related intellectual disciplines. Literature also provided a contiguous field of verification for psychoanalytical propositions. Freud was only too willing to borrow literary examples to prove analytical points. It is therefore not surprising that in the second half of this century psychoanalysis has emerged as a valid tool of literary criticism and gained wide acceptability among the critical and intellectual circles.

At present four widely practised psychoanalytic critical models are available. They base themselves on (a) the author and his unconscious sources; (b) the putative unconscious of the literary characters; (c) the unconscious response of the reader to the text; and (d) the formal construction of the literary work focusing on its textual and rhetorical aspects. Apart from these, other models such as the "transferential model" (Peter Brooks), "dream-work model" (Terry Eagleton) and "the psychoanalytic process model" (Meredith Anne Skura) are also suggested. Each model is effective depending on the object of attention and the critic's purpose.

What distinguishes psychoanalytic literary criticism from other approaches is that it usually takes into account those aspects of the work which have been thought of as unimportant by the conventional critics. Its practice of integrating these very "messy details"[3] into serious discourse has enabled it to come out with new interpretations of literary works. Through the pioneering efforts of scholars such as Shoshama Felman, Irvin Malin, Jean Baker Miller, Shlomith Rimmon-Kenan, etc., world classics had been brought under the psychoanalytic microscope and their continuing appeal was explained in scientific and psychological terms.

It is however disappointing to note that unlike the sociological approaches, which became popular with Indian critics with a surprising speed, psychoanalysis, in spite of its obvious relevance to India, has made little or no impact on Indian criticism in English. Except some stray studies such as the ones by Usha Bande, Darshan Singh Maini, K.C. Baral and R.S. Sharma no notable use of psychoanalytic concepts has been made in India to study our English literary works. Indian Writing in English seems to be in particular need of a new approach such as psychoanalysis for it certainly promises to earn it new respectability and wider acceptance on the world literary stage.

I therefore venture to suggest the possibility of making a

fruitful use of psychoanalysis, especially psychoanalytic character study, for creative and critical purposes.

II

As the noted Indo-Anglian novelist, Nayantara Sahgal, puts it "Fiction [and certainly Indian fiction in English]s is about people, basically about character [...] a novel is concerned with the characters it creates."[4] The characters in Indian fiction are shaped after the Indian personality structure which is extremely complex and has eluded all categorization until it has been studied from the psychoanalytic angle. Therefore, it becomes imperative both for the novelists and critics to understand this personality structure so as to authentically portray a character or to scientifically analyses it.

The Indian equivalent of the id, says Sudhir Kakar, is formed of a combination of the *chitta* and the *guna* constellation. Id is not viewed as a seething cauldron of instinctual drives but as aiming at altruism and moving toward the realisation of the purpose of human life. The new-born is believed to carry with him the three basic *gunas*: *suttva*, *rajas* and *tamas*. And if, in later life, *rajas* happens to be the dominant drive the individual has to expend large amounts of psychic energy to keep it in check for its free-pay amounts to practising *adharma*.

Indians have a "passive and less differentiated" ego in contrast with the "synthesizing and integrating activity" attributed to it in the West. In the Hindu scheme of things ego-reality (expressed in the West in terms of various ego functions such as a sense of reality, reality testing and adaptation to the environment) is of marginal importance. The whole of worldly experience is treated as a cosmic unreality. As against the classical psychoanalytic view of reality as tragic and ironic, the Hindu (more precisely the yogic) vision of reality is, in the words of Sudhir Kakar,

> a combination of the tragic and the romantic. Man is still buffected by fate's vagaries and tragedy is still the warp and woof of life. But instead of ironic acceptance, the yogic vision offers a romantic quest. The new journey is a search and the seeker, if he withstands all the perils of the road,

will be rewarded by an exaltation beyond normal human experience.[5]

Super-ego too seems to be weakly differentiated and insufficiently idealized in Indians. The tenets of *dharma,* the system of ideals, do not firmly entrench themselves in the individual's psychic stucture but exist deep within in close association with the other two sub-systems of personality. Whereas in the West an individual's behaviour is constantly regulated by the proscriptions of the super-ego, in a Hindu, it is regulated by what Sudhir Kakar calls "communal conscience." He explains that communal conscience which comprises family and *jati* norms "is a social rather than an individual formation: it is not inside the psyche. In other words, instead of having one internal "sentinel" an Indian relies on many external "watchmen" to petrol his activities and especially his relationships in all the social hierarchies."[6] This creates a situation in which clandestine infringement of moral standards is a thing not to be much worried about.

The above analysis of the Hindu personality structure in psychoanalytic terms gives one clear insight into certain commonly observable traits, and external manifestations of behaviour.[7] Most Indian are at least in theory religious in outlook. An unshakable belief in the rebirth theory seems to have given them a leisurely attitude toward everything. They do not easily get disturbed over delays and failures nor do they mind postponing things without much regret. Life is viewed as a continuum traceable to several births before and extendable to several births after the present one. As a natural result, the Indian concept of time defies all attempts of definition in the Western philosophical terms. The Indian concept of time seems to have historical origins too. Ancient India experienced long periods of peace and prosperity. People lived mostly in the open, in benevolent geographical surroundings enjoying nature's bounty in an easy and relaxed atmosphere. This, coupled with the joint family system and a weakly differentiated super-ego have integrated into the Indian personality ready hospitality, sharing attitude, love for peace, aversion for aggressiveness and tolerance for the expression of ambivalence especially when it is not detrimental to "communal conscience." An off-shoot of the religious outlook is fatalism which appears to have given the Indians the ego-strength to maintain equanimity even in the face of unpleasant happenings. But at the same time the low achievement motivation is also often attributed to this trait. While the high premium the Westerners place on the tension between the ego and the super-ego results in guilt feelings which are ultimately channelised into a "high potential for activity" an Indian is not induced into action by a strongly internalised agency. He can sit idly for hours and feel none the worse for it.

In their dealings with others, Indians often exhibit a strange admixture of inhibition and compromise on the one hand and communicative and intruding attitude on the other. The authoritarian joint family relations which made Indians depend on external authority figures to an excessive degree and the long periods of foreign domination account for the former and a readily accommodating nature and the basic trust in others may account for the latter. But surprisingly enough, centuries of subjugation has given them an unusual ability to survive through difficult times. Even in the face of oppressive and provocative circumstances Indians usually exhibit a forbearance rarely found elsewhere in the world.

On the negative side, Indians relatively lack integrity and honesty. The basic religious values of truth and honesty are rarely practised. Sincerity and direct statement of facts is generally disapproved of. The joint family atmosphere and the *jati* bonds have such profound influence on the individual that he begins to regard corruption, nepotism and dishonesty as mere abstract concepts. Immorality and illegality are irrelevant as long as one's acts do not vary from the "principle of primacy of relationships."

Dignity of labour is conspicuously absent in Indian society, especially among the people of middle class origin who are incidentally the protagonists of most of the Indian novels. The almost uncritical preference for jobs of a certain kind and open dislike for labour intensive occupations has much to do with the traditional *varnavyavasta* which sought to sharply divide people on the basis of their vocations that enjoyed various degrees of respect and prestige. Another manifestation of the caste-system is status consciousness generally found in public life but more pronounced in family life where elderly and male members invariably enjoy greater respect than others.

The foregoing theoretical understanding of Indian psyche will surely offer fresh insights into and brighten the dark corners of especially the novels which lend themselves to psychoanalytic interpretation. One often notes that the protagonists of such novels deviate from these common Indian norms and therefore their life becomes worthy of narration. Anita Desai, Arun Joshi, Bharati Mukherjee and Nergis Dalal of the second generation Indo-Anglian novelists have portrayed, often with full knowledge of the tenets of psychoanalysis, literary personages in their moments of intense psychic struggle. The works of these writers are unamenable for conventional critical approaches. The sensitively portrayed characters of these novels are best appreciated in the light of the formulations of depth psychology.

However, the Indian literary critic using the psychoanalytic formulations for critical purposes should do so with full knowledge of the fact that traditional psychoanalysis as it obtains in the West is not entirely applicable to the somewhat special literary and cultural environment of India. The Americans and the British too felt similarly and that is perhaps why native varieties of psychoanalysis such as Ego-psychology and Object Relations Theory have developed there and have been promptly assimilated by literary criticism.

Indians continue to be governed by group or *jati* norms. In other words, Indian society has not yet become an individualistic society. People are still viewed in relation to society rather than as separate entities in India. Therefore, while the sociologically oriented later Freudian "Metapsychology" continues to be relevant to the Indian conditions, it should be further qualified by the findings and theories of Sudhir Kakar, Erik Erikson and Erich Fromm because they have added a psycho-social dimension to psychoanalysis. Sudhir Kakar has transplanted psychoanalysis on the Indian soil. He discussed the psychology of Indians in terms of their myths, literature and popular culture in such of his works as *The Inner World, Shamans Mystics & Doctors* and *Intimate Relations.* His contribution to the discovery of Indian personality structure in psychoanalytic terms has already been discussed earlier in this chapter. Erikson's most significant contribution lies in the field of the psyhcho-social development of man from birth to death. In the words of Sudhir Kakar, "Erikson sees human development [...] as a series of predetermined steps [...] by which the individual seeks contact in an ever-widening radius with his society, which welcomes and regulates his 'unfolding.'" Erikson's different conception of ego marks a departure from Freud's "originological" emphasis on childhood experiences in determining later behaviour. He sought to place ego in a historic-cultural context, that is, historical and cultural influences too act as determinants of one's ego. Fromm brings a historical perspective to the relation between the individual's psyche and society. He assigns a creative role to society in shaping human nature. He thinks that society has experienced a long series of "historical dichotomies" by which he means the unconscious manifestation of ideology in society. The indefatigable nature of human mind always sought to resolve the incompatibilities occasioned by historical processes. The often passive acceptance of exploitative relationships between various classes of society, viewed in this light, fulfil an unconscious need. The self-preservative instinct compels man to grudgingly accept the conditions of his existence—the social norms, economic relations and other aspects. The introjection of societal standards makes him "desire" what is absolutely "necessary." In other words, the satisfaction of instinctual urges is culturally and socially determined. Fromm makes a powerful case for a synthesis between the biological and sociological forces. In their interaction man emerges as one who affects and is affected by history and social structure.

Thus, in view of the obvious relevance of the above three psychoanalysts, Indian psychoanalytic critics do well to bring their theoretical formulations to bear upon their literary discussions. In fact a selective and systematized body of views of these three would serve as a theoretical frame of reference to the Indian creative writers and critics alike.

The next important aspect of psychoanalysis from which Indian fiction and criticism in English can benefit is its deep insight into the operation of myths in the mental sphere. India is a fertile land as regards both religious and literary myths. Myths have been often but uncritically employed by Indian novelists to strengthen the structure of the novels. Apart from Meenakshi Mukherjee, who has a chapter on the literary use of myths in her pioneering work *The Twice-Born Fiction,* no Indian critic of note has focused attention on this aspect of Indian fiction.

In psychoanalytic terms, the creative process involves a fusion of the writer's dreams with the material drawn from the psychological heritage of his race. No other elements of this heritage are more authentic and amenable to his genius than the myths of the race. Freud contended that myths are projected onto the supernatural phenomena after they have originated under purely human conditions. While the dreams of the writer are more in the nature of a personal fantasy myths constitute a universal illusion and by judiciously mixing elements from both, which a skilled writer is certainly capable of, proceeds aesthetic pleasure. The recognition of a widely shared human experience in the personal fantasy of the writer is the hallmark of literary appreciation and a source of great pleasure. Peter Brooks thinks that every novelist works repetitions into his fictional product.[9] Myths are by nature repetitive and are applicable to a variety of people and circumstances. It can therefore be said that a psychoanalytic understanding of myths is doubly useful in the Indian context.

I would like to sum up my argument by stating that Indian fiction in English and Indian criticism in English are likely to be immensely benefited by incorporating psychoanalytic formulations into the creative and critical endeavour respectively. Psychoanalysis promises to introduce scientific spirit into the Indian literary critical effort which has been for long dominated by conventional and somewhat outmoded critical tools. Psychoanalytic criticism is scientific to the core and is therefore in keeping with the scientific spirit of the present age.

Notes and References

1. Meredith Anne Skura. *The Literary Use of the Psychoanalytic Process* (New Haven: Yale UP, 1981) 4.
2. Peter Brooks. "The Idea of a Psychoanalytic Literary Critcism," *Critical Inquiry* 13.2 (Winter 1987): 336-37.
3. Leonard Tennenhouse, ed. *The Practice of Psychoanalytic Criticism* (Detroit: Wayne State UP, 1976) 13.
4. Nayantara Sahgal in a letter to D. Ramakrishna, *Close Encounters with the Muse* (Eluru: Vecon Press, 1986), 86.
5. Sudhir Kakar. *The Inner World: A Psychoanalytic Study of Childhood and Society in India* (New Delhi: OUP, 1981) 6.
6. Kakar 28-29.
7. Some of these traits have been painstakingly compiled by Indu Dave, *The Typical Indian Personality as Perceived by Indians* (Udaipur: Himanshu Publications, 1984).
8. Sudhir Kakar, "The Traditional Hindu View and the Psychology of Erik H. Erikson," *Identity and Adulthood,* ed. Sudhir Kakar (New Delhi: OUP, 1979) 3.
9. Peter Brooks. "Freud's Master Plot," *Literature and Psychoanalysis The Question of Reading: Otherwise,* ed. Shoshama Felman (Baltimore: The Johns Hopkins UP, 1982) 280-300.

SECTION III

12

Introductory Notes on the Application of Art Criticism to Legal Research

DÁMASO JAVIER VICENTE BLANCO

> "Events are always to hand. But the coherence of these events—which is what we mean by reality—is an imaginative construction."
>
> John Berger, *The Sense of Sight*[1]

I

Law is an element of the culture in a society, and follows its ups and downs. If we take this premise as a starting point the connection between Art and Law will be simple to verify. The consideration of Law as cultural reality has been defended by multiple authorities.[2] Among these the work of Max Weber should be considered seminal in the examination of the genesis of Law as an element of social and cultural elaboration that responds to the character and rationalisation of each human community and civilization.[3] Paraphrasing Leonardo da Vinci in his reference to painting (*La Pittura è cosa mentale*), F. Rigaux has affirmed that Law "is an intellectual reality."[4] The constructed character or human creation of both disciplines (Painting and Law) is underlined in his statements. S. A. Sánchez Lorenzo has emphasized that Law follows the fortunes and the course of the cultural phenomena of each historical period: "Law is a cultural product. As such, it necessarily responds to the characteristics of a certain historical moment and it evolves in a parallel way to other manifestations or products of a particular culture."[5] Thus, Law is demarcated from the Natural Sciences (from causality) and it should be considered that its origin is not "solemn," but a fruit of the vicissitudes of life, of conflicts, accidents, relationships of force.

II

Certain social theorists have shown us that "reality" is built socially and that the law of a given society also responds to its own "construction," in which the collective mind has elaborated through time a system of organisation and social control.[6] From this perspective, the Law projects an *Imago Mundi,* made up entirely of sets of juridical rules and regulations that manifest a conception of things; it mimics an image of the preconceived world. Ronald Dworkin has made a clear parallel between the constructive model of the judicial criteria that sustain the Law and the work of a sculptor who starts from a given premise to elaborate his figure.[7]

III

The possibility of demonstrating a parallel between art criticism and legal research is justified by the conviction that it is this perspective that can best enrich the jurist's or law scholar's analysis. This allows them to verify if certain methods, techniques or approaches used by the art critic when analysing artistic creations can be used to complement the methods of study of those researching juridical phenomena.

IV

Is there anything in common between Art and Law or are they totally different? In his classic work "Spanish Civil Law," the famous Spanish civil lawyer Federico de Castro y Bravo offers a scathing criticism of Kelsen and the Pure Theory of the Law. As he puts it in his own particular rhetoric:

> The essence of the Law cannot be found simply in any one of its characteristics, even the most typical (the regulatory scheme), but, rather, in its entirety, in the profundity of its aims, although with this one has to take on qualities or contents that are common to other subjects (morals,

sociology, politics). The significance of this doctrine has been universal and it has even had influence on its opponents. The widespread acceptance that it has received is perhaps less because of its positive qualities than because it fits perfectly in the period from which it originates. The Days of Pure Poetry, of Cubist painting: no time could be more favourable to the fashion of a "Pure" Judicial Theory.[8]

Aside from a certain deliberate banalisation, by resorting in a crude and conventional way to the idea of fashion, the parallel between Cubist painting and Pure Theory of Law has a value that goes beyond the purely anecdotal; insofar as both movements, in painting and in Theory of Law, share more than a few characteristics and methodological foundations. Think about whether the following passages dedicated to cubism and Picasso by the art critic John Berger can be applied or not to the pure Theory of Law:

> The way of seeing [...]. They (the Cubists) hated the conventions that had forgotten their origins: the oil paint in love with itself. Yet they had to use conventions. So they preferred to use the simplest ones which our eyes can still accept innocently [...]. In their figure painting they approached the problem differently. It was not the presence of the figure as a person of flesh and blood which they now stressed: but the physical complexity of the structure of that figure. At first it may be quite difficult to find the person; and, when found, he or she may have little connection with the sensuous experience of a body. But the structural arrangement which the body is made as tangible and precise as the architecture of a town [...]. This austerity of approach in relation to the figure was at least partly the result of a reaction against excessive talk of the spiritual and soulful. By reducing the body to an organization, comparable with that of a city, they assert the unmetaphysical character of man.[9]

> [The cubists] expressed their consequent enthusiasm for the future in terms which are justified by modern science. And they did this in the one decade in recent history (1907-1914) when it was possible to possess such enthusiasm

> and yet ignore, without deliberate evasion, the political complexities and terrors involved. They painted the good omens of the modern world.[10]

Does a parallel not exist between the animosity towards oil painting for its own sake, the repudiation of historicism, and the repugnance of Natural Law towards the Pure Theory of Law? Is there not in positivism, in its rejection of the idea of Natural Law, the same reaction against the wordiness of the spiritual and the soul, affirming the human being's "anti-metaphysical character"? Is separating the Theory of Law from any theory of justice not equivalent to the withdrawal from painting of an ideal canon of beauty, in the search for another way of understanding reality? Was positivism not also the fruit of a historic moment fired by faith in progress and reason?

V

Such correspondence is neither gratuitous nor capricious, and in fact there are those who have spoken of a common origin of Art and Law:

> For millennia art was comparable to Law in common magic origins and in common strivings for eternity. It remained comparable to Law when, like Law, it was a means of creating the good. And when Law was an instrument which was to produce justice, art was a skill which was to produce beauty [...]. Both art and Law then served traditions of beauty and justice.[11]

This parallel between justice and beauty, between ethics and aesthetics, is at the base of the comparative possibilities between Art and Law, of the use of art criticism by jurists, of the correspondence between the history of art and the history of ideas and the Social Sciences, including Law. This is something that art critics who believed in a "pure," "unpolluted" idea of the arts have reviled furiously, instead of wondering about the true buried reasons why concepts like *vanguard* or *bourgeois* should have been used in the artistic war in the same way as in politics during the 19th and 20th centuries, or why in the sphere of the Social Sciences and in that of the Arts a parallel historical course can be followed.[12] Without a doubt an exact extrapolation of concepts and attitudes does not exist, but equivalent intellectual and vital predispositions are observed in the face of two distinct worlds. What interests us now, however, more than developing the parallel between justice and beauty, is to show something to which we have previously referred which is at the foundation of all art and in some measure is also common to Law: the mimetic character of the artistic activity. Law also acts by means of *mimesis.* Aristotle, in his *Poetics,* begins an entire interpretive process which, taken to its extreme consequences, would culminate in our century in analytical methods such as semiotics and allegorical analysis:

> Epic and tragic poetry, comedy too, dithyrambic poetry and most music composed for the pipe and the lyre, can all be described in general as forms of imitation or representation. However, they differ from one another in three respects: either in using different media for the representation, or in representing different things, or in representing them in entirely different ways.
>
> Some people, whether by art or by practice, can represent things by imitating their shapes and colours, and others do so by the use of the voice; in all the arts mentioned above the imitation is produced by means of rhythm, language, and melody, these being used either separately or in combination.[13]

VI

Mimesis is "imitation," but also echo, reflection, projection, *Imago Mundi,* representation. In Law, it is possible that mimesis does not always operate to the same degree, as we will see later, and without a doubt it does not serve the function—accepting, here, the functionalist perspective—that it possesses in any artistic phenomenon. It is with difficultly that one turns expressly for aesthetic enjoyment to juridical texts, even if Stendhal did daily read an article of the Napoleonic Civil Code to gain agility and spontaneity in writing. It is an entirely different matter if good linguistic expression is used, or if the indolent reader goes "looking for flowers among the thorns." And, if I am allowed an anecdote, my first university edition (1982) of the Spanish Civil

Code of 1889 still carries annotations to certain passages, such as these:

> "If before this time the town was an uninhabited wilderness [...]" (Article 515); "The environs of the banks of navigable or floatable rivers also have towpaths for the exclusive service of navigation and river flotation" (Article 553); "The owner of a swarm of bees shall be entitled to pursue it on land belonging to another, but shall compensate its proprietor for any damage caused. If the land is surrounded by a fence, he shall require the proprietor's consent to enter. Where the owner of the swarm has not pursued it or ceases to pursue it for two consecutive days, the proprietor of the land shall be entitled to seize or retain it. The owner of domesticated animals shall also be entitled to claim them during a period of twenty days after their being taken by another. At the end of that period, they shall belong to the one that has acquired them and looked after them" (Article 612).

An "uninhabited" town, navigable rivers, a swarm; tamed animals: are these not eloquent texts? Do we not imagine a tale, a story, behind the right to chase a swarm of bees on someone else's land? Or behind the right to keep a seized animal after twenty days? The specific regulation on the swarm—beyond its possible Latin origin—or that on the ownership of domesticated animals, speak of peasants' landholdings, of a rural world and a precarious economy whose law regulates aspects that later would be left marginalised by a mainly urban world and economy. The Law is eloquent and speaks of life, it uses language to understand reality and can do so in a more intense, even emotional way, or else with the technical indifference and coldness of naturalistic description. As Jürgen Habermas puts it:

> In some prominent places, the text of the legal itself reveals these implicit diagnoses of the times, for example, in the "bill of rights" section of constitutions that have emerged from political upheavals or revolutions. In contrast to the professionally formulated or developed law of legal scholars, even the style and wording of these declarations display an emphatic statement of will from citizens who are reacting

> to concrete experiences of repression and humiliation. Most articles in a bill of rights resonate with a suffered injustice that its negated word for word, as it were. What is obvious in those rare moments of the revolutionary founding of a constitution remains implicit in the everyday work of the legislature and the judiciary and so must be laboriously deciphered by the historian. Parliaments and courts can pursue the goal of realizing rights only in a context that their members interpret in view of actually allowed but limited possibilities of action. One can understand what actors respond to, and have responded to, with their decisions and reasons only if one recognizes their *implicit image of society* and only knows which structures, achievements, potentials, and dangers they ascribe to their own society at the time, in the light of their task of realizing the system of rights.[14]

We can refer here to the present, to a highly contemporary example: independently of all discussion of its legitimacy, one may wonder whether the attempt to apply Spanish law extraterritorially in order to extradite General Pinochet from the United Kingdom and put him on trial in Spain did not have at its base the collective imagination of Spanish society, in the context of its own recent political history and its past as regards human rights. One may wonder whether it is true that not only the norm, but judicial practice too, are facts of a collective experience.

VII

Mimesis and its forms, when manifested historically, marry Art and Law. This same historicity is expressed in the values that Law welcomes and the Arts reflect in their topics, attitudes and concerns. The historicity of the conception of time, of philosophical and ideological postulates, is reflected in both the artistic manifestations and the juridical norms and their judicial application in a given society. That common historicity explains the transposition possibilities of many studies of art criticism with regard to law, in what they reveal of the processes of change of all the common aspects of the two disciplines. In the interpretation that the Spanish art critic and architect Josep María Montaner makes of the changes in the arts between the end of the 19th century and beginning of the 20th, even though he employs a restricted concept of *mimesis*,[15] law could also be included as another of the disciplines that undergoes an identical transformation:

> The widespread concept of mimesis, which had its origin in Greece and reached maximum development in classicism and neoclassicism, has been at the base of the whole of the history of Art and Architecture. The different ways of looking at and representing the visible image of the world have been the motor of a continuous evolution. At the end of the 19th century and the beginning of the 20th century the great transformation occurred: the gradual abandonment of the mimesis of reality, the search for new types of expression in the world of the machine, of geometry, of materials, of the mind and of dreams, with the objective of breaking and diluting the conventional images of the world in favour of totally new forms. The basic resources of this transformation were the very diverse mechanisms that abstraction possesses as a way of supplanting mimesis in the representative arts: invention, conceptualisation, simplification, elementarism, juxtaposition, fragmentation, interpretation, simultaneity, action or collage.
>
> The modern artist who first appears with the autonomous individual of Romanticism, the creator who is not subject to the demands of a client, rebels arrogantly against the tyrannical subordination to mimesis and against the principle of representation. The crisis of the established vision of things and the negation of mimesis end up in the celebration of the senses: the new art will be based on stimulating the relationship between the work and the receiver from the point of view of the mechanisms of perception.
>
> Each artistic discipline will open up a limitless inquiry into its own materiality and dematerialisation possibilities: design and composition, lines and colours in painting;

> structures, elements and pure geometric forms in architecture. The works of Pablo Picasso, Vassily Kandinsky, Kasimir Malevich and Piet Mondrian will be seminal to this search for a hidden reality beyond appearances, revealing the most purely structural, formal and compositional aspects. This will have its correspondence in the writings of James Joyce, the music of Arnold Schoenberg and the philosophy of Ludwig Wittgenstein.[16]

Positivism, juridical realism, alternative uses of Law, analytic theories, jurisprudence of interests, neo-natural law theory [...] norms, "reality," facts, legislative politics, interests, values, immanent rights. Is a similar process not also applicable to Law? Has a decomposition of its multiple aspects not also taken place?

VIII

The thesis of secularisation claims that Western "civil" notions derive from the secularisation of theological concepts.[17] The interpretation of literary texts would then follow this path and evoke the interpretation of the "Text" par excellence—the sacred text, the Bible.[18] Juridical notions, as Carl Schmitt sustains in his *Political Theology,* would arise from secularised theological concepts: the characteristics of the State, for example, as a transfer of the attributes of God to an earthly power. The transposition from some fields of knowledge to others of methods, notions and constructions is not only not alien to our culture: it is in fact a characteristic feature of Western culture. The invitation made by Walter Benjamin, in his *Theses on the Philosophy of History,* to employ theology in the materialistic analysis of history is also a response to the idea of transposition, of using a tradition that was in danger of disappearing yet contained keys that could give us a better understanding of historical phenomena.[19]

IX

I shall now conclude, while still leaving many points untouched. The performative character of judicial law impedes or hinders the automatic transposition of the methods of art criticism to law. The role of Law, its position, function, and social purpose, are not those of Art. Nonetheless, there are multiple methods of art criticism which are capable of enriching the jurist's task. Some of these have not only been used, but have even been consolidated as methods of analysis of Law. This has been the case with the philosophy of language of Ludwig Wittgenstein, with the hermeneutics of Hans-Georg Gadamer (as explicitly responded to by J. Habermas[20] and R. Dworkin,[21] leading to an intensive debate on interpretation), and with semiotics.[22] Others have not been brought into general use. I could linger over the approaches, values and procedures of legitimisation of art—to have it considered as such, to identify and define a creative work as artistic—and the parallels with judicial legitimisation. Or one could go into the multiple possibilities offered by analogy as a means of reception of extrajudicial methods.[23] Or one could explore a very concrete perspective that I find especially fruitful: the transposition to Law of the method of *dramaturgical analysis* as a particular method of study of human conflicts that is, if only in derived fashion, a method of aesthetic analysis.[24] One might venture to claim that it is what the art critic contributes to the theory of knowledge that is capable of enriching juridical method and legal research.

Even though normative and jurisprudential analysis still remain at the heart of legal research, the possibilities are open. Meanwhile, the potentiality of the transposition of art criticism to legal research has not been exhausted. Walter Benjamin proposed such a task for the relationship between art criticism and philosophy:

> For the philosopher, the most interesting thing about fashion is its extraordinary anticipations. It is well known that art will often [...] precede the perceptible reality by years.[25]

But in some instances, as happens with a truth like that just cited, there are "realities" which are unquestionable but are also unusable in practice. In my own case (my field is the study of practical Law, and, in particular, private international law), that cannot be forgotten. Transposition, then, will also prove to have its precise limits.

Notes and References

1. John Berger, *The Sense of Sight* (New York: Vintage International, 1993) 279.
2. From Max Weber—who extended it to the group of the social sciences—to authors who apply it directly to Law, such as G. Radbruch, A. Kaufmann, or J.M. Broekman.
3. See Weber, "Law and Economy. Sociology of Law," in his great *Economy and Society,* as well as the Weber volume in Spanish translation, "*Sobre la Teoría de las Ciencias Sociales*" (Barcelona, Península, 1997).
4. In *Les Situations Juridiques Individuelles dans un Système de Relativité Générale, Collected Courses of the Hague Academy of International Law* 213.1 (1989): 45.
5. In "Posmodernismo y Derecho internacional privado," *Revista Española de Derecho Internacional* XLVI. 2 (1994): 557.
6. See J.I. Martínez García, *La imaginación Jurídica* (Madrid: Debate, 1992) 17 ff. C. Pérez Ruiz also adopts this position in his *La construcción Social del Derecho,* University of Seville, 1996. The principal works to be noted in this context are, in the sociology of knowledge, P.L. Berger and T. Luckmann, *The Social Construction of Reality,* 1966, and, in the field of Law, the contributions of J. Rawls, *A theory of Justice,* 1971, and R.D. Dworkin, *Taking Rights Seriously,* 1977. Particularly relevant are the deep corrections to Berger and Luckmann made by J.R. Searle in his *The Construction of Social Reality* (New York: The Free Press, 1995).
7. R. Dworkin, *Taking Rights Seriously* (*Los derechos en serio)* (Barcelona: Ariel, 1989) 247.
8. F. de Castro y Bravo, *Derecho Civil de España,* 1952, pp. 18-19.
9. John Berger, *Success and Failure of Picasso* (1965; London: Granta, 1989) 58-59. Strictly speaking, Berger's text makes a comparison with dialectical materialism, but, as shown, the comparison with Kelsenian positivism also offers clear similarities.
10. Berger 71.
11. A. Ehrenzweig, *Psychoanalytic Jurisprudence* (Leiden, 1971) 169.
12. F. Kaskell: "The Art of Language and Politics," *Pasado y Presente en el arte y en el gusto* (Berger: Alianza Editorial, 1989) 105 ff.

13. Aristotle, *Poetics,* trans. Penelope Murray and T.S. Dorsch, *Classical Literary Criticism,* ed. Penelope Murray (Harmondsworth: Penguin, 2000) 57-58.

14. Jürgen Habermas, *Between Facts and Norms. Contributions to a Discourse Theory of Law and Democracy,* trans. William Rehg (Massachusetts: MIT, 1996) 388-89.

15. Montaner employs a restricted concept of mimesis, opposed to "abstraction," in contrast to Aristotle's broad concept which both incorporates music in its scope and integrates within itself that same "abstraction," as a process that mimics "reality."

16. Josep María Montaner, *La modernidad superada. Arquitectura, Arte y Pensamiento del Siglo XX* (Barcelona: Gustavo Gili, 1997) 9-10.

17. See G. Marramao, *Cielo y Tierra. Genealogía de la Secularización* (Barcelona: Paidós, 1998).

18. See Umberto Eco, *Obra Abierta* (Barcelona: Ariel, 1979) 67; and "La línea y el Laberinto: estructuras del pensamiento latino," *Civilización latina* (Barcelona: Laia, 1989) 39 ff.

19. See Walter Benjamin, "Theses on the Philosophy of History" [1940], *Illuminations,* ed. and intr. Hannah Arendt, trans. Harry Zohn, (London: Fontana, 1973).

20. Jürgen Habermas, *Teoría de la Acción Comunicativa I* (Madrid: Tecnos, 1987) 182-89; *La lógica de las Ciencias Sociales,* pp. 277-306; *Factividad y validez,* pp. 263-309.

21. R. Dworkin, *Law's Empire,* Harvard University Press, 1986 (*El Imporio de la Justicia* (Barcelona: Gedisa, 1988) 47 ff; see also note 2, p. 48 and p. 293).

22. As regards the function of language in Law, numerous analyses exist. Particularly original is the study by E. García de Enterría, *La lengua de los derechos. La formación del Derecho Público europeo tras la Revolución Francesa* (Madrid: Alianza Editorial, 1994).

23. On analogy in Law and its different conceptions, one can turn to the studies of M. Atienza (*Sobre la analogía en el Derecho: ensayo de análisis de un razonamiento jurídico* (Madrid: Civitas, 1986), M.J. Falcón Tella (*El argumento analógico en el Derecho* (Madrid: Civitas, 1991) and J. Vallet De Goytisolo ("La analogía en el Derecho," *Anuario de Derecho Civil,* 1995, No 3, pp. 1039 ff.). It is necessary to mention in this respect the statement of Norberto Bobbio: "That something is governed on the same lines as something similar to it is a convention of juridical language. No reasoning by analogy exists that is valid in and for itself. It is valid where, under the fundamental rules of a certain language, its legitimacy is recognised and, therefore, its use is imposed. For a physicist analogy is weak reasoning; for a jurist it is

sure reasoning because it is, as it were, one of the rules of the game." *Contribución a la Teoría del Derecho*, ed. A. Ruiz Miguel (Valenci: F. Torres Editor, 1980) 194.

24. "In classical drama theory, the theatre has the object of presenting human actions and following the evolution of a crisis and the emergence and resolution of conflicts"—P. Pavis, *Diccionario del Teatro*, Paidós, Madrid, 1983, p. 92. On this subject, see: J.L. Alonso De Santos, *La Escritura Dramática* (Madrid: Castalia, 1998); J.A. Hormigón, *Trabajo dramatúrgico y puesta en escena*, published by *Asociación de Directores de Escena de España* (Madrid: 1991); J.H. Lawson, *Teoría y Técnica de la escritura de Obras Teatrales*, published by *Asociación de Directores de Escena de España* (Madrid: 1995); and G.E. Lessing, *La dramaturgia de Hamburgo*, published by *Asociación de Directores de Escena de España* (Madrid: 1993).

25. Walter Benjamin, "Fashion," Chapter B, Section B.1,9, *The Arcades Project*, trans. Howard Eiland and Kevin McLaughlin (prepared on the basis of the original German volume edited by Rolf Tiedemann), (Cambridge, Mass: Harvard UP) 63.

✪✪✪

13

Toward an Exemplary Relationship between the Judge and the Literary Critic

NOURI GANA

> Instead of noninterference and specialization, there must be interference, a crossing of borders and obstacles, a determined attempt to generalize exactly at those points where generalizations seem impossible.
>
> —Edward Said, "Opponents, Audiences, Constituencies, and Community" (30).

While Gadamer elects legal hermeneutics as the exemplary model for literary hermeneutics, Dworkin appoints literary interpretation as an indispensable paradigm for legal interpretation. Both steps, by Gadamer and Dworkin respectively, have provoked a lot of controversies and debates which have in turn fuelled an old skepticism about the nature and value of literature and law, not to mention their commingling. Since it would take some more pages to round out my working answer to these renewed challenges, it suffices now to mention that such an answer will proceed, in the context of this paper, by an exploration of the overlapping zones of literature and law, an exploration that will eventually open up other corridors for inquiry into their nature and value. Can law, therefore, by virtue of being a domain of praxis, rid literature of the accusations of vacuity, hollowness, parasitism and otiosity foisted on it by such inimical appraisers as J.L. Austin, John R. Searle as well as Judge Richard Posner? And can literature, by virtue of being a bounteous host and catalyst of different interpretations, instigate a vibrant and tolerant practice of interpretation in the legal field? These two questions presuppose a marriage between law and literature *via interpretation*, but although interpretation is the kind of nexus marshaled throughout this paper, it should not blind us to the many other spaces of interaction, overlap, and also tension between law and literature, such as in representations of law in fiction or in censuring fiction by law. Neither of these, however, will receive a special attention in the course of this paper. On the contrary, I will try to answer the two questions raised above propounding a normative relationship between the judge, the interpreter of legal texts, and the critic, the interpreter of literary texts, a relationship predicated on the dialectic of *proximity* and *distance*. The faculties of the critic and the judge should not, I will argue, operate strictly within the niche of literature and law respectively, but should distend and close elastically. In my examination I shall leave out of account all the antagonistic tendencies within the pale of each tradition, the literary tradition of criticism and that of legal studies respectively, and try instead to belabor my argument midway between the overlapping territories of the practices of the literary critic and the judge.

Before we plunge into the midst of these struggles, let's array ourselves in the armor of the insights of the most renowned interventions in what is known in the North American academic environment as the law and literature movement. Although the law and literature movement may seem at *prima facie* an unprecedented breakthrough in what Said deprecates as "disciplinary ghettoes," it can be argued that this movement is no more than a revival of an old tradition in which many—now autonomous—disciplines were herded under the rubric of philosophy. It can as well be argued that this interdisciplinary movement is simply a reactionary movement to the current "rigid" (Said 81), "atomized order of disciplines and fields" (Said 22) in which "the present continuation of the humanities depends," Said alerts us, "on the sustained self-purification of humanists for whom the ethic of specialization has become equivalent to minimizing the content of their work and increasing the composite wall of guild consciousness, social authority, and exclusionary discipline among themselves"

(Said 25). If we agree with Said on this somewhat diseased state of specialization, then the law and literature movement could best be seen as an antidote to the ubiquitous drive of specialization, as an immersion in the general waters of the humanities that would ultimately tally with, tessellate and temper, rather than vindictively wreak havoc in, the continued pursuit of the particularization of knowledge.

The debates over the usefulness of literature as a paradigm for law and particularly over the pertinence of literary interpretation as a guide for legal hermeneutics seem to have eclipsed discussions over the relevance of legal hermeneutics (in turn) to literary hermeneutics. Now, the relation between interpretation in law and interpretation in literature seems to have undergone a cyclic reversal: after having been appointed by Gadamer as the norm for literary hermeneutics, legal interpretation as practiced by Dworkin, James Body White and others is now taking after interpretation in literary fields. This reversal tempts one to ask two complementary questions: first, what is it that makes judges of particular interest to literary critics? Second, what is it that presses judges to want to learn from literary critics? While the answer to the first question will refer us to Gadamer, the answer to the second question will require an examination of Dworkin's as well as White's postulations. Before that, a remark is in order: although we have taken to heart Said's imperative "to generalize exactly at those points where generalizations seem impossible," and although we will loosely use the generic signifier of "literary critic" to refer to scholars belonging to different schools (hermeneutics, formalism, deconstruction, etc), we will not so much indulge in a massive obfuscation of all parametric differences between the practices and practitioners in each of these schools as pursue a genuine entanglement with convergences, meeting points, and ultimately elucidate those overlaps, interlinks, and the concrete interfaces between these perspectives—interfaces existent *ab initio* as much as *ex post facto* although they have been thrust into oblivion through our century's extraordinary fund in specialization. My focus on the practices of the judge within the American constitutional milieu should not, we hope, excuse us from the incumbent task to reach out far for judges everywhere.

I - The Exemplary Significance of the Judge

In his *Truth and Method*, Gadamer assigns himself the task of "redefining the hermeneutics of the human sciences in terms of *legal* and theological hermeneutics" (Gadamer 277, italics mine). Obviously, the project is ambitious inasmuch as it can kill two birds with one stone: it would not only serve to disassociate the human sciences from the classic accusations of being as useless as needless a branch of knowledge for everyday life, but would also give a thoroughly practical, albeit highly contested, dimension to this very field of the human sciences. Legal hermeneutics is of an "exemplary significance" to literary hermeneutics not only because it is characterized by the practice of interpretation, but most importantly because it is the archetypal field wherein "understanding [...] is always application" (275). For Gadamer, "the recognition of application as an integral element of all understanding" is a prerequisite to any attempt at connecting literary, theological and legal hermeneutics (see Gadamer 275).

Gadamer tries to collapse supposedly successive and distinctive activities into one. First, he fuses the phase of understanding with that of interpreting: "Interpretation is not an occasional additional act subsequent to understanding, but rather understanding is always an interpretation" (Gadamer 274). Second, he merges understanding (i.e. interpreting) with application: "application is neither a subsequent nor a merely occasional part of the phenomenon of understanding, but codetermines it as a whole from the beginning" (Gadamer 289). It is only through this very strategic process of amalgamating sequential or successional activities into simultaneous inquiries (understanding/interpretation, interpretation/application) that the affinities between literary, theological and legal hermeneutics begin to emerge. Indeed, the project of redefining literary hermeneutics in terms of legal and theological hermeneutics would not have been possible had Gadamer not established application as the common denominator among these schools of hermeneutics.

Notwithstanding the neatness of this interdisciplinary redefinition of literary hermeneutics, the degree to which application in literary hermeneutics resembles application in either theological or legal hermeneutics remains shrouded in ambiguity and haziness. In other words, if we concede that an interpretation in the literary field is necessarily an application as much as it so elsewhere, is that sufficient to hold that that application has also the same impact as an application in the legal or theological hermeneutics? This question urges us to dig deep into the nature of legal and theological interpretation/ application and compare it to that of literary interpretation/ application. Although from Gadamer's ontological[1] approach to literary, legal and theological hermeneutics, we can maintain that application is as native to interpretation as constrained by traditional practices; we can *hardly see* how a literary application/ interpretation, characterized by play, *can* earn the same status (i.e. decisiveness) as a legal or a theological interpretation, characterized by an *immediate* and *vécu* impact on life and on the world.[2] I am by no means suggesting that a literary application/interpretation has no effect on the interpreter's or/ and the reader's store of (lived) experiences and on his repertoire of knowledge in general; I am suggesting a difference in *degree*.

Contrary to literary application / interpretation, legal and theological application/interpretation can be a matter of life and death. It is precisely because a just and correct interpretation can save the lives of people that traditional hermeneutics was reserved to interpreting law and the scripture. Indeed, as E.D. Hirsch rightly argues, traditional "hermeneutical theorizing was confined almost exclusively to two domains where correct interpretation was a matter of life and death (or heaven and hell)—the study of scripture and the study of law" (Hirsch 19-20).

To integrate interpretation and application, and to open up interpretation to the restrictive play[3] of tradition such that tradition becomes practically the only player, leaves—however whole-hearted an attempt to avoid opportunism and subjectivism this might be—us totally unshielded vis-à-vis the vagaries of tradition, history, community, and the like. At this level, we are of course bordering on the Gadamer-Habermas debate—a debate whose ramifications ripple, though in miniatures, through the many scholastic debates between the communitarians (Fish) and the liberals (White, Dworkin). In point of fact, Fish's concept of "interpretive communities" is itself but a miniaturized adaptation, a carved out version, of the more pervasive concept of "tradition" in Gadamer's lexicon. Gadamer's elaboration of interpretation as a game that plays us at the very moment we are playing it is also, revealingly enough, the same trope Fish deploys to ensure a kind of embedded game-system that regulates in a quasi-*sous-entendu* manner the relations between the members of a given interpretive community, between their interpretations and the principles on the grounds of which their community has been edified. Thus, once a set of interpretive strategies is in place, performance, i.e. interpretation, will necessarily follow from within (Fish), and once an operative historical context is stated and a vibrant tradition articulated (Gadamer), the application of what our predecessors have handed down to us will be no less than a naturally-occurring ritual. Fish and, to a lesser degree, Gadamer verge on, if not inhabit the abode of, pragmatism such that they fall short of allowing a room with a view on the interpretive community (Fish) and on the tradition (Gadamer), i.e. the storehouses of interpretation, from which every interpretation ensues but is by no means thereby theoretically enabled to coil up at the pillars of community or tradition in such a manner as to bite, if need be, its own tail. Such a room and such a potentiality for biting one's own tail become all the more urgent especially when it comes to legal interpretation since what is at stake is, as Hirsch has pointed out, human life.

Gadamer's redefinition of literary hermeneutics in terms of legal hermeneutics, i.e. in terms of application, has to undergo the appropriateness test. Although I think it is perfectly plausible and admissible for a judge, or a literary critic to interpret in terms of application, I think that application in law has another dimension which has *pro tanto* to do with decision making. Gadamer's preoccupation with crossing the disciplinary boundaries *via* the generalization of the *subtilitas applicandi* to all forms of understanding within the literary and legal fields is pitched at the expense of the peculiarities and idiosyncrasies as well as differences in degree of application in the two fields mentioned above. One essential difference between the judge and the literary critic that Gadamer's theory of application does not tolerate is the fact that the judge has to adjudicate while the literary critic would not necessarily feel the need, let alone the pressure, to do so. First, how can the judge decide justly if he is volleyed within a given community with explicit and implicit principles and interests[4]? Second, would the literary critic tolerate the hue of decision-making under which the judge labors? I will come back to the first question when I deal with Fish, but I will now, relying on the dynamic dyad of *proximity* and *distance*, pave the ground for a possible fruitful chime between the judge and the literary critic.

To interpret in terms of application is plausible in legal hermeneutics inasmuch as application in this field is as immanent as imminent, but to interpret in terms of application in the literary field is not so much an unlikely practice as a not-necessarily the only possible, much less the primary, task to be sought and wrought by a critic. Literary critics do not only interpret, but also read for many other different purposes. Although the dividing lines between reading and interpreting have been blurred, and most often subsumed under interpretation, the activity of reading has endured throughout the last decades with an almost unconquerable persistency all the marginalizing propensities of literary criticism, which even the very school of Reader-Response is guilty of. This activity asks of us, as Coleridge has it, to willingly suspend our disbelief, and to plunge into the world of the text so as to be transported and entertained by it. Such a momentary uplifting from the world of reality into the world of fiction cannot be rendered in terms of application: application is subsequent to it. We certainly do not imagine a judge reading amendment fourteen of the American constitution in the way a literary critic would read *Hamlet*, for instance. While the judge has to simultaneously interpret and decide the meaning of the doctrine of "equal protection of the laws" in relation to the case at hand, the literary critic would read/interpret without necessarily feeling the urge to adjudicate on whether Hamlet (and behind him the intellectual at large) is capable of action or not.

Unlike the pressured judge who interprets/applies in terms of a final sole decision he has eventually to make, the less strained literary critic knows from the outset that his interpretation/application would be, no matter how highly he esteems it, only one among many coexisting, *possible*, if not 'equally acceptable' interpretations. The idea of coexisting plural interpretations, in what Wayne C. Booth calls the "critical commonwealth,"[5] cannot be embraced by a jurist whose objective is to reach a just and unfaltering decision. It is at the moment of decision-making that the judge ceases to be the exemplar for the literary critic.

The literary critic does not so much seek a *correct* interpretation—except in the case of absolute monists like E.D. Hirsch and, to a lesser degree, P.D. Juhl—as much as a *different* one. Grossly put, the literary critic is after a *new* interpretation that might complement, refine, or bounce the other interpretations of a given text—an interpretation that can hardly therefore pronounce the final word on the work under consideration. But the insistence on novelty and difference does not warrant one to seek novelty *in vacuum*: one has to *justify* the new ideas or hypotheses one comes up with; one has to build an *argument* in the hope that it might earn value, or command recognition. The new interpretation can by no means, however, annul the perspectival validity of the preceding interpretations, no matter how critically it can disarm their pre-emption, prominence, and predominance. Difference and novelty become the hobgoblin of little minds once they are vacuously looked for. Unlike the critic who might be more inclined toward, as Lessing had long ago stated in a fit of stark prophetic gloom, the *search after* truth rather than *truth itself*, the judge has no alternative but to establish the truth, the only deterrent against injustice(s).

The above description of the manner according to which a literary critic functions provides us with almost all the clues that draw him, in a strategically elastic manner, *near* and yet *far* from the judge. Inasmuch as the literary critic has to justify and defend his argument, his new interpretation, on a solid and rigorous basis, the judge would be of exemplary significance for him. The literary critic should think of his interpretation as an application not only ontologically (Gadamer), but also epistemologically—as an *application-prompting-interpretation.* He also should support his interpretation and not pontificate it in a blithely naïve manner. The critic must not dishonestly jockey for a position for his interpretation since a literary interpretation is in no position to purport to be the only correct interpretation, although it must be spurred by, and birthed from within, that very powerfully illusive aspiration and has thus to stand in the critic's mind *as if* it were so. The aspiration to provide the best interpretation makes the engine of the critic's interpretive faculties run at full throttle, but the aspiration has always to surpass, if not overlook, the concretization on which much of a judge's labor is predicated. The "as if" in the last but one sentence describes laconically but tellingly how much the literary critic can approximate the activities of the judge in a court and how much he remains at a strategic distance from them. Insofar as the literary critic seeks to solidify and justify his interpretation, he finds in the judge his idol, but insofar as he seeks to interpret in terms of difference and newness and not in terms of restoring or finding a sole correct interpretation, the judge would prove too rigorous to be emulated, much less trusted. This is not to say that the literary critic is oblivious to deciding upon the best interpretation he can proffer for a text, but that his interpretation would not so much aim at reiterating a previous interpretation that he finds correct (as is the case following the precedent in law) as to carve out a different interpretation from the already circulated plethora of interpretations, or to baroquely raise up one from the wreck those interpretations might have suffered. While the literary critic aims at "persuasion" (Fish); the judge strives for resolution. The judge familiarizes himself with the preceding cases in order to repeat what former judges have decided on a given case that offers itself anew; the literary critic should immerse himself in the tradition of literary criticism not so much to reproduce its moves wholesale as to give them a wide berth.

Unlike the judge who is compelled from the outset to end up with a single interpretation, the literary critic is asked to come up with a new one. The literary critic would not add anything to our knowledge of a work of art if he just ransacks all the previous interpretations of it in search of the correct one amongst them. While the judge may find the right interpretation of legal propositions in precedent, the literary critic would find in precedent a store of different interpretations that should enrich rather than hamstring his activities. In the gross, the literary critic is supposed to enhance and explore the plurality of a literary text while the judge is obliged to validly interpret the text of law in the light of the (particular) case at hand. Although there is still much exploration to be made and much to be discovered in the relation and regulation of the relation between the judge and the literary critic, it is my contention now that the literary critic can be in turn of exemplary significance to the judge. As an explorer of plurality and difference, the literary critic proffers an example for the judge, an example in thinking and deciding self-consciously of interpretive plurality, of perspectival differences, and thus of the slippery nature of truth—the only obviator of injustices.

II - The Exemplary Significance of the Literary Critic

In his "Law and Literature: A Relation Reargued," Richard Posner complains that "academic law in America is busily ransacking the social sciences and the humanities for insights and approaches with which to enrich our understanding of the legal system" (1996: 61). Of course, Posner alludes to, amongst others, James Boyd White, the initiator of the law and literature movement and to Ronald Dworkin, the stipulator of the "chain enterprise" metaphor. Unlike White and Dworkin who are adamant to transcend the fiefdoms of disciplinary demarcations, Posner, albeit "sympathetic" (1996: 85), is very skeptical about the necessity and relevance of literature, the field of fiction, aesthetics and the unconscious, to law, the field of reality, practice and consciousness.

As developed polemically in his *Law and Literature* (1988) and as concisely put in the above-mentioned article, Posner's argument against an interdisciplinary approach to law boils down to claiming that "the functions of legislation and literature are so different, and the objectives of the readers of these two different sorts of mental product so divergent that the principles and approaches developed for the one have no *useful application* for the other" (1988: 74, italics mine). By and large, Posner maintains that fiction is divorced from reality, "written in an unconscious blur," and "read for pleasure and to a lesser extent for instruction" (70). Consequently, he propounds two different approaches—the intentionalist approach, which he reserves for law, and the New Critical approach, which he reserves for literature. The former intentionalist approach would consist of retrieving the framers' state of consciousness, intentions or "spirit" and "vision," as Edwin Meese, an intentionalist much like Posner, puts it (Meese 29). Such an approach is in tune with Meese's "high objective: fidelity to our fundamental law" (Meese 25). The New Critical approach, however, is the rubric under which Posner groups, notwithstanding their differences, both the American New Critical practices and what he loosely calls "postmodernist," "poststructuralist," or "deconstructivist" practices whose most notorious representative in legal hermeneutics is Ronald Dworkin. According to Posner, this approach cannot be applicable for legal texts because it would distort the "consciousness" behind the text and open law to speculation, "chaos," and indeterminacy. He maintains, however, that this approach is very apt for literature because literary texts are "exceedingly enigmatic" and interminably "ambiguous" (1988: 71). I will come back later to these distinctions Posner makes between literature and the best approach to literature, on the one hand, and law and the right approach to it, on the other; suffice it now to announce that Posner is already revolving within the orbit of literary theory simply because the intentionalist perspective he advocates for the study of legal texts is itself a well-established *literary* approach.

Posner maintains that literature, unlike law, is divorced from reality and is read for pleasure and hardly for guidance. As will be patently clear, Posner's argument will prove untenable once the marriage between law and literature is built on the resemblance between the judge's and the literary critic's tasks and not between the jurist's and the reader's ones, as Posner took it to be. Posner's dismissal of literature as "otiose" and irrelevant is no more than a sheer visceral pontification about art and the role to be played by the literary critic. Would that be a result of confusing *reading*—as a willing suspension of disbelief—with *interpreting*, as a deliberate and conscious subsequent act? Most probably. Unlike the writer of fiction who can be at two removes from reality (Plato) and the reader who may be at more incalculable removes from reality, him/her being transported and elevated elsewhere by the fictive text, the literary critic comes into play to establish and elucidate the link(s), the intersection(s) and the affiliations between the fictionality (or unfamiliarity) of the fictive text and the reality of the world from within which the text is born, and to which it ultimately addresses itself.

The fictive text might be traversed by an imaginative discursive design complicitous with or critical of (or both) the dominant ideology, power, or imperium, and it is incumbent upon the critic to caution the reader against the surreptitious workings of such a design in the very banalization of fiction, a banalization that Posner inadvertently indulges in. The literary critic has to pursue ever more, in a world torn apart at the seams by struggling wills and hyper-intensified discourses, the role of the enlightener, the provider of the counter-discourse, or what E. Said famously calls, the contrapuntal discourse. Furthermore, it is a truism that the whole discipline of hermeneutics had emerged out of the need and desire to understand divine messages. Hermes is the mediator *par excellence*. The need for a Hermes, an interpreter or a critic, stems primarily, it bears repeating, from the fact that we are either in front of a divine, ambiguous message or a fictional, non-real one, a message that has, in both cases, to be interpreted *pro bono publico*. And it is the critic's devoir to do so.

It seems that we need fiction writers to transport us out of reality as much as we need literary critics to reawaken us to reality again, to strike the chord between fiction and reality, and to heighten our sensitization of reality in ways the author of fiction might not have envisaged. To enter the fictional world of the writer, we need to willingly suspend our disbelief although we need to regain it belatedly so as to be able to see, thanks to the literary critic, how the work of fiction relates to reality. This state of affairs is very commonsensical: if the function of literature is to defamiliarize us with the familiar, then it becomes, syllogistically speaking, the duty of the interpreter, the literary critic, to re-familiarize us with the unfamiliar. As Viktor Shklovsky beautifully puts it, "The technique of art is to make objects '*unfamiliar*,' to make forms *difficult*, to increase the difficulty and length of perception because the process of perception is an aesthetic end in itself and must be prolonged" (55, italics mine). The literary critic's task is then to interpret unfamiliarity in terms of familiarity and fiction in terms of reality, and, in so doing, to join the camp of the judge who, though concerned with reality writ large, has as well to mediate between different layers of reality; that is, the reality of the legal text as he now sees it and the distant reality in which it was composed. As Gadamer maintains: "The place between strangeness and familiarity that a transmitted text has for us is that intermediate place between being an historically intended separate object and being part of a tradition. The true home of hermeneutics is in this intermediate area" (Gadamer 263).

As it turns out, the literary critic offers a very pervasive paradigm for the judge: the literary critic relates the work of fiction not only to its historical context, that is, to its "historical horizon" (Gadamer), but also to reality in general. If the judge is to be mediating between two realities, between historical reality and present reality, the literary critic is supposed not only do that, but also to mediate between fiction and reality. Simply put, while the judge concerns himself with reality as such (past and present), the literary critic does not only bridge the gap between two distant realities, but also between these two and the fictional reality. This goes to say that the *scope* of the literary critic is wider than the scope of the judge and, thus, the critic would be of exemplary resourcefulness for the judge to broaden and sharpen the blade of his human knowledge, and to temper his particularized and fervent, if not blind, expertise in the legal field by those strategic immersions in the other overlapping fields. It is this very hope—which Posner dismisses as "the great false hope of law and literature" (1996: 66)—that inspires Dworkin, and impels him to explore the intertwined territories of both literature and law through the narrative metaphor of the "chain novel."

Although Dworkin makes the analogy between judges (here, the founding fathers of the American constitution) and authors in terms of writing, he does not exempt them, authors and judges alike, from the imperative to interpret, which tempts us in turn to explicate the exemplarity of the literary critic for the judge. Since interpreting is native to writing and vice versa, then the framers of the American constitution, for instance, must have been good interpreters as well. The judges, the latecomers, are not warranted to ignore the propositions of the constitution and strike in a new direction. They should, according to Dworkin, see themselves as authors in a "chain novel," as belonging to a narrative enterprise which they not only prize but also take seriously by committing themselves to it. For Dworkin, "every novelist *but the first* has the dual responsibilities of interpreting and creating because each *must* read all that has gone before in order to *establish*, in the interpretivist sense, what the novel so far created is" (1982: 262, italics mine). In his reply to Fish's criticism over giving the first novelist in the chain a freedom denied to others, Dworkin affirms that the foundational author is also on duty—busy interpreting while writing and vice versa.

Now this chain enterprise assigns judges, albeit discreetly, not only the task to interpret and write, but also to *create* the law. Of course, to warrant the judge to create the law would scandalize Posner and his colleagues: they would deprecate it as the most threatening, wayward and subjective project for a judge to embark upon. Although I do not deny that allowing the judge to create the law as he moves along interpreting it in the light of the case at hand might open the discipline to personal preferences, to opportunism and to political morality as the positivists (Hart) and intentionalists (Posner) would protest, I am not sure that doing otherwise—abiding by the literal meanings of the rules or by the authoritative guidance of precedent—is always adequate to the particular demands of concrete, hard cases (Dworkin), or penumbra (Hart). Propositions of law may be as "indeterminate"—allowing a plethora of interpretations—as "underdeterminate," i.e., lacking.[6]

Indeed, cases of underdeterminacy, which are often mistaken for cases of indeterminacy, do not cease to pop out. And every actually litigated case can be, according to Solum, treated as "constrained by the law, but not determined by it" (Solum 489). Solum's motivation, in making this distinction, is to soften the indeterminacy thesis—the claim that law is indeterminate. I cannot resist the temptation to soften this thesis further by reassuring Solum that indeterminacy cannot be différanced *sine die*; it is only an ephemeral and transitory moment toward determining—either by way of interpreting and writing, or creating—an otherwise, not eternally indeterminate, *determinable* law, interpretation, decision or what you will. A contingent decision should not to be mistaken for indecision, and a nomadic search for a determinable interpretation should not be reduced into a hopeless quest in the pale of indeterminacy.

If we take the example of the eighth amendment[7] to the American constitution, we cannot fail to note that the "cruel and unusual punishment" phrase is left unspecified and, therefore, open for controversy. Posner avers that "a responsible judge in the intentionalist tradition will want to find out what he can about what the framers actually intended, even if this means looking outside of the constitutional text" (1996: 68-69). To look outside is to go back to 1791, and to the historical context in which the eighth amendment was adopted, which nobody would gainsay. But, granted we do go back and enlist all the referred-to punishments, does that mean that these "unusual punishments" can be identified, determined and accepted? Can capital punishment be maintained? Actually, capital punishment, no matter how heinous and most unusual a punishment/crime, has been thought to be *per se* exempt of these characteristics of being cruel and unusual, and thus continues to enjoy the privilege of being applied, which means that there is an urgency for critical interpretation of law, and this we will come back to later.

In *Trop v. Dulles (1958)*, the Supreme Court ruled that the definition of "cruel and unusual punishments" is not permanently fixed and is subject to change over time as a result of "*evolving standards of decency*" in America—"the evolving standards of decency that mark the progress of a maturing society." It is patently clear that the Supreme Court has already departed from the constraints of the eighth amendment in order to keep with the evolution of the society. The Supreme Court has neither stuck to the framers' intentions nor to the historical context. In brief, the Supreme Court has reshaped, refashioned and recreated the eighth amendment. Even if the "cruel and unusual punishments" were unspecified by the framers, they were left determinable, and they always are determinable in the sense of being *creatively* recreatable. But, they would not have been so if the judges were *ir*responsible intentionalists, to rectify Posner. Texts of law remain, writ large, as Hart rightfully argues, "open textured" not only because of our "relative ignorance of fact" but also because of our "relative indeterminacy of aim," not only because of our inability to "regulate, unambiguously and in advance, some sphere of conduct by means of general standards to be used without further official direction on particular occasions," but also because of the ungetroundable fact that "human legislators have no such knowledge of all the possible combinations of circumstances which the future may bring" (1961: 125). As such, legislators are inextricably bound to cast a certain dark, haziness, and imprecision on the statements of the law they produce, a certain dark that the judge will, starting from the particular case at hand, see to its dawn. The judge becomes, in turn, inextricably bound to writing, articulating, and spelling out the threshold at which the legislators stopped. Otherwise, we would be living, as Hart expounds, in "a world fit for 'mechanical' jurisprudence" (1961: 125).

If re-writing the law becomes one of the judge's *sine qua non* prerogatives, then such creative re-writing will involve a certain adhocracy that the literary critic, thanks to his assiduousness and critical astuteness, can potentially be of significant modality for the judge who has to work through the adhocracies and intricacies of a *sui generis situs*, or a unique case. Having said that, I think that it is best to caution at the outset that the bulk of the critic's exemplarity to the judge in terms of scope, as we have earlier demonstrated, and in terms of re-writing, as we are now suggesting, does by no means imply that the judge would be given a "blank check to regulate criminal sanctions," as Posner scornfully pontificates, nor that he would be given free rein to rewrite the law ego-syntonically, much less that the judge would be recycled and reconfigured so as to *become* a judge *pro forma* and a literary critic *sub rosa*. I will come back to this later when I examine, once more, the regulative tie of proximity and distance which I think should punctuate the *in situ* relation between the judge and the literary critic. Now I will explore in more depth the relevance of the literary critic to the judge in terms of writing and rewriting, as possible modes of interpreting.

The literary critic's laudable talent to re-write the text under examination has been, it bears reminding, celebrated by, amongst many others, such monumental figures as Gadamer, in the hermeneutic tradition, and Roland Barthes, in the poststructuralist upsurge. In *Truth and Method*, Gadamer suggests that the interpreter does not interpret a text but creates another. In *S/Z* as well as in "The Death of the Author," Barthes deploys his interpretive acumen to clear a considerable space for the "modern scriptor" to write perennially in the "*here and now*" (170). Indeed, in *S/Z* Barthes had almost literally rewritten Balzac's "Sarrasine." But, what is this fuss (about rewriting) all about? One of the values of a modern literary text is its being a "writerly" as opposed to a "readerly" text, a text to which—to rephrase Barthes—we gain access to by several entrances, a text marked by plurality, studded by a galaxy of signifiers, and tessellated, or traversed by many discourses, all of which open it up for infinite digging (see *S/Z* 6). The modern text is as such a text nowhere to be found unless in instances of "*ourselves writing*" (*S/Z* 5). Needless to say that this writerly value of the literary text, if imported wholesale to the legal text, would destabilize any judge, no matter how lax he would claim to be. Yet, we have already seen how plural and indefinite the "cruel and unusual punishments" phrase could be since it can strictly be taken as referring to those punishments of 1791. What is more, the phrase can extend itself to other newly invented technologies of punishments, or shrink to declare that one of the punishments of 1791 is not "unusual." In all cases the phrase has traveled amorphously and become almost "ourselves writing" (Barthes) or ourselves composing (White) and arresting this phrase, albeit momentarily and contingently, in an ever-rejuvenated labor of interpretation.

To interpret such phrases, then, as the one of "cruel and unusual punishments" of the eighth amendment or an even more perspicuously ambiguous phrase, that of "equal protections of the laws," of the fourteenth amendment, necessitates the New Critical tool which Posner reserves for literary texts alone. Furthermore, a judge may be guided by the often decried and derided techniques of a deconstructive literary critic. As identified by Posner, "the deconstructionist assumes that [literature] is a mass of contradictions and looks outside the work to find the causes and consequences of these contradictions" (1996: 67); I would add: "and as such he illuminates and inspires the judge." Had a tool like deconstruction, which is becoming all the more common in legal practices nowadays, been at hand for all the judges and lawmakers on duty before the Civil War (1861-1865), the atrocities of that war and the many deaths would have been spared. A deconstructionist judge or lawmaker would not fail to put his fingers on the internal tensions and "mass of contradictions" of a constitution that promises liberty to people, all the while holding them slaves. It has actually taken too much time for texts of law to be deconstructed, though of course in a manner oblivious to deconstruction as now theorized and practiced. It took more than half a century for the massively contradictory doctrine of "separate but equal rights" of the *Plessy v. Ferguson* (1896) case to be debunked in *Brown v. Board of Education* (1954). But this is not to say, of course, that history would have simply taken another direction if legislators and judges were immersed in literary criticism: the fact that they were not so, combined with many other factors, might, however, belatedly help us understand the direction history had taken.

It is clear that the "separate but equal rights" doctrine cannot obtain because it is built on a paradox that a judge immersed and trained as a literary critic, a hermeneutician, or a deconstructionist would scarcely fail to critique. It is within the practice of deconstruction to identify binary oppositions and to proceed to show the privileged part of the binary as well as the underprivileged one so as to rehabilitate it, and re-establish justice. Although "separate" and "equal" do not form a neat binary, they hide racial and political agendas: keeping blacks and whites separate so that one group can be privileged to the detriment of the other. As Balkin asserts,

> Deconstruction is useful here because ideologies often operate by privileging certain features of social life while suppressing or de-emphasizing others. Deconstructive analyses look for what is de-emphasized, overlooked, or suppressed, in a particular way of thinking or in a particular set of legal doctrines (Balkin 368).

Deconstruction looks for what is suppressed to claim it back, to clear a space for it in the limelight. In *Of Grammatology*, Derrida rehabilitated the status of writing. In his article "The Force of Law: 'the mystical foundation of authority'," Derrida writes, "Deconstruction is justice" (qtd in Balkin 371). Certainly, justice is what a lawyer aims at, and this is why "deconstruction has proven to be a surprisingly adaptable concept serving many different purposes and supporting many different types of scholarship" (Balkin 373). Dispensing with the "separate but equal rights" doctrine is the labor of a deconstructionist rather than an intentionalist, the labor of a writer, composer, maker and re-maker, as James Boyd White would put it, rather than a single-minded partisan or monist. If Fish is right, Posner's fierce attack on the Critical Legal Studies Movement comes as a natural result of his being a partisan of Law and Economics[8]. The advent of critical theory, therefore, can only be very threatening to the economic welfare of an influential and famous judge like Posner.

If the law itself is, as the "separate but equal rights" doctrine shows, racial and tendentious, then it becomes a matter in a more urgent need of rewriting, remaking, and revision, rather than of application. As it turns out, the law as a system or construction is not actually very systematic and taxonomic: it is continually subject to the exigencies of exegesis, of interpretation, of recreation and "composition," all of which discursive practices might ultimately bring about its emendation. Indeed, composition is the law of law. This is the vein of thought that James Boyd White, the initiator of the literature and law movement, follows. White's thinking delves into the intricacies and "pretences" of judges who, although entitled to interpret, adjudicate and justify, tend often to harp on some system or structure: "One great vice of theory in law is that it disguises the true power that the judge actually has, which it is his true task to exercise and justify, under a pretence that the result is compelled by one or another intellectual system" (1996: 17). White's argument culminates in asserting that such pretences ought to be destroyed and that the law be redefined as "the work of individual minds, for which individuals are themselves responsible" (1996: 17). Actually, White redefines law, in many respects, in terms of that quality of "writerliness" much endeared by literary modernism: far from being a system or program, law is a *process* open to discovery, to reformulation and transformation, and remains, therefore, permanently tentative and presumptive (see 1996: 18).

As process, law becomes writing. This idea ripples across White's writings in variegated forms, the most recent of which is an article whose title alone—"The Life of the Law as a Life of Writing" (2001)—captures laconically but tellingly this very long standing idea of af*filiation* between law and writing. The bulk of White's earlier article, "The Judicial Opinion and the Poem" (1996), had also been reserved to reiterating the compositional nature of law. Like the student of literature, the student of law is asked to go beyond surface descriptions of the law, and to engage in generative and transformative practices:

> The task of the law student is not simply to understand and describe the law, but to make it and remake it in practice; the work of the critical reader is not merely to describe the poem but to give it a new meaning and a new place in his or her own world. The sort of education of which I speak, in law and in literature, constantly tells us to recognize that we are makers of texts and remakers of culture. This is in fact its major lesson (1996: 10).

White's destabilizing arguments are simply the right opposites of Posner's. Judging from the history of the American constitution and from the steady amendments made to it, I find White's arguments more commonsensical. White pretends neither to be able to fix the law nor to protect it from/against error, but only to approach it dynamically: to enter imaginatively into the spirit of the founding fathers of the American constitution, and in this spirit to develop the study of certain legal problems beyond the point at which they left them. As such, he opens the field of law to contingency and to radical uncertainty.[9] And though this is not a state to be afraid of, the saving grace remains within the hands of judges who should now give up the habit of shuffling off their responsibilities on systems and structures and start "doing law" (1996: 7).

Such a brief of White's emancipating argument foregrounds the compositional and the critical tasks that the judge has to learn to develop from his strategic immersions in the practices of the literary student or critic. But, what is put in a very straightforward manner is that human agency, rather than being shaped by law and culture, shapes and remakes them. For, "culture never exists in fixed and certain forms, but only in performances each of which involves both reaffirmation and transformation," which leads to the conclusion that "in looking at the relation between text and culture our emphasis will be on the modification, not the continuity" (1996: 21). Again and again, these arguments eventuate in endlessly debatable binaries between structure and agency, subjectivity and objectivity and to the stimulating as much as frustrating debate between Gadamer and Habermas. Such debates are far from being resolved. Although in this essay I am not primarily concerned with intervening in those debates, I have earlier introduced a model—the chain enterprise of Ronald Dworkin—that places itself in an intermediary position, halfway between determinism and relativism.

By now, it should have become clear that I am drawing on many antagonistic theories for the purposes of establishing an exemplary relationship between the judge and the literary critic. The first section has been dedicated to demonstrating the ways in which the judge can serve to enrich the literary critic by urging him to think and interpret in terms of practice, and this section has largely gone to promote the thesis that the judge may learn from the literary critic to interpret, to criticize and to create the law. In the gross, if the judge can be the prodigy of application and repetition, the literary critic may in turn be the prodigy of interpretation and creation. Judge and literary critic cannot exchange places, no matter how much their practices may intersect and overlap. They can, however, move back and forth, approximate and distanciate themselves from each other toward an exemplary relationship.

III - Toward an Exemplary Relationship between the Judge and the Literary Critic

In "Law as Interpretation," Dworkin propounds an aesthetic hypothesis that purports to be as applicable for law as for literature. This hypothesis contends that "an interpretation of a piece of literature attempts to show which way of reading (or speaking or directing or acting) the text reveals it as the best work of art" (1982: 253). Interpreting a literary or a legal text so as to make of it the best work of art is not, however, to be equated with *inventing* another radically different work. Dworkin imposes some constraints on the judge as well as on the novelist: the judge has to abide by precedent and the novelist by the genre within which he writes. Actually, the *withinness* of writing, of interpreting and of adjudicating becomes like the hidden hand that shapes everything from behind the scene. This is the hidden hand from which, as we have seen, White complains because it simply relieves judges from their responsibility to write the law. The best recent version of what we have just called withinness is perhaps Fish's "interpretive community." For Fish everything is accountable to a set of (principled?) principles that are always and necessarily in place before something takes place naturally. With Fish, we are placed in the farthest position possible from a state of *tabula rasa*. By and large, Dworkin goes half the way with Fish: he acknowledges that the judge or the critic is always *internally* constrained, but he leaves a spark of hope in the human agency—his belief that hard cases cannot be settled unless moral arguments come into play. But, Dworkin is not really very clear about his position, and he actually seems to occupy both ends of the binary of structure-agency which he set out to outflank at different times (see Fish 1989: 103, 356 and Fish 1982: 275).

In his influential book *Law's Empire* (1986), Dworkin follows on with his assay of "merging" the practices of judges with those of literary critics. I say "merging" because Dworkin does not really specify the moments or phases in which a judge's interpretation approximates a literary critic's and the moments in which they both diverge. Although one can gather elements that illustrate Dworkin's awareness of differences, one can hardly trace any attempt of his to regulate the relationship. He, however, specifies three phases of interpretation, which together reveal some details of the chain enterprise. I will examine these three phases, and I will try to show how they can be used to regulate the relation between the judge and the literary critic in terms of approximation and distance. Notwithstanding the power of the chain enterprise, I will try to show its shortcomings and develop a relation between literary critics and judges based on Foucault's distinction between "initiators of discursive practices" and succeeding theorists/authors.

Dworkin distinguishes between three stages of interpretation. First, there is the "'pre-interpretive' stage in which the rules and standards taken to provide the tentative content of the practice are identified." Second, there comes "the interpretive stage at which the interpreter settles on some general justification for the main elements of the practice identified at the pre-interpretive stage." Third, there emerges the "post-interpretive or reforming stage, at which [the interpreter] adjusts his sense of what the practice 'really' requires so as to better serve the justification he accepts at the interpretive stage" (1986: 65). Now, a certain familiarity with Dworkin's writings enables us to remark that these three new stages used to be collapsed under the dual of "fit" and "justification" (or "substance"). The former dyad is supplemented by the pre-interpretive stage which is now to provide the background against which a given interpretation takes shape. This stage is added probably in response to Fish's critical bites, especially that it is only at this stage that Dworkin introduces concepts such as "community," "consensus," "presuppositions," which are, largely speaking, the concepts on which Fish builds his theory of interpretive community. Though there is no space for it here, an argument could be made for the improvements that Fish's criticisms have introduced into Dworkin's theory. Once that argument is made, it would certainly illustrate further how much the literary critic can help the legal theorist, and from there the judge.

Dworkin presents us, albeit inadvertently, with a happy chime of the literary critic and the judge. The interpretive stage in which interpretation is at its peak can be very much enlightened by the literary critic as much as the post-interpretive stage, in which a decision has to be made, can instigate the literary critic to think about his interpretation in terms of its applicative relevance to the word, society, or culture it addresses itself to, or/and imbibes from, or both. The resulting interpretation—out of these three phases—which Dworkin calls the "creative" or "constructive" interpretation is very telling about the ways in which the judge, almost like the literary critic, creates another work of art instead of just interpreting the work at hand. The best cases that really encourage a creative interpretation are hard cases, cases in which the substance and justification of a given interpretation (in the absence of a precedent) becomes what is at stake: cases which usually transcend the notion of fit and come to be addressed, in the case of Dworkin, according to political morality. This latter argument for political morality has often been the target of positivist criticism because it has been thought to set the engine of legal relativism in full throttle. Positivists, alarmed by the unpredictable consequences of the conjunction between morality and law, adhere to the argument that the moral dimension of law is always "latent" within law and should therefore not to be used as a defensible ground for "intelligent decisions" at the penumbral level (see Hart 1996: 39). Notwithstanding those accusations, I think Dworkin's chain enterprise stops at the fringe of open texture, and remains largely binding not only by precedent (fit) but also by the withinness of the notion of what he identifies as "internal skepticism"—misgivings about assertions within a determinate position.

If, however, we decidedly gloss over the internal texture of the theory and concentrate on its aptness or non-aptness for the relationship I am establishing between literary critics and judges, it becomes necessary for me to rehearse it in terms of another, more practical relation that Foucault develops in his essay "What is an Author?" Foucault distinguishes "initiators of discursive practices" like Marx, Freud and Saussure from successive theorists such as Antonio Gramsci, Jacques Lacan, and Noam Chomsky, even if those last-named have by now earned the potentiality, if not the status, of initiators of discursivity. What Foucault found characteristic of the initiators of discursive practices is that they "produced not only their works, but the possibility and the rules of formation of other texts" (Foucault 145). This idea is spelled out in a long passage, part of which deserves quotation:

> Marx and Freud, as initiators of discursive practices, not only made possible a certain number of analogies that could be adopted by future texts, but, as importantly, they also made possible a certain number of *differences*. They cleared a *space* for the introduction of elements *other* than their own, which, nevertheless, remain *within* the field of discourse they initiated (145, italics mine).

Reading this definition, one finds it much more apt to call the founding fathers of the American constitution initiators of discursive practices rather than chain novelists. My reason for propounding this thesis is twofold: first, I find that the chain enterprise is too far-fetched and by no means applicable in literary or critical fields; second, I find that to approach the founding fathers and judges by way of analogy to initiators of discursive practices and successive theorists is much more practical and emancipating. What I am seeking to do, while remaining as faithful to Dworkin's interdisciplinary postulations as possible and seeking assiduously for any guidance which he has provided, is to extend the prudently hamstringing chain enterprise to a more spacious field, which he avoided treading with a great amount of trepidation. In pursuance of this aim I have to expose inconsistencies and contradictions where they seem to me to be ungetroundable.

First, Dworkin's narrative enterprise does not tell much about the potentially exemplary relationship between the judge and the literary critic. By making the analogy between judges and novelists, it already sets the rot in: it remains vulnerable and easily defeasible by the old-fashioned argument that novelists write fictions (i.e. not even constatives) while judges write actions (i.e. performatives). Although, as I have shown, the relation does exist between writing fiction and writing the law somewhere in the literary critic who translates fiction in terms of reality and thus joins the real world of the judge, there remains a lingering doubt about the two practices. Moreover, the analogy of the chain narrative itself is fictional and has nothing to do with the practice of writing and interpretation in the literary field. What I find ironic about Dworkin's appropriation of this supposedly literary exercise for law is that it is not quite truly a literary exercise. Indeed, Dworkin himself regards it as a "strange literary exercise" (1982: 263). This exercise is far from being the practice in the literary field wherein Dworkin claims to ground his theory of law. It seems that this exercise is much more plausible and obtainable in law than in literature. In other words, it does make sense in law, inasmuch as judges will always consider the chapters of the constitution before they make amendments or create complementary chapters, while in literature it is hardly the case that a novel can be written in that kind of chained and chaining way by otherwise free writers. What am I driving at? Dworkin pretends to use the literary field as a model for legal practice, but he ends up concocting a menu inspired by law, exports it to literature and finally imports it back from literature to law. It is not a *genuine* reliance on the literary field, to say the least.

Second, the Foucauldian model of initiators of discursivity substantiates better the relation between the judge and the literary critic. On the part of the literary critic, the relation with the judge becomes very proximal in terms of application, inasmuch as the literary critic would not only be applying

Freudian psychoanalysis, but also changing it, taking it to another stage, which may in turn change the conception of Freudianism itself. On the part of the judge, the relation with the literary critic would reach its apotheosis insofar as the judge would perceive of "cruel and unusual punishment" not as an indeterminate phrase but as a "space for the introduction of elements" other than the founding fathers' own, or elements the founding fathers were in no position to imagine. Furthermore, the model of the initiators of discursive practices allows "a certain number of differences" to be made. Although I cannot be conclusive in exploring all the potentially substantial arguments for this model in the space of this essay, I have at least shown that the implications of this Foucauldian model are much more promising for an exemplary judge-critic relation than those of the Dworkian model.

IV - Proximity and Distance

Although a judge—unlike a literary critic who might just be concerned with coming up with a different (but not necessarily an impossible) interpretation of a given work of art—must construct the best possible interpretation of a legal text, he can still always rely on the cooperative effort of the literary critic. The legal text might be as ambiguous as the fictional text, for the framers (of the constitution, for instance) could not have made pronouncements about every specific case that might arise in the future; on the contrary, they could only have made abstract and general pronouncements about how cases of a given sort should be adjudicated. They could have only made sweeping generalizations, which have to be tightened up and particularized according to the penumbral elements of a given case. As we have seen the legal text is already contaminated by the germ of indeterminacy as well as by that of underdeterminacy. In other words, the framers could not have written the constitution without having in mind the open-mindedness of their successors, without clearing some space for the labor of their successors. Otherwise, writing the constitution would have quite simply been impossible. The constitution is a text abstract enough to be comprehensive and, paradoxically, also abstract enough to be inconclusive and open to discursive, urgent or crucial amendments and transformations. The judge will not be able to transform the constitutional text, or to create another one whenever an urgent need to do so presents itself, unless he allows the literary critic to become his full-fledged *amicus curia*, and unless he himself strives to acquaint himself with the extraordinary fund of critical talent which the interpreter of literary texts houses—a talent which, when it does not create, will at least constantly stimulate the judge's productive and compositional impulse.

The question that a judge has to ask *ab initio* is: how would a literary theorist interpret such and such a statute or constitutional proposition? Such a question is very crucial at the early stage of litigating since it will free the judge from the compulsion or obligation to be accountable for one's interpretation, which alone can freeze his trepidations and fears of the community with which he is affiliated, and can ultimately unleash the empowering internal forces that would compel him to speak truth to power. *Once free, the judge can see better.* If, however, he feels pressured from the very outset and over-preoccupied with the decision he has to reach, or jump to, he will probably miss the point as he will be seeing with lenses of endings before he has even the time to strike new beginnings. As we have seen with White, the judge needs only to be responsible, to justify and to persevere in making and remaking the law in the manner in which a literary critic would act on a literary text.

Proximity relates, then, to the way in which a judge attempts to approximate the strategies of interpretation which characterize the literary domain. For example, before making a decision, a judge is supposed to examine the whole spectrum of possible interpretations of the propositions of law related to the case at hand. In this, he or she imitates the interpretive strategy of the literary theorist, taking account of the plurality of interpretive practices which characterize the literary domain. But unlike the literary critic who can tolerate a degree of indeterminacy (but not indeterminacy as *terminus ad quem*) when it comes to the question of interpretation and who may perceive of his interpretation as only one among many possibly incommensurable interpretations, a judge is concerned to reach one correct interpretation. Unlike the literary critic who may multiply ambiguities as he gets lured into and tangled in their jungle, the judge is concerned to resolve crises. He is thus required to maintain a distance from the 'vagaries' of interpretation. After all, the literary critic would not be as much pressured as the judge in coming up with a definite interpretation and even when he does he would hardly feel the urge to impose it on anybody, although he would certainly have to justify it. It is, in a sense, this very laxity and looseness (of the literary critic) that the judge has to lavish in order to see clearly and conversely that this is what he should avoid in the final analysis in order not to be dazzled.

I do not think this collaborative enterprise can be otiose (Posner) once the proximity/distance pair is well respected. Of course, the judge may always remain skeptical about what a literary critic may proffer as an interpretation, but skepticism is not a reason for abandoning the endeavor altogether: to preclude any attempt to rub the judge's nose in the supposedly muddy and slippery terrain of the literary critic is probably the hobgoblin of little minds. The judge should not, however, get too enmeshed within the intricacies, rhetoricity and indeterminacies of literary texts, and should maintain the adequate distance needed for him to decide on a case. This is not to say that legal texts may not be intricate, rhetorical or indeterminate and would therefore necessitate a literary-critical rationale to deal with them; on the contrary, it is because they are or can be so that the literary theorist is wanted and at the same time unwanted: wanted to crack the riddles and fill in the gaps of the text of law, and unwanted because he may suggest so many ways of filling in the gaps such that he may eventually fail to decide, and stray away in pursuance of intellection. But, really *it is precisely this ambivalence toward the literary critic that the legal theorist should explore rather than abhor.*

The legal theorist gains his status not in losing his own identity (as decision-maker) through a piecemeal defacement by, and assimilation into, the play world of the literary critic, nor through a radical silencing of his propensity to proliferate interpretations, but through a strategic partitioning of his efforts, as much for exploring the plurality of the legal text as for sifting through that very plurality in an all-encompassing attempt to decide upon the best interpretation possible. It would be no more than sheer naïvety if a judge decided not to venture into the world of the literary critic simply because it is a world where more than one interpretation is possible as well as permissible. Interpretation in the literary field, for all its uncertainties and for all its infamous practical vacancies, can be very fruitful for the legal theorist who knows how to mediate elastically and craftily between proximity and distance. But, "Perhaps the trouble with literary studies is not," as Fish succinctly puts it, that "they are irrelevant but that, at least potentially, they are too relevant" (1989: 309).

Notes

1. The conception of interpretation as application is deeply rooted in Gadamer's ontological approach to interpretation. For him, all understanding is interpretation, and, in turn, all interpretation is application. This point follows from the necessary situatedness of every act of understanding within an all-encompassing structure, perspective, point of view, or tradition, such that it becomes indissolubly bound to application. Here the analogy with the judge becomes very apt: understanding the law of capital punishment, for instance, must always occur in terms of possible ways of application. And hermeneutics, as Jean Grondin asserts in the preface to Papadopoulos's book, has nothing to lose if understood as Gadamer had suggested from a juridical vantage-point. Grondin goes on to affirm Gadamer's claim that the ideal field for practical hermeneutics is that of jurisprudence since it is the field where application is imperative.
2. Here, I do recognize that application in Gadamer's parlance is not, as David Couzens Hoy points out, the same kind of application involved in traditional epistemology, in which one is concerned with applying a theory or a concept to a practical situation. Application does not follow from understanding, but explains how understanding occurs at all: "Since understanding is always embedded in a situation, the problem is not of fitting preconceived notions to a situation, but of seeing in the situation what is happening and, most important, what is to be done" (Hoy 54). What I find lacking in Gadamer's ontological approach to understanding/application is the account of an application that proceeds, or follows, from a given interpretation.

Gadamer's application remains imaginative (in the sense that every interpretation has to be gauged with the *idea* of application in mind, rather than the application itself) and non-consequential: it does not take into consideration the aftermath of the actual application, nor does it distinguish between the "gravity" of application in legal hermeneutics and the "relative impact" of application in literary hermeneutics.

3. Gadamer analogizes the experience of a work of art with a game: "The 'subject' of the experience of art, that which remains and endures, is not the subjectivity of the person who experiences it, but the work itself" (92). In the same manner, "the actual subject of play is obviously not the subjectivity of an individual who among other activities also plays, but instead the play itself" (93). Just as a work of art (and behind it a tradition) is handed down to another generation, a game can pass from generation to generation, binding its players whenever/wherever they play. The nature of the game is that it has precedence over the players and therefore determines their moves by giving them the impression of moving freely. Thus, "all playing is a being-played. The attraction of a game, the fascination it exerts, consists precisely in the fact that the game tends to master the players" (95).
4. In *Doing What Comes Naturally*, Fish describes the judge's task in a way that I find too rigorous to be trusted: "The creative supplementing of the law that is involved is a task that is reserved to the judge, but he is subject to the law in the same way as every other member of the community. It is part of the idea of a legal order that the judge's judgment does not proceed from an arbitrary and *unpredictable* decision, but from the *just* weighing of the whole" (294, italics mine). If the judicial judgment can, by virtue of being anchored in a principled community, be predictable, this might threaten to undermine the idea of justice, and suppress the particularity of the cases whose precedence cannot be determined. It is true that situating the judge within a given context, a constraining community, in which he will be prudently hamstrung, can help to preclude opportunism, but it cannot justify any judge's judgment unless the contours of this community can be demarcated *ab ante*, which is quite unobtainable not only because the contours of a given community will have to remain relatively indeterminate, but also because even if we concede that the principles can be totaled and the contours demarcated, there is still the problem of the *concentric circles* within which the members of each community are gathered together in sub-communities. If a judge is to abide by the rules of the community—rules which make his judgment predictable—then his judgment would be unjust as long as it would be for or against the litigant depending on how near

or far he is to the sub-community of the judge, depending on his place in the schema of concentric circles.

5. In "'Preserving the Exemplar': or, How Not to Dig Our Own Graves," Booth calls for a "critical commonwealth" whose foundational premise is the toleration of conflicting interpretations. It is, however, an ambivalent commonwealth whose tolerance, willingness to reach out far, and "efforts to understand" would require it include even "Derridaesque *glasisme*" within the canon of pluralism. Regardless of whether it is relativistic or not, I believe that the current situation of literary interpretation is pluralistic at large, conflictually so. This view is magisterially edified by Paul Armstrong throughout his book *Conflicting Readings*.
6. In an article entitled "Indeterminacy," Lawrence Solum complains that "The distinction between indeterminacy and underdeterminacy is rarely observed in the indeterminacy debate" (490), which more often than not leads judges adrift to radical indeterminacy—the belief that any decision will be legally correct. Solum advances underdeterminacy as a more modest claim to indeterminacy, more defensible, and more critical in its bite: "A legal dispute may be constrained by the law, but not determined by it" (489). Solum subsumes actually litigated cases (i.e. cases that actually proceed to filing, trial, or appeal) under the rubric of underdeterminacy because their "outcome (including the formal mandate and the content of the opinion) can vary within limits" (489).
7. Amendment VIII: "Excessive bail shall not be required, nor excessive fines imposed, nor cruel and unusual punishment inflicted."
8. In an article entitled "Don't Know Much About the Middle Ages: Posner on Law and Literature," which forms along with other essays the body of his *Doing What Comes Naturally,* Fish unearths the underpinning *economic* motivations of Posner's dismissal of literary critical theory as "otiose" to legal studies: "Although Posner says nothing about economics, the effort he mounts [...] to deauthorize literary studies is intended to clear the field so that the authority of economics in the legal academy can be secured; and since members of the Critical Legal Studies are among the most prominent and forceful opponents of Law and Economics, Posner is obliged to disarm them, which is precisely what he will succeed in doing if he manages to discredit the discipline [literature] from which they take so much of their arsenal" (308). Fish goes on to argue that "Posner detects in the perspective offered by literary and deconstructive theory a danger to the [economic] program with which he is closely associated" (309). And I find this understandable, especially if we bear in mind that "It is, after all, a thesis of deconstructive theory that forms of representation, of which any system of currency is an instance, are

always agencies of power and manipulation and never simply stand in for natural forces like the market" (309).

9. White consoles his audience by reassuring them that they just have nothing to fear since they "have in fact always lived, and can only live, with radical uncertainty" (1996: 20). He then goes on to give an account of the security measures to be taken vis-à-vis this shifting and moving ground, measures which can only be contingent. White concludes: "We make the best sense we can of things, the best judgments we can make, always checking our account against experience, against our sense of our own dispositions to err, against the suggestions and imaginations of others. We are always tentative or presumptive, always revising; in all of this we are always making and remaking our culture. This is what we know how to do" (1996: 20).

Works Cited

Armstrong, Paul B. *Conflicting Readings: Variety and Validity in Interpretation.* Chapel Hill: North Carolina UP, 1990.

Balkin, J. M. "Deconstruction." *A Companion to Philosophy of Law and Legal Theory.* Ed. Dennis Patterson. Cambridge: Blackwell, 1996. 367-74.

Barthes, Roland. "The Death of the Author." *Modern Criticism and Theory.* Ed. David Lodge. New York: Longman, 1988.

——. *S/Z.* Trans. Richard Miller. New York: Hill and Wang, 1974.

Booth, Wayne C. "'Preserving the Exemplar': or, How Not to Dig Our Own Graves." *Critical Inquiry* 3 (1977): 407-23.

Bruns, Gerald L. "Law as Hermeneutics: A Response to Ronald Dworkin." *The Politics of Legal Interpretation.* Ed. W.J.T. Mitchwell. Chicago and London: U of Chicago P, 1982. 315-20.

Coleman, Jules L. and Brian Leiter. "Legal Positivism." *A Companion to Philosophy of Law and Legal Theory.* Ed. Dennis Patterson. Cambridge: Blackwell, 1996. 241-60.

Dworkin, Ronald. "Law's Ambitions for Itself." *Law and Morality: Readings in Legal Philosophy.* Ed. David Dyzenhaus and Arthur Ripstein. Toronto: U of Toronto P, 1996. 86-99.

——. *Law's Empire.* Cambridge: Harvard UP, 1986.

——. "Law as Interpretation." *The Politics of Legal Interpretation.* Ed. W.J. T. Mitchwell. Chicago and London: U of Chicago P 1982. 249-70.

——. "My Reply to Stanley Fish (and Walter Benn Michaels): Please Don't Talk about Objectivity Any More." *The Politics of Legal Interpretation.* Ed. W.J. T. Mitchwell. Chicago and London: U of Chicago P, 1982. 287-313.

Fish, Stanley. *Doing What Comes Naturally: Change, Rhetoric, and the Practice of Theory in Literary and Legal Studies.* Durham and London: Duke UP, 1989.

——. "Working on the Chain Gang: Interpretation in the Law and in Literary Criticism." *The Politics of Legal Interpretation.* Ed. W.J. T. Mitchwell. Chicago and London: U of Chicago P, 1982. 271-86.

Foucault, Michel. "What is an Author." *Critical Theory Since 1965.* Eds. Hazard Adams and Leroy Searle. Tallahassee: UP of Florida, 1986. 148-63.

Freeman, M.D.A., ed. *Lloyd's Introduction to Jurisprudence.* 6th ed. London: Sweet and Maxwell, 1996.

Guest, Stephen. *Ronald Dworkin.* Stanford: Stanford UP, 1991.

Hart, H.L.A. "Positivism and the Separation of Law and Morals." *Law and Morality: Readings in Legal Philosophy.* Ed. David Dyzenhaus and Arthur Ripstein. Toronto: U of Toronto P, 1996. 28-48.

——. *The Concept of Law.* Oxford: Clarendon Press, 1961.

Herald, Paul J., ed. *Literature and Legal Problem Solving: Law and Literature as Ethical Discourse.* Durham: Carolina Academic Press, 1998.

Hirsch, E.D. *The Aims of Interpretation.* Chicago: U of Chicago P, 1972.

Hogan, Patrick Colm. *On Interpretation: Meaning and Inference in Law, Psychoanalysis and Literature.* Athens: U of Georgia P, 1996.

Hoy, David Couzens. *The Critical Circle: Literature, History and Philosophical Hermeneutics.* Berkeley: U of California P, 1978.

Ledwon, Lenora. *Law and Literature: Text and Theory.* New York: Garland Publishing, 1996.

Levinson, Sanford and Steven Mailloux, eds. *Interpreting Law and Literature: A Hermeneutic Reader.* Evanston: Northwestern UP, 1988.

Michaels, Walter Benn. "Is There a Politics of Interpretation?" *The Politics of Legal Interpretation.* Ed. W.J. T. Mitchwell. Chicago and London: U of Chicago P, 1982. 335-46.

Marmor, Andrei. *Interpretation and Legal Theory.* Oxford: Clarendon Press, 1992.

Meese, Edwin. "Address Before the D.C. Chapter of the Federalist Society Lawyers Division." *Interpreting Law and Literature: A Hermeneutic Reader.* Ed. Sanford Levinson and Steven Mailloux. Evanston: Northwestern UP, 1988. 13-24.

Morawetz, Thomas. "Law and Literature." *A Companion to Philosophy of Law and Legal Theory.* Ed. Dennis Patterson. Cambridge: Blackwell, 1996. 450-61.

Murphy, Cornelius F. *Descent into Subjectivity: Studies of Rawls, Dworkin and Unger in the Context of Modern Thought*. Wakefield: Longwood Academic, 1990.

Nerhot, Patrick. *Law, Interpretation and Reality: Essays in Epistemology, Hermeneutics and Jurisprudence*. Dordrecht: Kluwer Academic Publishers, 1990.

Papadopoulos, Ioannis. *Pratiques juridiques interprétatives et herméneutique littéraire: Variations autour d'un thème de Ronald Dworkin*. Cowansville: Les Éditions Yvon Blais, 1998.

Posner, Richard. *Law and Literature: A Misunderstood Relationship*. Cambridge: Harvard UP, 1988.

——. *Law and Literature: Revised and Enlarged Edition*. Cambridge: Harvard UP, 1998.

——. "Law and Literature: A Relation Reargued." *Law and Literature: Text and Theory*. Ed. Lenora Ledwon. New York: Garland Publishing, 1996. 61-90.

Said, Edward. "Opponents, Audiences, Constituencies, and Community." *The Politics of Legal Interpretation*. Ed. W.J.T. Mitchwell. Chicago and London: U of Chicago P, 1982. 7-32.

Sampford, Charles. *The Disorder of Law: A Critique of Legal Theory*. Oxford: Basil Blackwell, 1989.

Schauer, Frederick. *Playing by the Rules: A Philosophical Examination of Rule-Based Decision-Making in Law and in Life*. Oxford: Clarendon Press, 1991.

Shklovsky, Viktor. "Art as Technique." *Contemporary Literary Criticism*. Ed. Robert Con Davis. New York and London: Longman, 1986. 52-63.

Skubik, Daniel W. *At the Intersection of Legality and Morality: Hartian Law as Natural Law*. New York: Peter Lang, 1990.

Solum, Lawrence. "Indeterminacy." *A Companion to Philosophy of Law and Legal Theory*. Ed. Dennis Patterson. Cambridge: Blackwell, 1996 488-502.

Taylor, Charles. *Human Agency and Language*. Cambridge: Cambridge UP, 1985.

White, James Body. "The Life of the Law as a Life of Writing." *The Edge of Meaning*. Chicago: U of Chicago P, 2001. 221-56.

——. "The Judicial Opinion and the Poem: Ways of Reading, Ways of Life." *Law and Literature: Text and Theory*. Ed. Ledwon-Lenora. New York: Garland, 1996. 5-28.

✪✪✪

14

Feminist Deconstruction and Reconstruction of Male Myths and Fairy Tales via Intertextuality

N. GEETHA

> Reject rejoice rejuvenate rejuvenate rejoice
> reject rejoice rejuvenate reject rejuvenate reject rejoice.
>
> —Gertrude Stein, "Patriarchal Poetry"

Intertextuality, a concept introduced by Julia Kristéva in the late 1960s in her discussion of the ideas of Bakhtin, refers to the way texts relate to one another. The notion of intertextuality is as old as time. However, it is T.S. Eliot's tool of "comparison," of comparing one literary work (or part of a work) with another, which helped to systematise the concept. Though Bakhtin is one of its source thinkers, Julia Kristéva is generally credited with having introduced the term "intertextualité" in French. Disputing the autonomous nature of a literary text, she writes that it is the "transposition of one or more systems of signs into another accompanied by a new articulation of the enunciative and denotative positions." She points out that "every text is the absorption and transformation of other texts" (Selden 417-18). There is no "master text," but a library of simultaneous texts (Harari 347). One text either echoes another or is linked to other texts by direct quotation or allusion or simply by being a text. Intertextuality can take different forms, such as parody, pastiche, imitation, appropriation or mimicry.

A text is thus a transformation of another. Even within a

single text there can be a continual "dialogue" between the text given and other texts (Wales 259). A text can literally wind itself upon a previous text, reinscribing it, giving it an entirely new context. Christopher Norris views it as a "series of figurative crossings and wild substitution which abolish all sense of textual autonomy" (Norris 115). Philip Thody points out that for Julia Kristéva and the critics who grouped themselves in the 1960s and 70s around a review called "Tel Quel," all "literature consists of texts and all texts are reflections or reproductions of different versions of other pre-existing texts" (Thody 86). Norman Fairclough notes that "texts [...] are heterogeneous in their forms and meanings the heterogeneity emanating from their intertextuality texts are constituted from other already produced texts and from potentially diverse text type [...] a complex and creative practice involving new combinations of genres and discourses" (Fairclough 2). He refers to various types of complex intertextuality in texts: sequential intertextuality, embedded intertextuality, mixed intertextuality. In sequential intertextuality different stages of generic schema are modelled in different genres; in embedded intertextuality one genre is embedded within another; but in mixed intertextuality it is impossible to ascribe different parts of a text to different genres, for even a single clause may be multi-generic (Fairclough 15).

Asserting the intertextual nature of any verbal construct, Culler affirms that any projects and thought which it implicitly or explicitly takes up, prolongs, cites, refutes or transforms must pose the problem of intertextuality (Culler 101). The concept of intertextuality is thus central to any structuralist or semiotic description of literary signification. According to Laurent Jenny intertextuality enables one to recognize pattern and meanings in texts. He says: "outside of intertextuality the literary work would be quite simply imperceptible in the same way as an utterance in an as yet unknown language" (Culler 104).

However, the complexity inherent in the use of intertextuality does not make it an easy tool to work with. For Bloom the intertextual is not a space of anonymity and banality but a heroic struggle between "a sublime poet, and his dominant predecessor" (Culler 108). Barthes, on the contrary, uses the word "intertext" to label writers who have influenced him (though he would not have it that these are influences). To him the "intertext is not necessarily a field of influences, rather, it is a music of figures, metaphors, thought, words, it is the signifier as siren" (Jackson 29). Gérard Genette focuses on "hypertextuality," meaning the relations of one text to an earlier one (Hutcheon 21). For Eco, intertextuality functions as an important "frame of reference which helps in the interpretation of the text" (Wales 259). Lodge calls intertextuality the "history of the appropriation, re-working and imitation of someone else's property—another's language, another's style, another's word" (Lodge 146).

Feminist writers and critics have identified a number of textual strategies to reinscribe and restore women to their rightful place in literature. The use of intertextuality is today a common feature of women's writing. Women writers have never had a literary history or a past, dominated by the patriarchal ideology that artistic creativity itself is a "male quality." The female tradition had been ignored, derided, or even taken over and replaced under this prevailing "phallocentric myth of creativity" (Moi 57). Most of what women wrote has escaped print, falling outside the sacred "canon" and dismissed as trivial and non-serious.

Women are thus forced to discover for themselves self-enhancing role-models who are "self-actualizing" and whose "identities are not dependent on men" (Moi 47). They have to either appropriate from the past writing via the use of intertextuality to recover the 'lost' tradition, or formulate an alternative 'canon' of women's writing. As their first field of activity feminist writers have resorted to rewriting and revising male canonical works. Popular patriarchal texts are raided, ripped off, recycled, imitated, parodied, rewritten and manipulated in as many ways as is possible. Intertextuality creates the very space for recharting existing male narratives or discourse, demolishing and exploding texts of male-established genres, reconstructing images and myths, recasting an entire range of male-conceived women characters: all these are recreated and reframed from a women's point of view and perspective. Moi contends that the "image" of women in literature is invariably defined in opposition to the "real person" whom literature somehow never quite manages to convey to the reader (Moi 44). Women characters who exist in male texts are basically of two types: positive roles which depict women as independent, intelligent and even heroic, or a surplus of misogynistic roles commonly identified as the bitch, the witch, the vamp and the virgin/goddess.

Feminist critics have through the use of intertextuality deconstructed the representations of women in cultures—the images, stereotypes and archetypes. They have found women as the beautiful Other, as aesthetic object of eros, glamour and fashion, as a mother whose will and power if checked and directed will succour; as a schemer whose will and power if unchecked will devour (Stimpson 117). Feminist criticism has been generally deconstructive: this dual activity of pulling down and putting up, negation and recreation, in part leads women to "demystifying a new world landscape that men were grandly mythologizing" (Stimpson 118). In his essay "'Ulysses' Order and Myth" T.S. Eliot advocated what he called the "mythical method." The modern writer is frequently faced with the chaos of modern history and is forced to find a "model" of order. Lacking a "coherent system of belief or a creditable idea of order," the modern writer, he suggested, must either "appropriate one from a past writing [...] or fabricate his own system" (Harari 346).

Feminist critics feel that the segregation of the public and private spheres has largely accounted for the silent subordination and the marginalization of women. The public life is man's domain; women belong to the invisible private sphere. This deliberate suppression of women had aided culture to invent its own representation of the gender; this fictional woman had for centuries appeared on stage in the myths and in the plastic arts "representing the patriarchal values attached to the gender while suppressing the experiences, stories, feelings and fantasies of actual women" (Case 7).

The feminist responses to "myths" constitute a crucial area

of critical discourse. Writing about myth, Simone de Beauvoir says:

> It is always difficult to describe a myth; it cannot be grasped or encompassed; it haunts the human consciousness without ever appearing before it in fixed form. The myth is so various, so contradictory, that at first its unity is not discerned [...] (Beauvoir 175).

Over the millennia women have been variously observed and understood and the derived wisdom recorded in literature, art and religion. These have often taken the form of strongly held beliefs which served to validate and to order experience. These mythic assumptions regarding women have concretized into a cluster of values and bundle of taboos placing women in a disadvantaged position. The deep-rooted myths about women the female and the "feminine" have not allowed women to lead an authentically free life. Juanita Williams points out that "man has always felt the need to explain and to codify woman, to come to terms with her presence on earth, and to accommodate her within his rational system" (Williams 1). Thus man made myths about women, just as myths were made to explain other phenomena of the universe.

Myths of the great mother formed part of the cosmic myth: the close analogy between women and the earth as sources of life inspired the myth. All the typical symbols used by nature mystics—ocean, sea, air, trees, water—are feminine both mythologically and psychologically. As an enchantress/seductress or a siren woman became a prize to be wrested, as in the abduction of Helen of Troy or Hoethcyn's kidnapping of the Swedish Queen. Woman became an object to perpetuate terrible warfare and bitter enmity. Still, woman was a necessary evil who could not entirely be dispensed with.

Mythology comprises a significant fibre of our existence. Lévi-Strauss says that myth is always the transformation of another myth (Carr 146). Feminist writers are employing the concept of intertextuality to recreate a positive female mythology—to create true, authentic "images" of women characters who can provide strong "models" for women to build their inner confidence and dissipate crippling fears.

Adrienne Rich, speaking of the vital importance of recasting the past tradition and creating a new history to restore women to their rightful place, says:

> Re-vision—the act of looking back of seeing with fresh eyes of entering an old text from a new critical direction—is for women more than a chapter in cultural history: it is an act of survival. Until we can understand the assumptions in which we are drenched we cannot know ourselves (Humm 181).

Intertextuality, which rests on the contention that all texts are dependent on other texts and are variations on previous models, has greatly helped women writers to realise their intentions. Efforts are on to recreate myths about women that are free from "the man-formed mythic maze" that is constructed to confuse and dominate women in general (Palmer 75). Feminist writers use myth as a newer means of generalising personal emotions and feelings. As a radical move toward the reconstruction of mythic women critics like Mary Daly, Annis Pratt and Cathy Davidson have broken away from the established Greco-Roman tradition to include a global mythic representation of women from different cultures. They look for a greater and wider range of myths which can be scrutinized and reinterpreted from a feminist perspective.

In most myths, visual or written, the politics of representation are inevitably the politics of gender. When viewed objectively it is true that women in mythology are well documented and discussed, but generally from a male perspective, hence the "wild zone" of women's experience has not been authentically articulated. Thus through the use of intertextuality women are introducing "mythic symbols to defy traditional feminine ideas of feminine passivity in an oblique way" (Humm 89). Mary Daly, Adrienne Rich Annie Pratt, Marta Weigle, and critics in the collection *The Lost Tradition*, edited by Cathy Davidson and E.M. Broner, see myth as a key critical genre.

Viewing myth as essentially a male construct, Susan Gubar considers Demeter or Ceres as the source of life and fertility, as the "central mythic figure for women" (Gubar 302). She points out that women writers must examine the extent to which patriarchal myths continue to reflect stereotypes and "seek to evade its tragic repetition" (Gubar 307). She speaks of the need to create an authentic voice for mythic female figures such as Circe, Leda. Cassandra, Medusa and Helen in women's writing. She warns that in deflating these destructive feminine stereotypes, they should not be replaced by equally debilitating stereotypes of masculinity (Gubar 310).

Literature is replete with stereotypes of images of women from Greek, Roman and Latin myths. Almost all these myths portray women as negative characters possessing a distorted and perverse personality. The Sirens of Greek mythology were women who could lure men to death through their song. "Siren" is typically used pejoratively of women who are alluring or seductive, meaning that their obvious sexuality is considered to be dangerous. Woman is often depicted as a courtesan, a temptress and an alluring object who, like Delilah the Philistine woman, could befool the strongest of all men, Samson. Women can be easily deceived, for they are greedy and avaricious like Atlanta, an Arcadian maiden who raced against her suitors but was eventually defeated by Milanion, who dropped golden apples on the course to delay her.

Hindu mythology has its fair share of the archetypal women who are often depicted as exemplary: Sita, Damayanthi, Draupadi, Maitreyi, Savithri and Kannagi to mention a few. Likewise there are the goddesses like Saraswathi, Lakshmi, Sakthi, Saranya, Rati and Manasa. The Indian female myth has been created and established by men or women writers of yore who dared not question this female myth:

> The woman was conceived of as "Grihalakshmi" symbolising prosperity of the home, "Sahadharmini" who identified herself with the dharma of her husband, "sati" whose life begins and ends with her husband, "Kshetra" which is an open field for her master's use, "Sakthi," the primal source of energy (Dutta 11).

A plethora of renewed images of mythic women, obviously fed on the previous models, have been created. These new mythic images of women have made women the "object" of their feelings instead of simply being viewed as the "other" and portrayed as objects of male desires and fears.

Hilda Doolittle, fascinated by the legends surrounding Helen, felt that Helen was viewed entirely from the male point of view and never allowed a chance to provide a defence of her actions. Always the object of man's act and the subject of his poem, she was herself always silent. If Helen did try to speak, would she even have a voice or a point of view? Based on this speculation Hilda Doolittle wrote her long meditative epic of more than 400 lines, "Helen in Egypt." In her feminist pacifist work "Cassandra" Christa Wolf rewrites Homer's tales of men and war, offering economic and political rather than romantic reasons for the Trojan war and telling the silenced story of the everyday life of the Trojan women ignored by the historical narratives written by the conquering foreigners—the Greeks. Cassandra herself is a creation of the male poets and hence was inscribed with their desires. The poet Louise Bogan uses the wild figures of Medusa and Cassandra in her poems "Tears in Sleep" and "The Dream" to widen the definition of a normal woman.

Mona Van Duyn, a women poet, in 1964 rewrote Yeats' canonical sonnet "Leda and the Swan." Demolishing Yeats's place as a regulator of cultural excellence and meaning, the two poems she writes on Leda are "both more carefully careless than the Yeats, more rhetorically casual and ordinary" (Stimpson 121). In the first "Leda" she gives her a history. She says that in men's stories Leda's life ends with the swan's loss. Van Duyn's Leda, however, brings forth her rape-engendered children. She becomes horribly depressed, recovers, and finally marries "[...] a smaller man with a beaky nose and melts away into the storm of everyday life" (Stimpson 121). In the second poem, "Leda Reconsidered," Van Duyn returns to the rape itself: Leda here is given here an "interiority, subjectivity, the capacity for choice" (Stimpson 121). In 1972 Adrienne Rich published another text simply titled "Rape." Much like Van Duyn, she rejects the temptations of transforming woman's pain into myth, into tragic grandeur. But unlike Van Duyn, she "austerely refuses to give women any choice about rape, that terrible formula for a man's exercise of power over a woman" (Stimpson 121).

Muriel Rukeyser, in *Beast in View* (1944), uses the rhyme schemes of myth to articulate the ambiguities of women's condition. Rossetti's *Goblin Market* is a feminized myth of Christian redemption. Marilyn Yalom refers to the mother-daughter icon in Atwood's novel *Surfacing* as a "radical feminist revision of the Christian myth" (Yalom 8). Angela Carter's *The Magic Toyshop* is an instance of her conscious and dexterous use of the device of intertextuality to explore femininity and female subordination as cultural constructs. Here she reworks episodes and motifs not from one text but from a total of three. These are the biblical story of the Garden of Eden, E.T.A. Hoffmann's *The Sandman*, and Freud's account of the psychic structures relating to the family unit. It also takes a revisionary look at the myth of Leda and the Swan. Her other novel *The Passion of New Eve* deconstructs and rewrites the biblical story of the creation of Eve. Michèle Roberts' *The Visitation* reworks popular motifs from myth and fairy-tale.

Deconstruction of myths and the feminist response to "myth" constitute a crucial area of critical discourse. Angela Carter chooses myth as the site of entry into a new "imaginary" (Mills 172). She perceives that some stories carry meanings that can be revised for feminism. Alicia Ostriker describes this feature of women's writing as a process of "revisionary myth-making" (Ostriker 172). Sylvia Plath has dedicated much of her prolific writing career to decry the inadequacy of Greek mythology as well as other facets of cultural ideology to represent human experiences. Her numerous poetic re-interpretations of Greek myths expose the confining gender stereotypes embodied in these tales. The surge of women's poetry specifically rewriting myths and fairy-tales—Hilda Doolittle, Anne Sexton and Stevie Smith are only a few of the names one could mention—is one very obvious example of this intertextuality.

Hindu mythology has not lacked its illustrious spread of women—self-sacrificing women who follow their husbands through tribulation and exile, women who plead with the gods to take on punishment or death intended for their husbands. Mahasveta Devi, a popular Bengali writer, has rewritten the mythic figure of Draupati in a short story of the same name.

Nabaneeta Dev Sen, another Bengali writer, takes up the task of retelling epic tales. Sita in her three short stories—"The Ur Ramayana," "The Trap of Immortality" and "Sita Enters the Netherworld"—is a person with an independent mind. Dev Sen remarks that the epic world does not allow freedom of speech to women. She sees the epic women as the "victims of male bonding: they are born to suffer to serve the epic purpose. They are used as pawns to prepare the ground for the heroic deeds" (Bhattacharya 1995). In a series of stories in which Dev Sen rewrites the epic women, a remarkable clan that includes Amba, Kaushalya, Sita, Surpanakha and Shakuntala.

A female thematics lies behind the efforts of women to create a distinctly female mythology. Women artists have made frequent use of traditional mythological figures—the Medusa, Demeter, the Spider Woman of certain Amerindian tribes and Lakshmi; they have also written new texts for these mythical figures, creating a matrilineal genealogy. Wittig's *Les Guerilleres* and the *Sultana's Dream* by Rokeya Sakhawat Hossein are prime examples of this kind of writing.

Any attempt to produce a literature for women that will be free of myth is near-impossible. As Ruthven says, "Every act of demythologising involves a corresponding act of remythologising" (Ruthven 79). The concept of intertextuality does provide women writers with a strategy for "remythologizing" the dominant patriarchal ideology implicit in these tales.

Feminist Rewriting of Fairy Tales via Intertextuality

The "institutionalizing" of the literary fairy tale began during the eighteenth century when aristocratic women gathered in salons and initiated it as a type of parlour game. A majority of writers and tellers of fairy tales were women, though at a later time men had appropriated them, using them to their advantage for social roles, socialization and as a "propaganda tool" (Cranny-Francis 198). For example it is said that it is Madame D'Aulnoy who prepared the way for the literary version of *Beauty and the Beast,* not Perrault.

A definite distinction can be discerned between the women's

tales and those written and told by men. In most of the male versions women characters subscribe to a standard precept: either they are piously good or wickedly bad. The images of women constructed by men are a strange composite of qualities: Cinderella is the incarnation of the highest good—young, beautiful, sacrificing and passionate, but a hopeless victim, passive, docile and timid; her step-mother and sisters belong to the other realm—wicked, foul-mouthed, cruel, destructive, but also powerful, scheming and ambitious.

The feminist dictionary defines the fairy tale as a "harmful cross-cultural educative story told to unsuspecting children that shows women as passive, opportunistic or cruel" (Cheris 149). Ruth Bottigheimer referring to it as a tale which praises demure heroines continues "powerful female figures in fairy tales were either deprived of (verbal) power or their power was transformed into the wickedness of witchcraft" (Bottigheimer 149). Fairy tales often present direct images of women as fearful objects—sirens. witches sorceresses and semi-supernatural creatures, able to transform men by spells. Often these threatening evil figures are deceptively beautiful—if not then old and ugly. In both the Western fairy tales and Eastern folk tales the wicked stepmother has no male counterpart. In contrast the male characters are depicted as strong, powerful, generous and courageous. What is praiseworthy in males is rejected in females.

Fairy tales are among the cultural forms which help to consolidate the belief that it is in the woman's best interest to get married and beget many children. As Karen E. Roe points out, they "perpetuate the patriarchal status quo by making female subordination seem a romantically desirable, indeed an inescapable fate" (Roe 195). These tales are mostly read by children who are powerless to intervene in things which happen in their best interest. Most children are fascinated by these tales and tend to internalize most of these aspirations "deemed appropriate to (their) real sexual function within a patriarchy" (Ruthven 80). Marcia R. Liberman calls them "training manuals for girls" which serve "to acculturate women to traditional roles" (Ruthven 80).

Feminists feel that it is wrong and dangerous to feed the

child readers' febrile imagination with sexist ideology and gender stereotyping that denigrate and marginalize women. For these fairy tales are not the value-free or harmless collection of childhood fantasy but are revealed "as carriers of conservative ideological discourses" (Cranny-Francis Cranny-Francis 90). Feminists concentrate on revising these traditional tales to "reveal the ideological content they encode, particularly their construction of a patriarchal reading position" (Cranny-Francis 197). Feminists have taken to rewriting these tales with the fiery zest of a mission, and their objective is to create corrective models of women who are autonomous, assertive, self-willed and independent.

Among the most popular traditional fairy tales "Cinderella" and "Red Riding Hood" have for decades fired the tender imagination of countless child readers. Generations of child readers have read and re-read these tales attracted by the romantic fantasy and magic charm present in these tales. However, feminists view these tales as repeatedly enforcing a patriarchal moral code and containing instructional material that is prescriptive in nature for women under patriarchy. Both Cinderella and Red Riding Hood are characters that are entirely passive, powerless, subordinate to men—acted upon rather than acting.

Feminists have attempted many intertextual versions of these two tales giving them a woman-centered perspective. Judith Viorst rewrites the story of Cinderella in a poem "And then the Prince knelt Down and Tried to put the Glass slipper on Cinderella's foot." The Cinderella recreated in this poem is a dynamic character and takes an active role in her destiny. She acts as an independent and autonomous subject. She rejects the prince both as a marriage prospect and as a male ticket. Tanith Lee also rewrites Cinderella in her story "When the clock strikes" published in the volume titled "Red as Blood or Tales from the Sister Grimmer." Ashella, the Cinderella of the fairy tale, takes revenge on the prince who is responsible for the murder of her family. There is no living happily ever after. Her quest complete, Ashella just disappears; the prince is killed by external enemies. The feminist intertextual version of the tale "confronts the popular fairy tale at every turn" and "elicits a continual comparison between the two versions, the text on the page and its absent referent" (Cranny-Francis 89).

Feminists see the fairy tale of Little Red Riding Hood as a patriarchal fable exhibiting the male desire to control women and circumvent them. Angela Carter rewrites this fairy tale in two stories, "The Werewolf" and "The Company of Wolves." In both the stories the little girls are active and assertive. In the first the girl, with the neighbour's help, kills her werewolf grandmother: now, "the child lived in her grandmother's house; she prospered" (Carter 136). This alternative Red Riding Hood, bold and courageous, "operates with the tools of patriarchy driving out the women who through her co-option by patriarchy has been operative in attempting to insert her granddaughter into that order as passive object" (Cranny-Francis 92). In the second, Carter depicts a girl who "outwolfs the wolf." Here again the girl instead of being terrified by the wolf asserts herself, and is thus freed from the wolf's domination; in the end they live together peacefully and amicably, as equals. Tanith Lee also rewrites "Little Red Riding Hood" in her story "Wolfland." Here a woman becomes a werewolf to deal with a brutal husband; when her granddaughter protests her grandmother's murder of her husband the latter expresses her lack of alternatives or choice.

Other popular fairy tales which have been rewritten include the stories of Bluebeard, Beauty and the Beast, the Vampire, the Elf-King and Puss-in-Boots. The indictment of fairy tales comes not merely from militant feminists. There are instances of objective male critique of these stories and the ideology implicit in them. John Zipes notes:

> The immanent meaning of the tales has little to do with providing suitable direction for a contemporary child's life. From a contemporary perspective the tales are filled with incidents of inexplicable abuse, maltreatment of women, negative images of minority groups, questionable sacrifices, and the exaltation of power (Zipes 1979: 170).

His book, *Don't Bet on the Prince: Contemporary Feminist Fairy Tales in North America and England* (1986), records the feminist revisions of traditional stories by a wide range of writers like Carter, Lee, Jane Yolen, Anne Sexton, Olga Browmas and Margaret Atwood. Many of these revised fairy tales can be used as substitutes for the traditional stories. These rewritten stories "construct a feminist reading position from which the anti-woman ideology coded in traditional fairy-tale becomes visible" (Cranny-Francis 94).

Among the child readers of these fairy-tales, girls particularly learn that they are by nature passive creatures and qualities like charity, kindness, patience, and self-discipline are expected of them. Like the legendary Sleeping Beauty or the incarcerated Rapunzel, they are to remain symbolically dead until brought to life by a man. Boys tend to identify themselves with the heroes in shining armour, valiant redeemers of beautiful but silently suffering women. To dismiss the fear or threat posed by these fairy tales as trivial is to undermine the tremendous influence these tales wield on the imagination of the child readers.

Feminist critical practice has decidedly justified the need for a revision of these popular fairy tales. But a few feminist writers in their over-riding concern to remove the in-built patriarchal biases and replace them with feminist attitudes and values often tend to lose sight of the fact that the readers of these tales are children. The efforts of the feminists are laudable as the chief aim is to desex traditional child reading practices by projecting stories of positive value that would introduce androgynous norms for the socialization of children. But most often feminists, while rewriting these stories, make them explorations into notions of female sexuality, phallic attraction, desire, etc., and in the process destroying the magical attraction these tales have held for children for ages.

Angela Carter, rewriting "Little Red Riding Hood" as "The Company of Wolves" transforms, it into a "story of the sexual maturation and potency of women who reject male domination" (Cranny-Francis 93). Although the feminist intentions are realised, the story does not read like one meant for young children, as can be seen by a reading of the following lines from the revised version:

> Her breasts have just begun to swell [...] she has just started her women's bleeding, the clock inside her that will strike henceforward once a month.
>
> [...] She is an unbroken egg; she is a sealed vessel; she has inside her a magic space the entrance to which is shut tight with a plug of membrane [...].
>
> [...].
>
> [...] The girl burst out laughing; she knew she was nobody's meat. She laughed at him full in the face. She ripped off his shirt for him and flung it into the fire in the fiery wake of her own discarded clothing (Carter 141-47).

There is an interesting debate on whether a "literature designed specifically for children should prepare them for the sexism of everyday life or shelter them from it" (Ruthven 82). It is true that children should not be encouraged to indulge in fruitless daydreams which only promote dissatisfaction, but should encounter and examine the world as it really is. They should be acquainted with the realistic situations, the regular occurrence, of sexism. But at the same time children have a right to their childhood, their innocence, their dreams and fantasies, without the adult world impinging upon theirs with its notions about sexism, gender justice, etc.

Fairy tales have to be generated in a manner that does not perversely distort a child's imagination. Children should be sensitized and made aware of their different sex roles. Non-sexist stories from the child's point of view adopting its voice and attitude should be written, for as Julia Briggs rightly points out, "Adopting the child's voice allowed her not only to locate her own position as a woman in a male-dominated society but also to escape from the pressure to write like a man" (Briggs 248). Perhaps, as Roe suggests, there is the need for a completely new set of fairy tales, along the lines of Alison Lurie's "Clever Gretchen and other Forgotten Folk Tales" (Roe 1980).

In India, unlike in the West, children's literature has never really come of age. India has had a rich oral tradition but much of it has unfortunately escaped print. There are the traditional regional folk tales and other stories, but the fairy tale, a Western genre, is an imported one. For decades Indian children have read and enjoyed these tales. The revised feminist versions have to undergo a cultural adaptation so as to be acceptable to the vast child readership of India. Intertextuality as textual strategy can be exploited to write Indianized versions of these fairy tales—keeping intact the feminist ideology, of propagating equality between the sexes.

Intertextuality as a feminist literary technique has given an opportunity for women writers to scrutinize, re-assess and rewrite the male canonical texts. Feminists aver that the only way to right the wrongs of the past is to proceed backwards, before they create a future for themselves and tell their own kinds of stories.

Works Cited

Arkin, Marian and Barbara Shollar. 1989. *Longman Anthology of World Literature by Women 1875-1975*. London: Longman.

Avery, Gillian and Julia Briggs. 1989. *Children and their Books: A Celebration of the Work of Iona and Peter Opie*. Oxford: Clarendon Press.

Beauvoir, Simone de. 1949. *The Second Sex*. Trans. H.M. Parshley. Harmondsworth: Penguin.

Bhattacharya, Santwana. 1995. "Nabaneeta Deb Sen: Retelling Epic Tales." *Indian Express* 16 July.

Bloom, Harold et al. 1979. *Deconstruction and Criticism*. London: Routledge and Kegan Paul.

Carr, Helen. 1989. *From My Guy to Sci-Fi: Genre and Women's Writing in the Post Modern World*. London: Pandora Press.

Carter, Angela. 1979. *The Bloody Chamber and Other Stories*. London: Gollancz.

Case, Sue Ellen. 1988. *Feminism and Theatre*. U.S.: Routledge.

Cheris, Kramarae and Paula A. Treichler. 1985. *A Feminist Dictionary*. London: Pandora Press.

Cranny-Francis, Anne. 1990. *Feminist Fiction*. Oxford: Basil Blackwell.

Culler, Jonathan. 1981. *The Pursuit of Signs: Semiotics, Literature, Deconstruction*. London: Routledge and Kegan Paul.

Davies, Bronwyn. 1989. *Frogs and Snails and Feminist Tales: Preschool Children and Gender*. London: Allen and Unwin.

Dutta, Ujjal. 1986. "Women in Bengali Fiction—An Enquiry." *Women in Fiction and Fiction by Women*. Ed. C.D. Narasimhaiah et al. Mysore: Dhvanyaloka.

Fairclough, Norman. 1995. *Critical Discourse Analysis: The Critical Study of Literature*. New York: Longman.

Gubar, Susan. 1979. "Mother Maiden and the Marriage of Death: Women Writers and an Ancient Myth." *Women Studies* 6.3.

Harari, Josue V., ed. 1979. *Textual Strategies: Perspectives in Post-Structuralist Criticism*. London: Methuen.

Humm, Maggie. 1986. *Feminist Criticism: Women as Contemporary Critics*. Great Britain: The Harvester Press.

Hutcheon, Linda. 1985. *A Theory of Parody: The Teaching of Twentieth Century Art Forms*. London: Methuen.

Kristéva, Julia. 1984. *The Revolution in Poetic Language*. Trans. Margaret Waller. New York: Columbia UP

Lee, Tanith. 1983. *Red as Blood or Tales from the Sisters Grimmer*. New York: Daw.

Jackson, Leonard. 1991. *The Poverty of Structuralism: Literature and Structuralist Theory*. England: Longman Group.

Lodge, David. 1988. *Modern Criticism and Theory: A Reader*. London: Longman.

Mills, Sara, et al. 1989. *Feminist Readings Feminists Reading*. London: Harvester Wheatsheaf.

Moi, Toril. 1985. *Sexual/Textual Politics: Feminist Literary Theory*. London: Methuen.

Norris, Christopher. 1982. *Deconstruction: Theory and Practice*. London: Routledge.

Palmer, Paulina. 1989. *Contemporary Women's Fiction: Narrative Practice and Feminist Theory*. London: Harvester Wheatsheaf.

Roe, Sue, ed. 1987. *Women Reading Women's Writing*. London: The Harvester Press.

Ruthven, K.K. 1984. *Feminist Literary Studies: An Introduction*. Cambridge: Cambridge UP.

Selden, Roman, ed. 1988. *The Theory of Criticism: From Plato to the Present*. England: Longman House.

Stimpson, Catherine R. 1988. *Where the Meanings are: Feminism and Cultural Spaces*. London: Routledge.

Thody, Philip. 1996. *Twentieth Century Literature: Critical Issues and Themes*. London: Macmillan.

Wales, Katie. 1989. *A Dictionary of Stylistics.* London: Longman.

Williams, Juanita H. 1974. *Psychology of Women: Behaviour in a Biosocial Context.* London: W.W. Norton.

Young, Robert. 1981. *Untying the Text: A Post-Structuralist Reader.* London: Routledge and Kegan Paul.

Zipes, Jack, ed. 1979. *Breaking the Magic Spell: Radical Theories of Folk and Fairy Tales.* London: Heinemann.

——. 1986. *Don't Bet on the Prince: Contemporary Feminist Fairy Tales in North America and England.* Aldershot: Gower.

✪✪✪

15

THE PASSAGEWAYS OF PARIS: WALTER BENJAMIN'S ARCADES PROJECT AND CONTEMPORARY CULTURAL DEBATE IN THE WEST

CHRISTOPHER ROLLASON

> A Klee painting named "Angelus Novus" shows an angel looking as though he is about to move away from something he is fixedly contemplating. His eyes are staring, his mouth is open, his wings are spread. This is how one pictures the angel of history. His face is turned toward the past. Where we perceive a chain of events, he sees one single catastrophe which keeps piling wreckage upon wreckage and hurls it in front of his feet. The angel would like to stay, awaken the dead, and make whole what has been smashed. But a storm is blowing from Paradise; it has got caught in his wings with such violence that the angel can no longer close them. This storm irresistibly propels him into the future to which his back is turned.
>
> —Benjamin, "Theses on the Philosophy of History" (1940)[1]

I

The arcades of Paris should need no introduction to the contemporary scholar. As a social, historical and cultural phenomenon they have been immortalised by the celebrated German-Jewish writer Walter Benjamin (1892-1940), in his immense unfinished study of nineteenth-century Paris entitled *Das Passagen-Werk* [*The Arcades Project*], which occupied his attention across the 1930s and today appears to many as one of the key books of the twentieth century.[2]

Drafted between 1927 and 1940, this monumental work finally saw German publication in 1982,[3] over four decades after its author's death: the English version did not appear until 1999. *The Arcades Project* is, then, a posthumous work; its enormous bulk (the English edition runs to 925 pages, editorial matter excluded) contrasts with the nature of Benjamin's published output in his lifetime, which consisted for the most part of essays and fragments. He is remembered as a member of the Institute for Social Research (also known as the Frankfurt School), alongside Theodor Adorno (1903-1969), his collaborator and fellow philosopher who outlived him by three decades and helped establish his posthumous reputation. The manuscripts of *The Arcades Project* are the collected fruit of Benjamin's painstaking investigations, financed in the later years by the Institute for Social Research, in the National Library of Paris in the very heart of the arcades quarter itself. They form the draft of the book that would have crowned his life's work; at the same time, however, they consist of a long sequence of fragments, albeit interconnected and organised according to a master plan. The volume as we have it appears as a compromise between two opposite concepts of writing—the finished work and the discrete fragment. A large part of Benjamin's text actually consists of blocks of quotations from other writers, mostly nineteenth-century, in either French or German; these quotations, generally brief, are arranged in sections, and are interspersed throughout with segments of critical commentary, again for the most part brief, by Benjamin himself.

History decreed that the project would never attain its final form. Forced by the rise of fascism to flee Germany in 1933, Benjamin based himself in Paris until the second world war and its consequences made his presence in France impossible.[4] The Gestapo, alerted to the anti-fascist tenor of his writings, asked for Benjamin's expatriation in February 1939; on 3 September of that year France declared war on Germany, and that month Germans living in France were interned. Benjamin was sent to an internment camp in the small Burgundian town of Nevers, but was released at the end of November thanks to the intercessions of friends. He provisionally returned to his researches and to Paris, where he remained until June 1940, when he had to abandon the French capital, leaving his precious manuscripts behind as Hitler's troops closed in on the city of the Enlightenment. Benjamin concluded that safety lay in emigration to the US, via fascist but neutral Spain and Portugal, and crossed the Pyrenees on foot, as an illegal migrant but with a legal American visa in his passport, in the hope of reaching Spanish territory in safety. On the night of 26 September 1940, in the locality of Port-Bou just across the Spanish side of the border, having been stopped in his tracks by General Franco's border guards, Benjamin took morphine and ended his life.

Despite this tragic finale, it is usually thought that the finished *Arcades Project* would have had much the same appearance—a mosaic of fragments, quotations and commentaries—as the draft that has come down to us, reconstructed from the manuscripts. The text that we have, although written in the first half of the twentieth century, has, paradoxically, to be seen as a recently released cultural phenomenon that still needs to be absorbed by historians, literary critics, art critics, philosophers and sociologists: if the German edition did not appear till well into the twentieth century's second half, the book burst on the English-speaking world only as the century was in its death-throes. In the brief time of its existence so far, the English version, published by Harvard University Press, has been received with near-universal enthusiasm and admiration by readers and critics;[5] nonetheless, in view of the short time-lapse involved, it will be useful, before examining the wider theoretical dimensions of Benjamin's enterprise, to introduce and explain its central image in some detail.

II

What is an arcade? In its classic sense, the term denotes a pedestrian passage or gallery, open at both ends and roofed in glass and iron, typically linking two parallel streets and consisting of two facing rows of shops and other commercial establishments—restaurants, cafés, hairdressers, etc. "Arcade" is the English name: in French the arcades are known as "passages," and in German as "Passagen."[6] The modern arcade was invented in Paris, and, while the concept was imitated in other cities—there are particularly fine mid-nineteenth century examples in Brussels—the Parisian arcades remain the type of the phenomenon. Benjamin quotes a passage from the *Illustrated Guide to Paris,* a German publication of 1852, which sums up the arcades' essence: "These arcades, a recent invention of industrial luxury, are glass-roofed, marble-panelled corridors extending through whole blocks of buildings, whose owners have joined together for such enterprises. Lining both sides of the corridors, which get their light from above, are the most elegant shops, so that the arcade is a city, a world in miniature, in which customers will find everything they need."[7]

The construction that is generally accepted as the first example of the Paris arcade proper was the Passage des Panoramas, opened in 1800 when Napoleon Bonaparte was First Consul, and still in existence.[8] There had been earlier partial precursors in Paris. The "Galeries de Bois" or Wooden Galleries inside the Palais-Royal—the former Royal Palace and residence of the Orléans branch of the royal family—offered, from 1790 until their demolition in 1828, a traffic-free space where a multitude of traders served thronging crowds under a wooden roof, and which, in literature, is the subject of a celebrated description in *Illusions perdues* (*Lost Illusions*), Balzac's classic fictional exposé of Parisian society published in 1843.[9] However, the Passage des Panoramas was certainly the first of the purpose-built glass-roofed arcades, and, therefore, of the arcades proper. This arcade, situated just off the rue Vivienne near the Bourse or Stock Exchange, to this day contains a multitude of small shops and restaurants, and culminates in the back entrance to the Théâtre des Variétés. Most of its successors were constructed between 1800 and 1830, i.e. through the Napoleonic period and under the post-1815 Bourbon monarchy, as restored after Napoleon's defeat at Waterloo; a further handful saw the light during the "bourgeois monarchy" of Louis-Philippe and the Second Empire under Napoleon III, the last being built in 1860. All these arcades—in their heyday they numbered between twenty and thirty—were located within a relatively small area of the city, on the right bank of the Seine. In the process that gave rise to them, landowners—aristocrats, bankers or large-scale traders—bent on speculation bought up and demolished old or empty properties, thus creating substantial vacant lots between streets, on which the arcades were constructed. In many cases the empty properties had earlier been private residences, but certain sites had been occupied by former convents, dissolved at the Revolution.[10] The latter connection allows the arcades to appear as a product and manifestation of secularisation from one angle, but from another as a locus for the displacement of one religion by a second one: to compulsory Christianity there succeeds the worship of the commodity.

The evocative list of their names includes the Passage Jouffroy, the Passage Verdeau, the Galerie Vivienne, the Galerie Colbert, the Galerie Véro-Dodat and the Passage Choiseul (the last-named, which is considered the best-preserved, is the home of the comic-opera theatre known as the Théâtre des Bouffes). The great majority, including all the above-named, still exist and are still used for their original purpose, the most significant exception being the Passage de l'Opéra, pulled down in 1925.[11] Running between and parallel to the visible world of the streets, and in some cases virtually abutting on one another, the arcades offered the Parisians of the nineteenth century an alternative universe of consumption, in which they could walk free from the deafening noise of horse-drawn carriages and the discomforts of rain, snow or mud outside. As one commentator, Amédée Kermel, put it in 1831, the arcades were "a shelter from showers, a refuge from winter wind or summer dust, a comfortable and seductive space to wander through," and also "a route that is always dry and even, and a sure means of reducing the distance one has to walk."[12] The presence from the early days of theatres, in more than one arcade, is no accidental detail, for the arcades themselves created a new form of spectacle. Idling, window-shopping and observing became an art, summed up in the French verb "flâner," meaning to stroll, which, with its derivatives "flâneur" (stroller) and "flânerie" (the activity of strolling), became inextricably bound up with this special form of urban space. The arcade was a paradise for—again in Kermel's words—the race of "determined 'flâneurs,' [...] sheltered from the caprices of the weather under an all-protecting vault."[13] In our own time, the arcades are, while not the most obvious of Paris' tourist attractions and, indeed, frequented more by Parisians than by outsiders, a subject of discreet attention to the more discerning of international visitors to the French capital, who may window-shop and browse to their heart's content among the milliners,' jewellers,' stamp-dealers, vendors of antique dolls, second-hand bookshops and traditional bistros, thanks to which the nineteenth-century structures have preserved (or re-created) their highly particular character. As in the past, organised diversion is not lacking: the Passage Jouffroy even houses the Musée Grevin, the city's waxworks museum. The arcades' contemporary fame is, in no small measure, due to the impact of the remarkable work of Walter Benjamin. Today, as the German architectural historian J.F. Geist wrote in 1987, "following the publication of Benjamin's significant fragments on the arcades, bringing in their wake interpretations and, already, a whole series of colloquies," we are living in a time when "the arcade is seen not only as a historical object but also as a contemporary possibility."[14]

III

Arguing that the arcades constitute "the most important architecture of the nineteenth century,"[15] Benjamin reads them as a phenomenon of extreme cultural ambivalence. All history, he believed, is double-faced, and in this connection he quotes an aphorism from the nineteenth-century writer Maxime du Camp: "History is like Janus: it has two faces."[16] For Benjamin, the arcades, as significant historical object and "dream- and wish-image of the collective,"[17] are Janus-faced too: what he calls the "ambiguity of the arcades"[18] constitutes them as, in the suggestive term employed by his associate and commentator Adorno, a "dialectical image,"[19] pointing in two directions at once and expressive of both oppression (by the ideology of consumption) and liberation (into a utopia of plenty).

The arcades are, certainly, a "primordial landscape of consumption"[20]—temples of the commodity, with their seductively displayed, endlessly varied wares: "binoculars and flower seeds, screws and musical scores, makeup and stuffed vipers, fur coats and revolvers."[21] They were created for purposes of profit, or indeed sheer speculation, offering the buildings' owners unrivalled financial opportunities by concentrating so many rent-paying undertakings within a small space.[22] Seen from one point of view, then, they are archetypal manifestations of the expanding market economy—creations of private enterprise and sources of profit, and most certainly not part of any public works project. The goods displayed are commodities—objects existing for profit above utility, manifestations of exchange value rather than use value: for Benjamin, they participate in the "fetishism of the commodity," the mystificatory conversion of human-made products into objects of irrational worship, which Marx classically analysed and denounced in the first volume of *Capital*. Benjamin speaks of the commodity in terms very close to those of Marx: "The property appertaining to the commodity as its fetish character attaches as well to the commodity-producing society [...] as it represents itself and thinks to understand itself."[23] He also cites Adorno's uncompromising definition of the commodity as "a consumer item in which there is no longer anything that is supposed to remind us how it came into being."[24] Seen from this vantage point, the arcades and the goods in them would do no more than prostrate the consumer before the idol of consumption.

And yet the arcades have their other face. In their glass and steel design, they both reflect and inspire the utopias projected by the social visionaries of the nineteenth century, embodying the "anticipation and imaginative expression of a new world."[25] In that last formulation—the notion of a "new world"—Benjamin is actually quoting Marx, who used that phrase in a letter of 1866;[26] and this reference opens up the utopian dimension of the arcades—their other face, contrary to the face of the commodity whose contours Benjamin also found in the pages of Marx. The existence of a utopian element in Marx's thought is evident enough, as in his critique of alienation in the early *Economic and Philosophical Manuscripts* of 1844 and in the famous passage of *The German Ideology*, co-written with Engels in 1846, which rather lyrically sketches out the communist future where "society regulates the general production and thus makes it possible for me to do one thing today and another tomorrow, to hunt in the morning, fish in the afternoon, rear cattle in the evening, criticise after dinner, just as I have a mind."[27] It would, however, be a mistake to limit consideration of the nineteenth century's utopian visions to those of Marxism alone, and indeed Benjamin also gives considerable space to the very different utopian vision of Marx's decidedly non-materialist predecessor, the French political writer Charles Fourier (1772-1837), whose dreams of a new world are placed in significant conjunction with the arcades. Fourier's projections of the future centred round what he called the "phalanstery," the model of a self-sufficient ideal community. Actual attempts to create such a community were made by his followers, notably in the US at Brook Farm in Massachusetts—an experiment which lasted from 1841 to 1847, and left its mark on literature in the ironic chronicle offered by Nathaniel Hawthorne in his novel of 1852 *The Blithedale Romance*.

The utopian dimension of the arcades is implicit in the womb-like protection which they offered to the pedestrians who used them. The glass roofing and the insulation from the discomforts of the street created the sensation of an ideal, fairy-tale world existing in parallel to the muddy and noisy world outside. The shop-windows with their agglomerations of discrete objects on one level represented the apotheosis of the commodity as fetish, yet at the same time offered the passer-by images of a dream-world beyond the confines of the existing society: as one of Benjamin's interpreters, Susan Buck-Morss, has put it, in the arcades the "desire for pleasure" becomes a "form of resistance."[28] The glass-roofed passages conjure up visions of utopia. Fourier took the utopian connotation of the glass medium further, imagining entire future cities that would be built on rational principles of social organisation and would be protected from the elements under a single, overarching glass covering. He could thus write of the ideal phalanstery, in a passage quoted by Benjamin in *The Arcades Project*: "The street-galleries are a mode of internal communication which would alone be sufficient to inspire disdain for the palaces and great cities of civilisation [...] The Phalanx[29] has no outside streets or open roadways exposed to the elements. All portions of the main edifice can be traversed by means of a wide gallery which runs along the second floor of the whole building."[30] What the phalanstery was in Fourier's dream of a new world, the arcades at least part-anticipated in reality.

IV

Marx and Fourier preside over *The Arcades Project* as its twin philosophical deities, opposed yet parallel. The section on Marx runs to 21 pages, that on Fourier to 31, and both are repeatedly cited in passing. Around the central metaphor of the arcades, to which the text inevitably returns, gravitate other themes and images—exhibition halls, railway stations, panoramas—and figures presented as social archetypes—the gambler, the "flâneur," the collector. Also highlighted throughout—for Benjamin was, be it not forgotten, not only a philosopher and historian but also a literary critic—is the literature of the nineteenth century, and, notably, the three figures who may be considered the most important French writers of their time: Balzac, Hugo, and, above all, Baudelaire.

In his commentaries on all this diverse subject-matter, Benjamin endeavours to make sense of the collective dreams of the nineteenth century. On one level, he is convinced that the arcades are a source of deceptive illusion: "houses, passages having no outside. Like the dream"[31]—of a collective alienation that seeks to deny history, reducing it to a bland continuum: "The dreaming collective knows no history. Events pass before it as always identical and always new."[32] Yet on another level, the arcades are an eminently material reality whose study holds the key to authentic historical understanding, to the interpretation of the dream: "In order to understand the arcades from the ground up, we sink them into the deepest stratum of the dream."[33]

The arcades also have an essential formal role to play in Benjamin's imaginative reconstruction of their century. They are not just the core subject-matter of the book: they are also the expression of its organising principle. The material that makes up *The Arcades Project* is arranged not as a sustained discursive argument but as a series of fragments, be they quotations from Benjamin's sources or his own commentaries. It is for the reader to place the fragments in a broader context by linking up one to another, and not necessarily in the sequential order in which they appear in the book's pages. Benjamin declares of his own method: "To write history thus means to *cite* history. It belongs to the concept of citation, however, that the historical object in each case is torn from its context,"[34] and one of his more perceptive readers, Hannah Arendt, goes even further when she evokes "Benjamin's ideal of producing a work consisting entirely of quotations, one that was mounted so masterfully that it could dispense with any accompanying text."[35] This mode of construction has the effect of aligning Benjamin's text with the arcades themselves. The fragmentary, piecemeal arrangement of the textual material is analogous to the arrangement of the diverse goods of multiple origins, thrown together pell-mell and cheek-by-jowl, in the windows of the shops in the arcades; and again, on the next level up, to the heterogeneous succession of shops and businesses encountered by the "flâneur" who perambulates through an arcade. As the frequenter of the arcades perceives things object by object and shop by shop, so Benjamin's reader assimilates the book's contents piece by piece, fragment by fragment, to be inducted en route into new forms of historical and cultural awareness by the shocks and flashes of unexpected juxtapositions and connections.

Benjamin believed the past is of use to us if we can make it illuminate the present. In this spirit, it will now be of interest to consider some of the ways in which his book can shed light, not only on the nineteenth-century universe which is its declared subject, but also on some of the cultural phenomena and associated debates of our own time. It will also be useful at this point to place *The Arcades Project* in its relation to some of the most significant of Benjamin's other writings; and here too, we find that across his work, considered as a totality, one text enters into dialogue with another, sometimes in unexpected ways—even if not all of the ideas always point in quite the same direction.

V

One dimension of Benjamin's work on which critics have signally failed to agree over the years concerns his relationship to Marxism. This polemic is unlikely ever to be resolved to the satisfaction of all: apart from anything else, Benjamin's Jewishness and his close friendship with the Jewish theologian Gershom Scholem are invoked to justify the position that his work contains an irreducible element of Jewish esoteric and messianic thinking that cannot simply be assimilated to the Marxist-materialist world-view. Commentators as distinguished as Hannah Arendt and Susan Sontag have sought to downplay the Marxist element in Benjamin's thought. Arendt calls him "probably the most peculiar Marxist ever," and finds large parts of his writings "remote [...] from dialectical materialism,"[36] while Sontag argues that his work should not be tied down to any one ideological position: "It was important for him to keep his many 'positions' open—the theological, the Surrealist/aesthetic, the communist [...] he needed them all."[37] Conversely, Terry Eagleton, in a study published in 1981, assimilated Benjamin's more vanguardist notions to the politics of Trotsky and the theory of permanent revolution; while, more recently, Lloyd Spencer has firmly stressed the consistent "militancy of Benjamin's thinking."[38] Adorno, himself a Marxist, praised Benjamin for "his capacity to reveal incessantly new aspects of things [...] by linking straight to their internal organisation," and claimed that, thanks to this revelatory method, "through the power of his words, everything he touched became radioactive."[39] Whether Benjamin's method of illumination, of making things radioactive, may be assimilated to the classical Marxist model of causation is, however, open to question: with hindsight, it seems by no means certain from the text of his magnum opus that Benjamin—for all that he quotes Marx in generous proportions, both as a nineteenth-century source writer and a methodological precursor—was always or necessarily a Marxist in any conventional sense. Certainly, his method cannot be assimilated in any pointblank or unqualified fashion to the classical Marxist base-and-superstructure model, according to which the economic base determines the ideological and cultural productions of a society.[40] Benjamin writes in *The Arcades Project*: "It is not the economic origins of culture that will be presented, but the expression of the economy in its culture,"[41] and, again: "The economic conditions under which a society exists not only determine that society in its material existence and ideological superstructure; they also come to expression."[42] It seems that for Benjamin the relationship between the economic and the cultural was less one of "causation," as in classical Marxism, than one of "expression"—a concept which, surely, points towards a model grounded in the notion of interrelation, in a world where all objects are related to all others and stray details can, when the moment calls, suddenly flare up into significance.

This still-open debate raises the question of the status within Benjamin's oeuvre of his most engagedly "Marxist" texts, notably "The Work of Art in the Age of Mechanical Reproduction" (1936). That essay was written under the influence of Brecht and his theory and practice of socialist theatre. It takes the form of a critique of nineteenth-century aestheticism and an exploration of the possibilities of film as they appeared in the 1930s, and is the most famous of Benjamin's productions in his ultra-materialist mode: indeed, it has been described, as recently as 2000, as the text for which Benjamin "remains best known."[43] To it may be linked the texts collected (in English) under the title *Understanding Brecht*, notably the essay "The Author as Producer," and a number of other writings focusing on visual technology and/or progressivist artistic movements, such as "Surrealism" and "A Small History of Photography." This fistful of essays has gained Benjamin a widespread reputation—it may be, especially among those who have not read him or have read only those texts—as an ultra-left ideologist of mass culture. A comment from a representative reference book, *The Penguin Dictionary of Literary Terms and Literary Theory* (1992 edition), may be cited as an example of this view: "Benjamin surveyed the importance of technology in 19th and 20th-century urban and industrialised society, and also the enormous development of the media. As a Marxist he is interested in 'mass culture' and in the way in which culture is packaged and consumed by the masses. In his view the media [...] has the power to eliminate the ritual and bourgeois elitism of art and literature [...] In his essay 'The Work of Art in the Age of Mechanical Reproduction' he suggests that modern technical innovations [...] have radically transformed the whole idea of a work of art."[44] These comments are typical of a whole vein of Benjamin criticism, albeit often of the potted variety. Quite how representative the handful of "Brechtian" writings are of Walter Benjamin's work as a whole is another matter.

In the "Work Of Art" essay Benjamin argues that the incursion of the technology of reproduction into the sphere of art, first through photography and then in the film, has radically changed the nature of the artwork and eliminated its false autonomy—or, in the arresting image he uses, *destroyed the aura*. The "aura" is Benjamin's metaphor for the alleged self-sufficient, self-referential character of the artwork, conceived by nineteenth-century idealism as the object of a quasi-religious devotion. He defines the aura as "the unique phenomenon of a distance," and declares: "That which withers in the age of mechanical reproduction is the aura of the work of art."[45] By contrast, he affirms the positive value of film as a new and demystificatory form of art, grounding his argument in two features of cinema: its piecemeal production and its collective consumption. On the making of films, he writes: "The camera that presents the performance of the film actor to the public need not respect the performance as an integral whole. Guided by the cameraman, the camera continually changes its position with respect to the performance. The sequence of positional views which the editor composes from the material supplied him constitutes the completed film."[46] The technical process of film-making would thus tend to destroy the illusory unity of the finished product. On the circumstances of cinematic consumption, he argues that watching a film in the picture house is a "simultaneous collective experience" which should favour the awakening of a radical mass consciousness: "individual reactions are predetermined by the mass audience response they are about to produce, and this is nowhere more pronounced than in the film."[47]

Benjamin's analysis in this essay has been fervently taken up by media evangelists and proponents of popular culture, but Adorno was less enthusiastic, viewing it as excessively marked by Brecht and his avant-garde-cum-didacticist performance theory. In his comments to Benjamin on the "Work of Art" essay, Adorno warns against an excessive faith in the transformational potential of cinema, arguing that "reification has no more disappeared from the cinema than it has from the great works of art." Doubting whether the conservative spectator will become avant-garde "solely by the skills acquired while watching a Chaplin film," he cautions against Benjamin's uncritical embrace of the notion of piecemeal construction, noting that when he actually spent a day observing what went on in a film studio, "what struck me the most was to discover how little they care about montage or about the state-of-the-art techniques which you point up in your essay; instead, reality is constructed mimetically in a jejune fashion and then 'photographed.'"[48] Balancing Adorno against Benjamin, it may indeed appear reasonable to side with Adorno and conclude that the positive value attributed by Benjamin to the fragmentary production technique of film is in practice cancelled out by the conditions of illusory coherence and continuity under which the medium is typically consumed. It may be true that the piece-by-piece composition process undercuts the autonomy of the film as artwork from the production end, but the consumer sitting in the cinema generally perceives the film in its formal aspect as the illusion of a seamless and unproblematic totality, seemingly three-dimensional and unfolding in a deceptively "natural" linear sequence. The aura destroyed in production is re-created in consumption. Equally, the collective consumption celebrated in Benjamin's texts does not necessarily have any kind of progressive result: the collective mass-cultural experience can quite as easily lead to the imprisonment of the masses in cliché, stereotype and conformity as to their creative awakening. In this connection, it is interesting to note that the stray references to film in *The Arcades Project* lack the Brechtianevangelical fervour of the "Work of Art" essay, as in this rather ambiguous statement: "Film: unfolding result of all the forms of perception, the tempos and rhythms, which lie preformed in today's machines."[49] A art-phenomenon which replicates the rhythms of machine production may offer either the transcendence of the machine or a new form of enslavement to it.

The publication of *The Arcades Project* in English may in fact serve as a corrective to those who would unhesitatingly enlist an imperfectly understood Benjamin as a paid-up member of the pro-audiovisual, anti-literature cultural tendency. The voices of Baudelaire, Hugo, Balzac and others that resonate across the *Arcades Project* do not sound like the siren songs of a fraudulent or burnt-out high culture. Indeed, if Benjamin's book has a hero, it is neither Marx nor Fourier, but Baudelaire, to whom he devotes his longest section (all of 160 pages), and who himself wrote of the "heroism of modern life" as he observed it on the streets of Paris.[50] The Baudelaire section of *The Arcades Project* was, in fact, the only part of the project which Benjamin developed in more conventional form in other published work. This material forms the basis of the essays on Baudelaire—pieces of sustained criticism rather than fragments—which appeared in English in 1973 as a single volume, under the title *Charles Baudelaire: A Lyric Poet in the Era of High Capitalism.*[51] In that book, Benjamin defines the nineteenth century as an era when "the shock experience has become the norm,"[52] and concludes that Baudelaire placed that experience "at the very centre of his artistic work."[53] From both the organised argument of this volume and the juxtaposed fragments in *The Arcades Project*, it is clear that Benjamin affirms Baudelaire, as lyric poet, prose-writer and art critic, as a new type of modern-day hero, thanks to the strategies developed in his writing for resisting and surviving the disorienting pressures of modern life. This presentation of the artist, while it certainly centres, here too, on the death of the aura, by no means rings the requiem bells for traditional high culture.

Benjamin sees the central theme of Baudelaire's work as "the disintegration of the aura in the experience of shock,"[54] and shows how this is unforgettably dramatised in the short prose piece "Perte d'Auréole" ("The Lost Halo"). In this text, a poet complains of the loss of his halo, blown off his head as he ran to avoid a carriage when crossing the boulevard: "Mon auréole, dans un movement brusque, a glissé de ma tête dans la fange du macadam. Je n'ai pas eu le courage de la ramasser" ("In a brusque movement, my halo slipped off my head into the mud of the tarmac. I didn't dare pick it up").[55] The loss of the halo is, indeed, the falling-off of the aura; but Benjamin also makes it clear that Baudelaire, in his poems and prose writings, evolved new aesthetic instruments to enable the modern writer to "parry the shocks"[56] that rose up from the streets to destroy the aura. Impelled by the struggle to survive, the Baudelairean city artist creates new personae such as the poet-fencer who, in the poem "Le Soleil" ("The Sun"), defiantly proclaims: "Je vais m'exercer seul à ma fantasque escrime" ("I go out alone to fence fantastically"), affirming writing as a mode of struggle.[57] In *Le Peintre de la Vie Moderne*, his key essay of 1863, Baudelaire calls, as art critic, for new urban forms of aesthetic expression which will reflect the rhythms of modern life: "La modernité, c'est le transitoire, le fugitif, le contingent" ("Modernity is the transitory, the fugitive, the contingent");[58] as poet, he evolves a new lexicon of imagery drawn from the modern urban environment, in a heroic endeavour to make sense of that battery of "transitory" and "fugitive" sensations which confusedly constitute the modern. The great achievement of Benjamin's reading of Baudelaire is, precisely, to show how art throws up new strategies of survival to adapt to the changed conditions imposed by industrial society.

If we take *The Arcades Project* and the Baudelaire book and balance them against the "Work of Art" essay and the other "Brechtian writings," it should emerge that Benjamin, in his work as a whole, is not advocating replacing high culture by mass culture as an object of study—but, rather, that his aim is to seek out the hidden connections that would raise certain phenomena of popular culture (as exemplified by the arcades) to the same level of significance and seriousness as is traditionally associated with high-cultural artefacts. In this connection, the essay entitled "Eduard Fuchs, Collector and Historian" appears as an interesting pendant to the *Arcades Project.* This text, written in 1937, starts out from the figure of Fuchs, a German art collector who would be little-remembered today were it not for Benjamin's tribute. Benjamin concludes that, as the collector redeems the objects he accumulates from the weight of history, so it is the task of the radical critic of culture, not to destroy or marginalise the existing products of high culture, but to absolve them from their past exclusive ownership by society's rulers by making them accessible to everyone: "Cultural history [...] may well increase the burden of the treasures that are piled up on humanity's back. But it does not give mankind the strength to shake them off, so as to get its hands on them."[59] These words of Benjamin's can be read today as implying the proposition that, whatever the failings of the conventional "cultural history" which he criticises, there **are** ways of creating universal access to the time-honoured objects of the cultural heritage, of enabling the mass of the population to "get its hands on them," rather than iconoclastically destroying the objects as the Taliban smashed the Buddhas of Bamiyan.

VI

If we are to seek Benjamin's traces in today's Western society in a more general sense, we may conclude that his true inheritors are in fact not the McLuhanite high priests of the image and detractors of the book, nor those who would drive high culture out of universities in the name of mass culture. Nor are they the deconstructionists and postmodernist theorists who, to quote the dissident US academic Morris Berman from his polemical book of 2000 *The Twilight of American Culture*, promote "a philosophy of despair masquerading as radical intellectual chic," while generations of students are taught that canonic literature "has no intrinsic meaning and is nothing more than the cultural expression of a wealthy class of dead, white, 'colonialist' males"—at a time when, in today's officially literate US society, "we cannot expect [...] to make a mythological allusion any more, or use a foreign phrase, or refer to a famous historical event or literary character, and still be understood by more than a tiny handful of people."[60] Benjamin should in no way be held responsible for any such cultural wasteland of semi-literacy and half-baked dogma. His authentic heirs are, rather, those cultural critics who have developed and systematised his dynamic concept of modernity, or else pursued his strategy of taking up stray objects from popular culture and coaxing out their wider cultural significance.

Among these continuators is another US academic, Marshall Berman (no relation to his namesake Morris Berman), the author of *All That Is Solid Melts Into Air* (1983), a remarkable study of the nineteenth-century roots of twentieth-century modernity which, consciously following in Benjamin's footsteps, evokes Marx, Baudelaire and Nietzsche as founding fathers of the restless, dynamic, open-ended way of being which he believes to be the essence of the modern. In his words: "To be modern is to find ourselves in an environment that promises us adventure, power, joy, growth, transformation of ourselves and the world—and, at the same time, that threatens to destroy everything we have, everything we know, everything we are. Modern environments and experiences cut across all boundaries of geography and ethnicity, of class and nationality, of religion and ideology: in this sense, modernity can be said to unite all mankind. But it is a paradoxical unity, a unity of disunity: it pours us all into a maelstrom of perpetual disintegration and renewal, of struggle and contradiction, of ambiguity and anguish. To be modern is to be part of a universe in which, as Marx said, 'all that is solid melts into air.'"[61]

Also worthy of mention as an inheritor of Benjamin is Eric Lott, lecturer at the University of Virginia and author of the remarkable study *Love and Theft: Blackface Minstrelsy and the American Working Class* (1995), which, in a sense, follows the trail blazed by *The Arcades Project* by teasing out the contradictions and ambiguities of what might seem a trivial or contemptible manifestation of popular culture, namely the nineteenth-century American "blackface" shows in which white performers "blacked up" and imitated African-Americans on stage. In Lott's words, "it was cross-racial desire that coupled a nearly insupportable fascination and a self-protective derision with respect to black people and their cultural practices";[62] this identification of a dialectic of "fascination" and "derision," utopia and reification, using a method that seeks to restore meaning to cast-off cultural products, clearly bears Walter Benjamin's seal. Equally, the writings of one of today's foremost American essayists, Greil Marcus, are impregnated with the spirit of Benjamin's endeavour to establish links between objects from both popular and elite cultures (ranging, in Marcus' case, from the Mississippi blues to seventeenth-century Puritan sermons) in a form that raises up the one without destroying the other—seeking out the hidden, non-official sense of history's discarded shards and fragments, pointing up their connections and redeeming them from oblivion for appropriation by the future. In the introduction to his book of essays *The Dustbin of History* (1995), Marcus writes: "There are those moments in history when possibilities quickly lost to us, if we acknowledge only the official record, once loomed up; there are those moments when, as we reconstruct a place and time, things that truly did happen, that have irrevocably shaped us, nevertheless seem like impossibilities." Such significant, isolated moments are, for Marcus as for Benjamin—whose presence is clearly acknowledged in his pages[63]—illuminated and connected through the "impulse to reveal what seems to lie beneath the surface of ordinary history."[64]

VII

If these transatlantic appropriations of Benjamin's work have been striking, it is also worth drawing attention to another facet of the *Arcades Project*, namely its exemplary Europeanness. This characteristic is unfortunately somewhat obscured in the English edition by comparison with the original. It is customary to speak of the "German original," but in fact a good half of Benjamin's text, as published for the first time in Germany in 1982, is not in German at all but in French. The majority of Benjamin's sources are French originals (the rest are mostly from German-language writers), and in the manuscripts he almost invariably quoted his sources in the original. This practice is respected in the published German version, and the result is what might be called a linguistically bi-coloured or piebald text, with abundant passages in French interleaved with others in

German. Benjamin's original is, then, "not" a bilingual text. It should, rather, be called a macaronic text—that is, one which operates on the lines of the medieval carols which alternate Latin and English (as in the well-known *In Dulci Jubilo*: "Ubi sunt gaudia/If that they be not there?" etc). This striking characteristic of Benjamin's text is, however, not reproduced in the English—or, rather, American—version, which, no doubt in deference to the limited foreign-language knowledge of its presumed Anglophone readership, translates everything into English. The English version consequently appears as both more homogeneous and less European than the original. The latter remains, in its material aspect, an exemplary instance in practice of Franco-German collaboration and, therefore, a tribute to the interrelated character of the common European cultural heritage. *The Arcades Project*, working against the grain of the dark period of Europe's history in which it was written, in this sense anticipates the post-war movement of European cooperation, guided by the likes of Jean Monnet and Robert Schuman, which led to the placing of the French and German coal and steel industries under a common authority, and subsequently to that much broader and deeper process of European integration which has only this year borne its latest fruit in the material emergence of a single European currency. This pan-European dimension of Benjamin's text today seems more evident with hindsight, and may seem particularly appropriate if we recall the presence in his pages, not only of visionary utopians like Fourier but also of Victor Hugo, whose bicentenary marked 2002, the year of the euro, and who is today seen as one of the spiritual fathers of today's European Union. Hugo, indeed, in an essay of 1867 entitled *Paris*, written for the world's fair held in that year, expressed his vision of a United States of Europe, with a single currency to boot, whose spiritual nerve-centre would be the French capital: "Au XXe siècle, il y aura une nation extraordinaire [...] Elle sera illustre, riche, pensante, pacifique [...] Elle s'appellera l'Europe" ("In the twentieth century, there will be an extraordinary nation [...] It will be illustrious, rich, thinking, peaceful [...] It will be called Europe").[65]

VIII

Utopias, then, can crop up in unexpected places. However, despite Benjamin's palpable empathy with diverse dreams of a visionary future, whether those of Marx or Fourier or those imprisoned in the glass and steel of the arcades, he was most certainly no acolyte of the doctrine of progress. This doctrine was, as is well-known, an article of faith for the triumphalist ideologies of the mid-nineteenth century. The literature of Victorian England contains a classic exposition in Tennyson's poem "Locksley Hall," published in 1842, with its celebrated lines: "Forward, forward let us range,/Let the great world spin for ever down the ringing grooves of change."[66] Of the writers who feature most prominently in *The Arcades Project*, Baudelaire, despite his call on artists to embrace the modern, openly repudiated "la loi fatale, irrésistible du progrès" ("the fatal and irresistible law of progress"), seeing it as no better than a "grande hérésie" (an "enormous heresy").[67] Both Marx and Hugo, however, in their different ways embraced a certain concept of linear or ultimate progress. For Marx, capitalism represented a linear progression over feudalism, to be superseded in its turn by socialism;[68] for Hugo, history was a "vaste évolution humaine vers la libération universelle" (a "great human evolution towards universal liberation"),[69] in accordance with an obscure law which he claimed to bring to light in such visionary lines as: "Le jour où nos pillards, nos tyrans sans nombre,/Comprendront que quelqu'un remue au fond de l'ombre" ("The day when those who pillage us, our numberless tyrants, will realise that in the depths of the darkness there is someone stirring").[70]

Benjamin, by contrast—writing in the 1930s and under the looming shadow of Nazism—draws a firm line under this nineteenth-century concept of progress, and, indeed, rejects the whole notion of linear development: as his editor Rolf Tiedemann has suggested, "the concept of progress [...] must have appeared untenable to Benjamin in the light of the experience of the twentieth century."[71] What Benjamin wishes to formulate is, he says in *The Arcades Project*, "a philosophy of history that at all points has overcome the ideology of progress."[72]

He declares: "In the course of the nineteenth century [...] the concept of progress would increasingly have forfeited the critical functions it originally possessed [...] the doctrine of natural selection [...] popularised the notion that progress was automatic";[73] and, again: "As soon as it becomes the signature of historical process *as a whole*, the concept of progress bespeaks an uncritical hypostatisation rather than a critical interrogation."[74]

If the notion of "progress" appears as unsatisfactory because it supposes an "automatic," linear evolution towards an inevitable goal—thus encouraging that "uncritical" acceptance of reality from which Benjamin wishes to distance himself—then an alternative model of history is required. If "progress" can be likened to a straight line, that straight line may have to be replaced by a different image. Here Benjamin devises the arresting image of the *constellation*. This motif makes a number of key appearances in *The Arcades Project*, as symbol of the relationship which emerges when the historian places a number of apparently unrelated historical events in significant conjuncture. The constellation links past events among themselves, or else links past to present; its formation stimulates a flash of recognition, a quantum leap in historical understanding. For example, the French revolutions of 1789, 1830 and 1848 and the Paris Commune of 1870 would all be placed in a constellar relation, as events separated in time but linked by a common insurrectionary consciousness. Thus Benjamin writes: "what has been comes together in a flash with the now to form a constellation,"[75] and again: "the concern is to find the constellation of awakening [...] the dissolution of 'mythology' into the space of history [...] the awakening of a not-yet-conscious knowledge of what has been."[76] The constellar image marks the transition from "mythology," or illusion, into an authentic understanding of history. The task of the critical historian is, Benjamin argues, positioning himself against the ideology of "progress," "to root out every trace of 'development' from the image of history and to represent becoming [...] as a constellation in being."[77]

The critique of linear "progress" and the image of the

constellation,[78] as present in *The Arcades Project*, are further expounded in the last text Benjamin ever wrote, the "Theses on the Philosophy of History" which he drafted in 1940.[79] This brief, cryptic but endlessly suggestive document systematises his radically non-linear model of history, grounded not in sequence but in interrelation. It may be seen, on one level, as Benjamin's reply to an even briefer text by Marx, the celebrated "Theses on Feuerbach" of 1845 which stake out the territory of the materialist reading of history in two pages of highly compressed argument. At the same time, however, Benjamin's "Theses," though generally read as a stand-alone text, were consciously planned as a methodological complement to *The Arcades Project*;[80] and Benjamin himself stressed "the hidden but revealing relationship between these observations and my previous works—it (the "Theses" text) expresses itself concisely on the method of these."[81] They are, furthermore, indelibly coloured by the urgency of the time when they were written, both for Benjamin the individual and for the collective victims of the period; as he wrote in one of his last letters, "Every line we succeed in publishing today—no matter how uncertain the future to which we entrust it—is a victory wrenched from the powers of darkness."[82]

In the "Theses," Benjamin, breaking with "a conception of progress which did not adhere to reality but made dogmatic claims" and was "regarded as irresistible, something that automatically pursued a straight or spiral course," argues that "the concept of the historical progress of mankind cannot be sundered from the concept of its progression through a homogeneous, empty time."[83] This is an anti-historical time that denies the possibility of linking up epochs or reconstituting authentically radical traditions. Benjamin counter-argues: "History is the subject of a structure whose site is not homogenous, empty time, but time filled by the presence of the now [...] Thus, to Robespierre ancient Rome was a past charged with the time of the now which he blasted out of the continuum of history. The French Revolution viewed itself as Rome incarnate."[84] This link between France in 1789 and ancient Rome is clearly a case of a historic constellation in the sense employed in *The Arcades Project*, and at the end of the "Theses" that image does indeed make its appearance. Benjamin affirms that a particular event may acquire dynamic historical significance only "posthumously [...] through events that may be separated from it by thousands of years. A historian who takes this as his point of departure stops telling the sequence of events like the beads of a rosary. Instead, he grasps the constellation which his own era has formed with a definite earlier one."[85]

Lloyd Spencer comments: "A constellation is made up of some stars that are nearer, others further away. It is only from our perspective, that of the here (and now), that they appear to take on a significant configuration. Benjamin's use of the word 'constellation' [...] expresses in a precise and evocative way an aspect of a new kind of thinking about history."[86] Marx ended his "Theses on Feuerbach" with the celebrated aphorism: "The philosophers have only *interpreted* the world, in various ways; the point is to *change* it."[87] Benjamin's theses change the form of that challenge by shifting it on to a non-linear plane. At a time when classical Marxism no longer exerts the influence and attraction it once did, and from the viewpoint of the applicability of Benjamin's ideas and images to our own day, I would wish to argue for the continuing value and utility of Benjamin's constellar model.

The image of the constellation can now be appropriated as a key element for the construction of a dynamic model of history that would stand in profound opposition to the crude and parodic versions of linearist progressivism which have in recent decades all too often taken over the collective mind. The notion of history as a continuum—what Benjamin calls "a sequence of events like the beads of a rosary," an irreversible and unstoppable linear flow—does not stand up to one minute's rational examination. Nonetheless, ideologists and publicists of diverse hues present whatever social or economic tendency they wish to promote as inevitable or irreversible. Examples here might include free-market deregulation, the global reach of Hollywood cinema or the exponential growth of road transport. Those who propound such ideologies typically cast their opponents in the role of Don Quixote tilting at windmills or King Canute trying to hold back the tide. In the world of education, this syndrome can produce situations such as that in which a "reform" of university humanities courses, implying contamination of the critical function of higher education via a lethal dose of compulsory vocationalism, would typically be presented in the language of "progress" and "modernity," with the imposition of positivist values served up as an allegedly necessary and inevitable "integration of arts faculties into the modern world." Linearist arguments of this kind are based on simplistic notions of history as a one-way pendulum and of the "modern" as an irresistible tide. To such intellectually and educationally dangerous reductionism may be opposed Benjamin's dynamic conception of the modern and his non-linear, relational interpretation of history as imaged in the constellation. Viewed through the prism of his extraordinary *Theses*, history ceases to be a continuum, and can reassume its authentic character as a battleground of contending forces in a world where all advance is provisional.

The model of history advanced in the "Theses" has the principle of interrelation at its core. Furthermore, the reader returns from the "Theses" to *The Arcades Project* with a heightened sense of how that principle infuses not only Benjamin's thought but the very structure of his magnum opus. The *Arcades Project* is organised on the relational principle, to the point where the book itself may be perceived as a great constellation of constellations. As Adorno observed, "his thought [...] turns the fragment into a rule."[88] The fragments that make up the text appear on the page in linear sequence, but they generate their meanings through relations of dialogue and cross-reference across the entire book, illuminating each other in a complex and dynamic totality. One fragment lights up another fragment; one section, or collection of fragments, lights up another section. Conversely, no one fragment and no single section acquires its full potential for generating meaning unless placed in relation with the larger whole. What we find in Benjamin is not fragmentation for its own sake, not the reduction of the cultural heritage to a mass of rubble, but, rather, a breaking-down of history into fragments which it is for the reader to reassemble into a qualitatively new whole—a new constellation to illuminate the future.

IX

Benjamin's constellar model of history, based as it is on interrelation rather than linear flow, may also be viewed with hindsight as anticipating one of the more promising developments of our time—namely that eminently non-linear phenomenon which is the Internet. The system of relations which he constructs bears, in its organising principles, a visible resemblance to the decentralised electronic network that came into being at the end of the twentieth century.

There is a curious convergence between certain technical characteristics of Fourier's utopia, as relayed by Benjamin, and today's Internet. According to Benjamin, "Fourier speaks of a *transmission miragique* which will make it possible for London to have news from India within four hours."[89] In this connection, he quotes both Fourier himself: "A certain vessel from London arrives in China today; tomorrow the planet Mercury, having been advised of the arrivals and movements of ships by the astronomers of Asia, will transmit the list to the astronomers of London,"[90] and one of his commentators who, writing in 1901, saw Fourier as prefiguring radio broadcasting: "We have here an extraordinary anticipation. For what he means to say is precisely this: the planet Mercury is there to represent a force, as yet unknown, which would enable the transmission of messages—a force of which he has had a presentiment."[91] Taken a step further, this becomes an anticipation of the modern-day "transmission of messages," via—not "the planet Mercury," but the human-made constellation called the Internet.[92]

The nexus thus formed between utopian dreams and network technology is arresting. If we recall the utopian dimension of the arcades themselves, we may further speculate that the "arcade-like" construction of Benjamin's text, where fragment speaks to fragment and the complete sense of any given citation or commentary is created out of its relations with the rest, in certain aspects anticipates the architecture of the

Internet.[93] The discrete blocks of text that make up *The Arcades Project* illuminate each other as the reader is jolted into awareness of their hidden connections: text connects to text as if through a hidden hyperlink. In Benjamin's writing as on the Internet, no message ever reaches a final destination: the generation of meaning is as much a function of the relations between texts as of the texts themselves. The interconnection of Benjamin's fragments offers a formal anticipation of the mode of structuring of the World Wide Web, where page speaks to page within a site and site speaks to site across the network. The acquisition of knowledge becomes a continuous, never-ending process, based not on the straight line but the constellation; to the constellation of textual fragments in Benjamin's pages corresponds, on a larger scale, the constellation of texts that is the Internet. Benjamin's way of seeing in *The Arcades Project* here emerges with hindsight less as Marxist than as pointing, in an unexpectedly pioneering sense, to something after and beyond Marxism. The utopian discourse of classical Marxism, based on an essentially linear model of human advancement, gives way to an alternative utopian vision, enabled by technological breakthrough but not confined by technicist horizons, which permits the creation of new, dynamic forms of human intervention based on the principle of interrelation.[94]

Every epoch creates its precursors: if Benjamin's greatest work has been revealed in English, the lingua franca of the new electronic networks, only at the very end of the twentieth century, that historic timing also points up the unexpected ways in which that same work now proves to anticipate the dynamic of that networking mode of being which offers the human race its best hope for the twenty-first century. By reading Walter Benjamin, by retracing his steps through the arcades, by re-creating the constellations of meaning that he plotted, we can come to a clearer understanding of our own new and emergent way of seeing.

Notes

1. Benjamin, "Theses on the Philosophy of History" IX/259-60.
2. In this paper, (1) all fragments cited from the English translation of Benjamin's *The Arcades Project* are identified by both editorial

reference number and page number, in that order; (2) the policy adopted regarding translations of non-English quotations, both for texts quoted by Benjamin himself and for those from other sources, is as follows: the original is given alongside the English translation in the case of citations of particular literary value, e.g. those from Baudelaire and Hugo; otherwise, only the English version is given.

3. Benjamin, *Das Passagen-Werk*, ed. Rolf Tiedemann (Frankfurt am Main: Suhrkamp Verlag, 1982).
4. For many of the details in this paragraph, I am indebted to Lloyd Spencer's article "On the Concept of History."
5. For representative reviews, see Lucas, "Parisian Dialectics," Mannes-Abbott, "Gone Shopping" and Nygren, "Life in the Jaws of the Crocodile."
6. A comprehensive multilingual definition is offered by Geist (*Le Passage*, 11-12).
7. The German title of the guide cited is *Illustrierte Pariser Führer* (Benjamin, *The Arcades Project* A1,1/31).
8. Those elements of factual information in this and the following paragraph which are not from Benjamin are taken either from Geist (op. cit.) or from de Moncan and Mahout, *Le Guide des passages de Paris*.
9. See Geist (305-09).
10. For the convent connection, see Geist (297) and, for the Passage Choiseul, de Moncan and Mahout (122).
11. See Benjamin, *The Arcades Project* section A [31-61], *passim*; Geist 318-23.
12. Amédée Kermel, "Les passages de Paris" (1831), quoted in Geist (298; my translation from French).
13. Kermel.
14. Geist 298 (my translation).
15. *The Arcades Project*, D,7/834. Kermel anticipates Benjamin in praising the arcades' architectural originality: 'I who, in my grateful imagination, have judged the person who first had the idea of the arcades and the audacity to construct them as being the equal of (the architects) Larochefoucault or Mansard' (loc. cit.; my translation).
16. *Arcades Project*, S1,1/543.
17. *Arcades Project*, "Materials for the Exposé of 1935, No 5"/905.
18. *Arcades Project*, loc. cit. 903.
19. For the "dialectical image," see Adorno, *Sur Walter Benjamin* 142-45, 148-52.

20. Adorno. "First Sketches"/827.
21. Adorno. "First Sketches"/828.
22. see Geist loc. cit.
23. *Arcades Project* X13a/669.
24. Adorno, "Fragmente über Wagner," 1939; quoted by Benjamin (loc. cit).
25. Adorno. W10a,1/637.
26. Marx, letter to Ludwig Kugelmann, 9 October 1866 (see Benjamin, loc. cit.).
27. Marx and Engels, *The German Ideology, Part One*, 54.
28. Buck-Morss 64.
29. "Phalanx" is an alternative name for "phalanstery."
30. Fourier, quoted by Benjamin, *The Arcades Project* A5,4/44.
31. *Arcades Project*, "First Sketches"/839.
32. *Arcades Project*, S2,1/546.
33. *Arcades Project*, H1a,5/206.
34. *Arcades Project*, N11,3/476.
35. Arendt, "Walter Benjamin: 1892-1940" 47.
36. Arendt, "Walter Benjamin: 1892-1940" 11, 12.
37. Sontag, "Introduction" to Benjamin, *One-Way Street and Other Writings* 27.
38. Spencer, "On Certain Difficulties."
39. Adorno, *Sur Walter Benjamin* 9 (here and elsewhere I have provided my own renderings into English from the French versions of Adorno's texts [originally written in German]).
40. cf. Marx, "Preface to *A Contribution to the Critique of Political Economy*" 425-426.
41. *Arcades Project*, N1a,6/460.
42. *Arcades Project*, M,14/854.
43. Mannes-Abbott, loc. cit.
44. Cuddon 529 (entry: "Marxist criticism").
45. Benjamin, *The Work of Art in the Age of Mechanical Reproduction* III/224, II/223.
46. Benjamin, *The Work of Art in the Age of Mechanical Reproduction* VIII/230.
47. Benjamin, *The Work of Art in the Age of Mechanical Reproduction* XII/236.

48. Adorno, *Sur Walter Benjamin* 170, 172, 173.

49. *Arcades Project*, K3,3/394.

50. See Baudelaire, "De l'Héroisme de la Vie Moderne" (*Salon de 1846*, section XVIII), *Œuvres complètes* 949-952.

51. The larger part of this material (i.e. the essay "On Some Motifs in Baudelaire") was published in German in 1939.

52. Benjamin, *Charles Baudelaire* 116.

53. Benjamin, *Charles Baudelaire* 117.

54. Benjamin, *Charles Baudelaire* 154.

55. Baudelaire, "Perte d'Auréole" [*Le Spleen de Paris*, XLVI], *Œuvres complètes* 299-300 (my translation); cf. Benjamin, op. cit. 152-154.

56. Benjamin, op. cit. 117.

57. Baudelaire, "Le Soleil" [*Les Fleurs du Mal*, LXXXVII], in *Oeuvres complètes* (line 5; my translation); cf. Benjamin, op. cit. 68, 118.

58. Baudelaire, *Le Peintre de la Vie Moderne, Oeuvres complètes* 1152-1192 (1163; my translation).

59. Benjamin, "Eduard Fuchs, Collector and Historian" 360-361.

60. Morris Berman, *The Twilight of American Culture* 63, 57, 55.

61. Marshall Berman, *All That Is Solid Melts Into Air* 15; the quotation which gives his book its title is from Marx and Engels, *Manifesto of the Communist Party* (10).

62. Lott, *Love and Theft*, 6. Lott's book avoids mentioning Benjamin by name, but it is impregnated by his influence: significantly, to figure the ambivalence of the minstrel shows he uses the Janus image, as employed by Benjamin for the arcades: "the early minstrel show was a Janus-faced figure for the cultural relationship of white to black in America, a relationship that even in its dominative character was far from self-explanatory" (ibid. 30; cf. note 16 above).

63. Marcus twice quotes Benjamin's remark that "history is a matter of seizing 'hold of a memory as it flashes up at a moment of danger'" ("Theses on the Philosophy of History," VI/257), in *The Dustbin of History* (37, 143).

64. Marcus, op. cit. 9, 8.

65. Hugo, *Paris* 25, 33 (my translation).

66. Tennyson, "Locksley Hall" lines 181-182.

67. Baudelaire, "Notes nouvelles sur Edgar Poe" 180 (my translation).

68. See Marx and Engels, *Manifesto of the Communist Party*: "The weapons with which the bourgeoisie felled feudalism to the ground are now turned against the bourgeoisie itself [...] Overthrow of the bourgeoisie

lays the foundation for the sway of the proletariat" (12, 15). This sequential model can perfectly well be read as an embodiment of the doctrine of linear progress.

69. Hugo, op. cit. 97.
70. Hugo, "La Caravane"; quoted by Benjamin, *Charles Baudelaire* (64; the translation is mine). For an account of Hugo's concept of "progress," see Pena-Ruiz and Scot, "Une philosophie critique du progrès" *passim.*
71. Tiedemann, "Dialectics at a Standstill" 941.
72. *Arcades Project,* O5/857.
73. *Arcades Project,* N11a,1/476.
74. *Arcades Project,* N13,1/478.
75. *Arcades Project,* N2a,3/462.
76. *Arcades Project,* N1,9/458.
77. *Arcades Project,* H,16/845.
78. In relation to this text, Lloyd Spencer explains that "constellation" is a literal rendering of the German "Konstellation" (see his "On Certain Difficulties with the Translation of 'On the Concept of History'").
79. Also known as "On the Concept of History." For the background to this text, see Spencer's two articles.
80. See Eagleton, *Walter Benjamin* (120).
81. Benjamin, letter to Gretel Adorno, 7 May 1940; quoted in Spencer, "On Certain Difficulties."
82. Benjamin, letter to Gershom Scholem, 11 January 1940; quoted in Spencer, "On the Concept of History."
83. Benjamin, "Theses on the Philosophy of History" XIII/262-263.
84. Benjamin, "Theses on the Philosophy of History" XIV/263.
85. Benjamin, "Theses on the Philosophy of History" A/265.
86. Spencer, "On Certain Difficulties."
87. Marx, "Theses on Feuerbach" XI/423.
88. Adorno, *Sur Walter Benjamin* 27.
89. *Arcades Project* W11a,3/639.
90. Fourier, quoted by Benjamin, ibid. W9a,3/636.
91. Charles Gide on Fourier [1901], quoted by Benjamin, loc. cit.
92. A surprising anticipation of the Internet appears in the pages of another writer frequently cited by Benjamin, Louis-Auguste Blanqui (1805-1881). Blanqui, a far-left political activist, wrote *L'Éternité des Astres* [*Eternity of the Stars*] (1872) when imprisoned following his

involvement in the Paris Commune. Benjamin considered this (little-known) text to be a work of major philosophical significance, declaring in *The Arcades Project*: "This book completes the century's constellation of phantasmagorias with one last, cosmic phantasmagoria which implicitly comprehends the severest critique of all the others" ("Exposé of 1939"/25). Blanqui's text, best described as a piece of cosmological speculation, alternates rather restlessly between a dark vision of the universe as endless repetition —a series of "duplicates produced by the billion"—and a somewhat more hopeful notion of the cosmos as a set of elaborately graduated combinations and variations. Benjamin reads this book as an overpowering nightmare; other readings are, however, possible, and one approach could be to foreground its incessant oscillation between the rival notions of standardisation (paralleling industrial mass-production) and variation (pointing to a utopian future). Today's Internet partakes in both phenomena: it permits the infinite reproduction of the same text and its diffusion to a potentially unlimited number of recipients, while also allowing multiple discourses to bloom worldwide. In a strange passage that suggests a cosmic utopia of communication between like-minded beings over huge distances, and thus curiously foreshadows the Internet, Blanqui declares: "It scarcely matters whether our doubles are our neighbours. Even if they lived on the moon, the conversation would be no less comfortable and it would be just as easy to get to know each other" (quotations from Blanqui, 123-124; my translation).

93. The Benjamin/Internet link has, it seems, been posited by Irving Wohlfahrt, in a paper entitled "Awakening from the Twentieth Century," given at the International Walter Benjamin Society Conference held in Barcelona in September 25-27 2000. This paper is summarised in Esther Leslie's report on the conference (see Works Cited), but her summary is too brief to give a clear idea of the nature of Wohlfahrt's analysis.

94. It is no accident that Benjamin is one of those writers for whose work multiple and fast-expanding Internet resources are now in place. Among the specialist websites may be noted the Walter Benjamin Research Syndicate at: http://www.wbenjamin.org

Works Cited

Adorno, Theodor W. *Über Walter Benjamin* [essays 1950-1968, collected 1970]. Translated into French by Christophe David as *Sur Walter Benjamin*. Paris: Gallimard (Folio), 1999 (includes: "Portrait de Walter Benjamin" [1950], 9-30; "Autour de 'Paris, capitale du XIXe siècle'" [letters to Benjamin and Max Horkheimer, 1935], 133-65; "Autour de

'L'Oeuvre d'Art à l'époque de sa réproduction technique'" [letter to Benjamin, 18 March 1936], 166-76).

Arendt, Hannah. "Walter Benjamin: 1892-1940." Introduction to Benjamin, *Illuminations* [1970] (1-58).

Baudelaire, Charles. *L'Art romantique.* Paris: Gallimard (Folio), 1968 (includes "Notes nouvelles sur Edgar Poe" [1857], 175-92).

Oeuvres complètes. Paris: Gallimard (Pléiade), 1961, repr. 1971 (includes: *Les Fleurs du Mal* [1861], *Le Spleen de Paris* [1869], *Salon de 1846* [1846], *Le Peintre de la Vie Moderne* [1863]).

Benjamin, Walter. *Charles Baudelaire: A Lyric Poet in the Era of High Capitalism* [1935-1939]. Trans. Harry Zohn and Quentin Hoare. London: New Left Books, 1973.

Illuminations. Trans. Harry Zohn [1970]. London: Collins (Fontana), 1973 (includes: "The Work of Art in the Age of Mechanical Reproduction" [1936], 219-53; "Theses on the Philosophy of History" [written 1940, published 1942], 255-65).

One-Way Street and Other Writings. Translated by Edmund Jephcott and Kingsley Shorter. London: New Left Books, 1979 (includes: "Surrealism" [1929], 225-39; "A Small History of Photography" [1931], 240-57; "Eduard Fuchs, Collector and Historian" [1937], 349-86).

The Arcades Project [written 1927-40, published 1982]. Trans. Howard Eiland and Kevin McLaughlin. Cambridge, Mass.: Harvard UP, 1999.

Understanding Brecht. Trans. A. Bostock [1973]. London: Verso, 1983 (includes "The Author as Producer" [written 1934, published 1966], 85-103).

Berman, Marshall. *All That Is Solid Melts into Air: The Experience of Modernity* [1982]. London: Verso, 1983.

Berman, Morris. *The Twilight of American Culture* [2000]. London: Duckworth, 2001.

Blanqui, Louis-Auguste. *L'Éternité par les Astres* [1872]. Paris and Geneva: Éditions Slatkine, 1996.

Buck-Morss, Susan. "Walter Benjamin—Revolutionary Writer." *New Left Review* 128 (July/August 1981). 50-75 and 129 (Sept.–Oct. 1981). 77-95.

Cuddon, J.A. *The Penguin Dictionary of Literary Terms and Literary Theory.* 3rd ed. Harmondsworth: Penguin, 1992.

De Moncan, Patrice and Mahout, Christian. *Le Guide des passages de Paris: Guide pratique, historique et littéraire.* Paris: Éditions Seesam, 1991.

Eagleton, Terry. *Walter Benjamin or Towards a Revolutionary Criticism.* London: Verso, 1981.

Geist, J.F. *Le Passage: Un type architectural du XIXe siècle* [1969, 1982]. Trans. Marianne Brausch. Liège (Belgium): Pierre Mardaga, 1987.

Hugo, Victor. "La Caravane," *Les Châtiments* [1853]. Paris: Gallimard [Classiques de Poche], 1998.

Paris [1867]. Paris: Bartillat, 2001.

Kermel, Amédée. "Les passages de Paris" [1831]. Reprinted in Geist, J.F. *Le Passage* (q.v.), 298-302.

Leslie, Esther. "Crossing Borders; Walter Benjamin Conference in Barcelona, September 25-27 2000," 2000. Walter Benjamin Research Syndicate, http://www.wbenjamin.org/crossing.html

Lott, Eric. *Love and Theft: Blackface Minstrelsy and the American Working Class.* New York: OUP, 1995.

Lucas, Paul. "Parisian Dialectics: Review of Walter Benjamin's *The Arcades Project." Logos,* 1.1, Winter 2002, http://logosonline.home.igc.org/benjamin.rev.htm

Mannes-Abbott, Guy. "Gone Shopping: *The Arcades Project.*" *New Statesman,* 13 March 2000; revised version at: http://www.g-m-a.net/docs/c_benjamin.html

Marcus, Greil. *The Dustbin of History* [1995]. London: Picador, 1997.

Marx, Karl. "Preface to *A Contribution to the Critique of Political Economy*" [1859], *Early Writings,* trans. Rodney Livingstone and Gregor Benton, intr. Lucio Colletti. Harmondsworth: Penguin, 1975, repr. 1992 (424-28).

"Theses on Feuerbach" [written 1845, published 1886], *Early Writings* (q.v.) (421-23).

Marx, Karl and Engels, Frederick. *The German Ideology, Part One* [1846]. Ed. and intr. C.J. Arthur. London: Lawrence & Wishart, 1970, repr. 1999.

Manifesto of the Communist Party [1848]. London: William Reeves, 1888, repr. (facsimile edn.), Trier (Germany): Karl-Marx Haus, n.d.

Nygren, Bill. "Life in the Jaws of the Crocodile: Walter Benjamin's Last Project." *West by North West* (Spring 2000). http://www.westbynorthwest.org/spring00/bookreviews.html

Pena-Ruiz, Henri and Scot, Jean-Paul. "Une philosophie critique du progrès." *Magazine Littéraire* (Jan. 2002) [special edition on Victor Hugo], 30-33.

Sontag, Susan. "Introduction" to Benjamin, *One-Way Street and Other Writings* [1979] (7-28).

Spencer, Lloyd. "On Certain Difficulties with the Translation of 'On The Concept Of History,'" 2000. http://www.tasc.ac.uk/depart/media/staff/ls/WBenjamin/TranslWB.html

"On the Concept of History: Some of the background to Benjamin's 'Theses,'" 2000. http://www.tasc.ac.uk/depart/media/staff/ls/WBenjamin/THESES.html

Tennyson, Alfred Lord. "Locksley Hall" [1842], *Selected Poems.* Ed. Aidan Day. Harmondsworth: Penguin, 1991.

Tiedemann, Rolf. "Dialectics at a Standstill: Approaches to the *Passagen-Werk* [1982]. Trans. Gary Smith and André Lefevere. Postface to Benjamin. *The Arcades Project* (1999) (929-45).

Special Note

This article is a revised version of a paper first given by the author in February 2002, at Kakatiya University, Warangal, and the Central Institute of English and Foreign Languages (CIEFL), Hyderabad.

16

Invisible Natures: On Italo Calvino's *Invisible Cities*

VIRGÍLIO AUGUSTO FERNANDES ALMEIDA

> Marco Polo describes a bridge, stone by stone.
> "But which is the stone that supports the bridge?"
> Kublai Khan asks.
> "The bridge is not supported by one stone or another," Marco answers,
> "but by the line of the arch that they form."
> Kublai Khan remains silent, reflecting.
> Then he adds:
> "Why do you speak to me of the stones?
> It is only the arch that matters to me."
> Polo answers:
> "Without stones there is no arch."
>
> —Italo Calvino, "Invisible Cities"

The starting-point is a short and disturbing sentence: "Our society lives after the end of nature." These are the words of the British economics professor and thinker Anthony Giddens, in his recent book *Runaway World.*[1] What exactly is the meaning of this uncomfortable affirmation? The "end of nature" does not necessarily mean the end of the physical world. The point is more that until very recently nature was still not affected by human intervention. We still do not know exactly what is natural and what is the result of human action. Global warming, flooding and drought in different regions of the planet, genetically modified foodstuffs: are these things natural or artificial phenomena? The "end of nature" could also lead us to think of cities concreting over the landscape, rainforests being felled or governments that despise the natural world. However, it is not my intention to go over this well-trodden ground once again: my concern in this paper is not the end of nature, but, rather, the growth of forms of invisible nature, which take possession of time and space like huge spider's webs.

Something is in process of exceeding nature, enveloping it in invisible fashion: that something consists of the networks which are the collective representation of the relations between humans and machines, between the human and the non-human. Rather than describe these relations in scientific or technical language, I believe that we may turn to literature as a means of deciphering at least some parts of this technological and social imbroglio. I shall use as my guide in this essay the sequence of short narratives which make up Italo Calvino's work of fiction *Invisible Cities* (1972).[2] In these narratives, Marco Polo, the celebrated Venetian oriental traveller, offers the emperor Kublai Khan an account of his presumed visits to a series of imaginary cities, each of which bears a woman's name. In their lightness, swiftness and multiplicity, Calvino's narratives work on the reader's imagination to generate means of capturing the similar "invisible natures" of today's world: "A Ersilia, per stabilire i rapporti che regono la vita della città, gli abitanti tendono dei fili tra gli spigoli delle case, bianchi o neri o grigi o bianco-e-neri a seconda se segnano relazioni di parentela, scambio, autorità, rappresentanza" ("In Ersilia, to establish the relationships that sustain the city's life, the inhabitants stretch strings from the corners of the houses, white or black or gray or black-and-white according to whether they mark a relationship of blood, of trade, authority, agency").[3] This tangle of stretched strings offers us a first glimpse of those "invisible natures." The network of relationships that is the Internet is a metaphor for connectivity in time and space.

"Se volete credermi, bene. Ora dirò come è fatta Ottavia, città-ragnatela. C'è un precipizio in mezzo a due montagne scoscese; la città è sul vuoto, legata alle due creste con funi a catene e passerelle [...] Sospesa sull'abisso, la vita degli abitanti d'Ottavia è meno incerta che in altre città. Sanno che più di tanto la rete non regge" ("If you choose to believe me, good.

Now I will tell how Octavia, the spider-web city, is made. There is a precipice between two steep mountains: the city is over the void, bound to the two crests with ropes and chains and catwalks [...] Suspended over the abyss, the life of Octavia's inhabitants is less uncertain than in other cities. They know the net will last only so long").[4] These words of Calvino's Polo suggest the fashion in which we ourselves are becoming ever more connected to the "invisible natures," even if we fail to notice what is happening. The spider-web which sustains our modern life is created through cellphones, computers, faxes, television and communication networks. And yet, at the same time, we remain unaware of the limits and the risks. Instant electronic communications, the Internet and computers are not just means of transmitting news and information faster. They are much more than that: they are phenomena which are radically altering the tissue of society. When the image of the US President is more familiar to us than our neighbour's face, it seems that the daily life of everyone, rich or poor, is being altered for good by technology—by the invisible nature of the communication and information networks. When we realise that an economic disturbance in South Korea, Thailand or Indonesia can almost instantaneously impact on prices and daily life in Brazil, we can be sure that we need to reach a clearer understanding of these networks and the invisible natures which they create.

"Quale linea separa il dentro dal fuori, il rombo delle ruote dall'ululo dei lupi?" ("What line separates the inside from the outside, the rumble of wheels from the howl of wolves?").[5] Such is the question raised in Calvino's text by the city of Zoe, the place of indivisible existence. The reader has the eerie sensation that the thin line that divides the real from the artificial is in process of collapse. In fact, we are experiencing the real and artificial at one and the same time. The signs of the real that we once recognised—contours, irregularities, texture, odour—are, perhaps, becoming things of the past. Gradually they are being replaced by information, in the form of images and sounds. In today's world, television, videos, the radio, digital cinema and the web of computers and cellphones are pushing out nature and taking over its space. Modern urban life is becoming intoxicated with artificial images, and it would come as no surprise to find today's children replacing the fantasies of the imagination and nature with Nintendo-type characters and scenes.

Artificial nature is invisible, yet it weighs on us. It weighs us down through its universal excess: the sources of images and information produce overdoses of news and fictions originating from all corners of the planet and on all possible subjects. The vastness of the empire of Kublai Khan should make us reflect on the culture of excess of the contemporary world: "Il Gran Kan contempla un impero ricoperto di città che pesano sulla terra e sugli uomini, stipato di ricchezze e d'ingorghi, stracarico d'ornamenti e d'incombenze, complicato di meccanismi e di gerarchie, gonfio, teso, greve. 'È il suo stesso peso che sta schiacciando l'impero,' pensa Kublai" ("The Great Khan contemplates an empire covered with cities that weigh upon the earth and upon mankind, crammed with wealth and traffic, overladen with ornaments and offices, complicated with mechanisms and, hierarchies, swollen, tense and ponderous. 'The empire is being crushed by its own weight,' Kublai thinks").[6] Are we too not being crushed by a universal excess, under the information overload of the Internet?

"Del carattere degli abitanti di Andria meritano di essere ricordate due virtù: la sicurezza in se stessi e la prudenza. Convinti che ogni innovazione nella città influisca sul destino del cielo, prima di ogni decisione calcolano i rischi ed i vantaggi per loro e per l'insieme della città e dei mondi." ("As for the character of Andria's inhabitants, two virtues are worth mentioning: self-confidence and prudence. Convinced that every innovation in the city influences the sky's pattern, before taking any decision they calculate the risks and advantages for themselves and for the city and for all worlds").[7] In Andria, life flows with the calm of the movement of the heavenly bodies, and acquires the necessity of phenomena not subject to the human will. By contrast with Andria, the collective nature of the modern communication and computer networks creates environments which are unstable and liable to accelerated change. Share-price anxiety can sweep across the whole planet. The networks create the possibility of immediate action, with capital movements following headlong on the heels of information, generating panic or euphoria. The invisible natures foster instability and generate innovation, thanks to the swiftness, interactivity and all-encompassing scope of the networks.

Information, knowledge and news are diffused in a near-instantaneous and unpredictable fashion, via the "electronic word-of-mouth" which characterises the networks of which the invisible natures are made. In the traditional media—television, radio, newspapers—information essentially flows one way only. In the new networks, information flows with the tide, and everyone can act on it, receive it and pass it on, like the stevedores and gondoliers recalled by Calvino's Marco Polo: "'Io parlo parlo,—dice Marco—ma chi m'ascolta ritiene solo le parole che aspetta. Altra è la descrizione del mondo cui tu presti benigno orecchio, altra quella che farà il giro dei capanelli di scaricatori e gondolieri sulle fondamenta di casa mia il giorno del mio ritorno, altra ancora quella che potrei dettare in tarda età, se venissi fatto prigioniero da pirati genovesi e messo in ceppi nella stessa cella con uno scrivano di romanzi d'avventura. Chi comanda al racconto non è la voce: è l'orecchio'" ["'I speak and speak,' Marco says, 'but the listener retains only the words he is expecting. The description of the world to which you lend a benevolent ear is one thing; the description that will go the rounds of stevedores and gondoliers on the street outside my house the day of my return is another; and yet another, that which I might dictate late in life, if I were taken prisoner by Genoese pirates and put in irons in the same cell with a writer of adventure stories. It is not the voice that commands the story: it is the ear'"].[8] The networks rapidly disseminate knowledge, information, legends and rumours.

Italo Calvino writes: "Nella vita degli imperatori c'è un momento, che segue all'orgoglio per l'ampiezza sterminata dei territori che abbiamo conquistato, alla malinconia e al sollievo di sapere che presto rinunceremo a conoscerli e a comprenderli; un senso come di vuoto che ci prende una sera con l'odore degli elefanti dopo la pioggia e della cenere di sandalo che si raffredda nei bracieri [...]" ("In the lives of emperors there is a moment which follows pride in the boundless extension of the territories we have conquered, and the melancholy and relief of knowing we shall soon give up any thought of knowing and understanding them. There is a sense of emptiness that comes over us at evening, with the odor of the elephants after the rain and the sandalwood ashes growing cold in the braziers [...]").[9] Is this not an image of a legitimate desire on the part of today's human beings to disconnect from the invisible natures that surround them—the desire to be unreachable by television, telephone, fax or email—the desire to reconnect with real nature, to breathe in its odours, contemplate its forms and hear its sounds and its silence? Are we not confronted here with an image of the perplexity of present-day humanity in the face of the uncertainty brought about by the overfast advance of technology and science?

Notes and References

1. Giddens' text (*Runaway World*, second lecture) may be found at: http://news.bbc.co.uk/hi/english/static/events/reith_99/week2/week2.htm
2. Italo Calvino, *Le città invisibili* (Torino: Einaudi, 1972). Trans. William Weaver [1974] as *Invisible Cities* (London: Vintage. 1997).
3. Calvino, op. cit. Italian edn. 82, English edn. 76.
4. 81, 75.
5. 40, 34.
6. 79, 73.
7. 157, 151.
8. 143, 135.
9. 13, 5.

Translated from the Portuguese by Christopher Rollason

✪✪✪

CONTRIBUTORS

Almeida, Virgílio Augusto Fernandes : Department of Computer Science, Universidade Federal de Minas Gerais, Brazil.
E-mail: virgilio@dcc.ufmg.br

Gadgil, Gangadhar: 4, Abhang, Sahitya Sahawas, Bandra (East), Mumbai 400 051 India.
E-mail: beacons@bom3.vsnl.net.in

Gana, Nouri : Département d'Études anglaises, Université de Montreal, CP 6128 succursale Centre-Ville, Montreal QC H3C 3J7, Canada.
E-mail: ganan@MAGELLAN.Umontreal.ca

Geetha, N. : Department of English, Mother Teresa Women's University, Kodaikanal 620 101 Tamil Nadu, India.
E-mail: ptsekaran@yahoo.com

Jones, Christine : Department of English, University of British Columbia, Vancouver, Canada.
E-mail: jonesc@interchange.ubc.ca

Kalu, Anthonia C. : Department of Africana Studies, University of Northern Colorado, Greeley, Colorado, USA.
E-mail: ackalu@bentley.unco.edu

Mittapalli, Rajeshwar : Department of English, Kakatiya University, Vidyaranyapuri, Warangal 506 009 Andhra Pradesh, India.
E-mail: rajeshwar9@yahoo.com

Mund, Subhendu : JO 9, Ravenshaw College Qtrs, Malgodown Area, Cuttack 753 003 Orissa, India.
E-mail: subhendu_mund@sify.com

Pandurang, Mala : Department of English, Dr BMN College of Home Science, 338 Rafi Kidwai Road, Matunga, Mumbai 400 019 Maharashtra, India.
E-mail: mpandu@yahoo.com

Pradhan, Prakash Chandra: Department of English, Godavans Mahavidhyalaya, Barpur, Khurda 752 031 India.

Raveendran, N.V. : Department of English, SVR NSS College, Vazhoor, Kottayam Dist., Kerala, India.

Ravichandran, T. : Department of Humanities & Social Sciences, Indian Institute of Technology, Roorkee, Roorkee 247 667 Uttaranchal, India.
E-mail: drtrcfhs@isc.rurkiu.ernet.in

Rollason, Christopher : 17, avenue Foch, F-57000 Metz, France.
E-mail: rollason@9online.fr

Ruiz Moneva, María Ángeles : Department of English and German Studies, Faculty of Philosophy and Letters, University of Zaragoza, c/ Pedro Cerbuna, 12, 50009 Zaragoza, Spain.
E-mail: mruiz@posta.unizar.es

Vicente Blanco, Dámaso Javier : Lecturer in Private International Law, University of Valladolid, Spain.
E-mail: damaso@portu.der.uva.es

✪✪✪